THE
WILD
TRUTH

THE
WILD
TRUTH

The secrets that drove
Chris McCandless into the wild

CARINE McCANDLESS

HarperElement
An imprint of HarperCollins*Publishers*
77–85 Fulham Palace Road,
Hammersmith, London W6 8JB

www.harpercollins.co.uk

First published in the US by HarperOne 2014
This UK edition published by HarperElement 2014

1 3 5 7 9 10 8 6 4 2

All photos are from the author's collection, with the exception of insert
p. 6 (bottom), insert p. 7 (top left, top right, middle), p. 264 and
p. 278 © Dominic Peters; insert p. 8 (top) © Jon Krakauer.

Material quoted on p. vii from *All Said and Done* © Simone de Beauvoir;
p. ix, "Dying in the Wild" © *The New York Times*; p. 15, "I Go Back to
May 1937" © Sharon Olds; p. 107, *Growing Wings* © Kristen Jongen;
p. 187, *Doctor Zhivago* © Boris Pasternak.

While every effort has been made to trace the owners of copyright material
reproduced herein and secure permissions, the publishers would like to apologise
for any omissions and will be pleased to incorporate missing
acknowledgements in any future edition of this book.

A catalogue record of this book is available from the British Library

ISBN 978-0-00-758513-7

Printed and bound in Great Britain by Clays Ltd, St Ives plc

CONTENTS

For Chris

I tore myself away from the safe comfort of certainties through my love for truth; and truth rewarded me.

—Simone de Beauvoir, *All Said and Done*

FOREWORD

FOREWORD

On September 14, 1992, I got a phone call from Mark Bryant, the editor of *Outside* magazine, who sounded unusually animated. Skipping the small talk, he told me about a snippet he'd just read in the *New York Times* that he couldn't stop thinking about:

DYING IN THE WILD, A HIKER RECORDED THE TERROR

Last Sunday a young hiker, stranded by an injury, was found dead at a remote camp in the Alaskan interior. No one is yet certain who he was. But his diary and two notes found at the camp tell a wrenching story of his desperate and progressively futile efforts to survive.

The diary indicates that the man, believed to be an American in his late 20's or early 30's, might have been injured in a fall and that he was then stranded at the camp for more than three months. It tells how he tried to save himself by hunting game and eating wild plants while nonetheless getting weaker.

One of his two notes is a plea for help, addressed to anyone who might come upon the camp while the hiker searched the surrounding area for food. The second note bids the world goodbye.

An autopsy at the state coroner's office in Fairbanks this week found that the man had died of starvation, probably in late July. The authorities discovered among the man's possessions a name

that they believe is his. But they have so far been unable to confirm his identity and, until they do, have declined to disclose
the name.

Although the article raised more questions than it answered,
Bryant's interest had been piqued by its handful of poignant details.
He wondered if I'd be willing to investigate the tragedy, write a
substantial piece about it for *Outside,* and complete it quickly. I was
already behind schedule on other writing assignments and feeling
stressed. Committing to yet another project—a challenging one, on
a tight deadline—would add considerably to that stress. But the story
resonated on a deeply personal level for me. I agreed to put my other
projects on hold and look into it.

The deceased hiker turned out to be twenty-four-year-old
Christopher McCandless, who'd grown up in a Washington, D.C.,
suburb and graduated from Emory University with honors. It quickly
became apparent that walking alone into the Alaskan wilderness
with minimal food and gear had been a very deliberate act—the cul-
mination of a serious quest Chris had been planning for a long time.
He wanted to test his inner resources in a meaningful way, without
a safety net, in order to gain a better perspective on such weighty
matters as authenticity, purpose, and his place in the world.

Eager to receive whatever insights into Chris's personality his
family might be able to provide, in October 1992 I mailed a letter to Dennis Burnett, the McCandlesses' attorney, in which I
explained,

> *When I was 23 (I'm 38 at present) I, too, set off alone into*
> *the Alaskan wilderness for an extended sojourn that baffled and*
> *frightened many of my friends and family (I was seeking challenge,*
> *I suppose, and some sort of inner peace, and answers to Big*
> *Questions) so I identify with Chris to a great extent, and feel*

like I might know something about why he felt compelled to test himself in such a wild and unforgiving piece of country. . . . If any of the McCandless family would be willing to chat with me I'd be extremely grateful.

My letter resulted in an invitation from Chris's parents, Walt and Billie McCandless, to visit them at their home in Chesapeake Beach, Maryland. When I showed up on their doorstep a few days later, the intensity of their grief staggered me, but they graciously answered all of my many questions.

The last time Walt or Billie had seen Chris or spoken to him was May 12, 1990, when they'd driven down to Atlanta to attend his graduation from Emory. Following the ceremony, he mentioned that he would probably spend that summer traveling, and then enroll in law school. Five weeks later, he mailed his parents a copy of his final grades, accompanied by a note thanking them for some graduation gifts. "Not much else is happening, but it's starting to get real hot and humid down here," he wrote at the end of the missive. "Say Hi to everyone for me." It was the last anyone in the McCandless family would ever hear from him.

Walt and Billie were desperate to learn everything they could about Chris's activities from the moment he performed his vanishing act until his emaciated remains were discovered in Alaska twenty-seven months later. Where had he traveled and whom had he met? What had he been thinking? What had he been feeling? Hoping that I might be able to find answers to such questions, they allowed me to examine all the documents and photos that had been recovered after his death. They also urged me to track down anyone he'd met whom I could locate from these materials, and to interview individuals who were important to Chris before his disappearance—especially his twenty-one-year-old sister, Carine, with whom he had had an uncommonly close bond.

When I phoned Carine, she was wary, but she talked to me for twenty minutes or so and provided important information for the 8,400-word article about Chris, titled "Death of an Innocent," published as the cover story in the January 1993 issue of *Outside*. Although it was well received, the article left me feeling unsatisfied. In order to meet my deadline, I had to deliver it to the magazine before I'd had time to investigate some tantalizing leads. Important aspects of the mystery remained hazy, including the cause of Chris's death and his reasons for so assiduously avoiding contact with his family after he departed Atlanta in the summer of 1990. I spent the next year conducting further research to fill in these and other blanks in order to write a book, which was published in 1996 as *Into the Wild*.

By the time I began doing research for the book, it was obvious to me that Carine understood Chris better than anyone, perhaps even better than Chris had understood himself. So I phoned her again to ask if she would talk to me at greater length. Highly protective of her absent brother, she remained skeptical but agreed to let me interview her for a couple of hours at her home near Virginia Beach. After we started to talk, Carine determined there was a lot she wanted to tell me, and the allotted two hours stretched into the next day. At some point she decided she could trust me, and asked me to read some excruciatingly candid letters Chris had written to her—letters she had never shown to anyone, not even her husband or closest friends. As I began to read them I was filled with both sadness and admiration for Chris and Carine. The letters were sometimes harrowing, but they left little doubt about what drove him to sever all ties with his family. When I eventually got on a plane to fly home to Seattle, my head was spinning.

Before Carine shared the letters with me, she asked me not to include anything from them in my book. I promised to abide by her wishes. It's not uncommon for sources to ask journalists to treat certain pieces of information as confidential or "off the record," and

I'd agreed to such requests on several previous occasions. In this instance, my willingness to do so was bolstered by the fact that I shared Carine's desire to avoid causing undue pain to Walt, Billie, and Carine's siblings from Walt's first marriage. I thought, moreover, that I could convey what I'd learned from the letters obliquely, between the lines, without violating Carine's trust. I was confident I could provide enough indirect clues for readers to understand that, to no small degree, Chris's seemingly inexplicable behavior during the final years of his life was in fact explained by the volatile dynamics of the McCandless family while he was growing up.

Many readers did understand this, as it turned out. But many did not. A lot of people came away from reading *Into the Wild* without grasping why Chris did what he did. Lacking explicit facts, they concluded that he was merely self-absorbed, unforgivably cruel to his parents, mentally ill, suicidal, and/or witless.

These mistaken assumptions troubled Carine. Two decades after her brother's death, she decided it was time to tell Chris's entire story, plainly and directly, without concealing any of the heartbreaking particulars. She belatedly recognized that even the most toxic secrets could possibly be robbed of their power to hurt by dragging them out of the shadows and exposing them to the light of day.

Thus did she come to write *The Wild Truth,* the courageous book you now hold in your hands.

Jon Krakauer
April 2014

PROLOGUE

Those who cannot remember the past are condemned to repeat it.

—George Santayana, *The Life of Reason:*
Reason in Common Sense

THE HOUSE ON WILLET DRIVE looks smaller than I remember. Mom kept the yard much nicer than this, but the haunting appearance of overgrown weeds and neglected shrubs seems more appropriate. Color returns to my knuckles as I release the steering wheel. I hate this fucking house. For twenty-three years I managed to steel myself while passing these familiar exits of Virginia's highways. Several times I wrestled with the temptation to veer off, wanting to generate memories of time spent with the brother I miss so terribly. But pain is a cruel thief of childhood sentiment. People think they understand our story because they know how his ended, but they don't know how it all began.

Once a carefully tended mask, the house's facade now appears to have been abandoned. Unruly thickets of sharp holly stab at the foundation, their berries like droplets of blood drawn from its bricks. The wood siding sags, forgotten and pale, lifeless aside from the mildew creeping across its seams. Gone are the manicured flower beds;

the front yard is now adorned with random papers and bottles from passersby. It's as if the dwelling has utterly expired, worn out from too many years as the lead in a grueling play.

The knot in my stomach quickly transforms into nausea, and I scramble out into the crisp October air to hunch over and wait, patiently. But the relief doesn't come.

The concrete driveway lies vacant, broken and stained. But I realize the house is not deserted. Someone had to roll the trash cans to the street, and a neatly covered Harley is tucked under the carport, a single wheel exposed just enough to be identified.

I stagger back to my Honda Pilot and crawl inside to make my escape. But just before my key strikes the ignition, a large Chevy pickup flashes in my rearview mirror and lumbers up the driveway. A woman steps out of the truck and begins to unload a few items from the cab. As she suspiciously eyes my SUV parked in front of her house, I rebuke myself for not parking on the opposite side of the street. With a few encouraging breaths and a burst of energy, I find myself back at the bottom of the long, sloped driveway. Her expression asks what the hell I am doing there.

"Hello, ma'am? My name is Carine McCandless. I grew up in this house." I watch her furrowed brow soften into acknowledgment. "Do you know the history?"

"Yes. Well, a little," she wavers.

I hastily assume her next reply as I walk up the incline. "May I come up to talk to you?"

She puts down her purse and packages on the truck bed and shakes the hand I have offered. "Marian."

Marian is tall, nice looking, with a strong build and sturdy handshake. Her long strawberry-blond hair reminds me of Wynonna Judd, and her bright pretty blouse and casual black pantsuit are what you might expect to see on an underpaid social worker. Amongst the delicate necklaces around her neck hangs a heavier chain with a distinctive silver and black Harley Davidson emblem. Her expression is warm yet tentative.

I press on. "I was hoping you wouldn't mind if I looked around a little bit?"

She gestures at her disheveled yard and balks. "Well, I don't know what you would gain from that. It certainly doesn't look the same as it did when you lived here."

There is a long pause, and it remains unspoken, yet obvious, that Marian is not prone to welcome visitors. Eventually she looks back at my hopeful face and relents. "Well, you're gonna have to give me a minute to let my dog out before he pees all over the house." She smiles and hoots, "He's an ole boy, that Charlie!"

As we walk around the backyard, the wiry chocolate Labrador keeps his head low while he examines me through the tops of his eyes. Harmless growls emerge from his graying muzzle like the rumblings of an old man disturbed from his routine. While urinating about the yard, Charlie ensures that either I am securely entangled in his extensive leash or he is standing between the house and me. Marian ignores the gaps in the dilapidated fence, apologizing as she liberates my legs again and again. "Charlie could just jump right over that."

While I struggle to maintain my balance, I scan the areas where Chris and I would seek our refuge. No evidence remains of the massive vegetable garden we picked beans in every summer. Aster and chrysanthemum no longer grace the fallen leaves. The beautifully landscaped beds that Mom had so carefully lined with large stones now appear as mouths agape with crooked teeth, coughing up snarled knots of condemned shrubs and weeds. The railroad ties that had been systematically placed to create steps between the multilevel beds are barely defining the slope of the yard.

Free for the moment from Marian's canine guardian, I make my way to the higher level of the backyard. In the left corner is a generous slope where Chris and I imagined ourselves as archaeologists and where he refined his considerable storytelling skills as an adolescent.

Our neighborhood was developed among a complex grouping of small hills and valleys where minor rivers had meandered centuries earlier to service tobacco plantations. The houses on our street were built along a strand of dehydrated streambeds. Looking down the back rows of neighbors' chain-link fences, I can still trace the forgotten path of running waters. And those waters left behind a great deal of storytelling material.

I tell Marian how Chris and I would haul up our wagon full of plastic shovels and buckets—and the occasional soup spoon swiped from the silverware drawer—to dig section by section, getting filthy, eager to discover relics of the past. We didn't come across anything that would be of significance to anyone else. But to Chris, everything we unearthed was legendary. Some of our greatest finds became our secret collection. Between the effortless detection of widespread oyster shells, we were thrilled whenever the excavation revealed ceramic shards of glazed white china. Arms raised in victory, we would run down to the spigot and wash off the mud and dirt until we could see a pattern we had come to recognize: depictions of oriental houses in soft blue-violet hues. Then we would sift through the shoe box in which we stashed our trove, looking to match the remnants together like puzzle pieces.

Our proudest days were those when our score completed an entire plate. Then we would sit and relish our accomplishment, gazing back up at the dig site while Chris weaved intricate stories about how the pieces had come to rest there. He told of ancient Chinese armies—the soldiers coming under surprise attack while enjoying meals in their dining tents—defenseless against superior forces while their dinner plates shattered and fell beside them, only to be discovered years later by the fantastic archaeological duo Sir Flash and his little sister, Princess Woo Bear.

Our dig site now lay covered with scattered piles of yard debris. The pleasant scent of late-season honeysuckle drifts over from the yard next door, and I recall hopping the fence like scavengers to suck the nectar from its delicate summer blooms.

On the days when our instincts led us to flee to greater distances, Chris would take me running down Braeburn Drive to Rutherford Park, where active streams could still be found. We ventured along the creek beds, soaking our sneakers with failed attempts to jump across the clear, cold rush at wider and wider points, skipping rocks, singing Beatles songs, and reenacting scenes from our favorite television shows. Chris was brilliant at creating diversions, and nature was always his first choice of backdrop. And even if the chosen scene from *Star Trek, Buck Rogers,* or *Battlestar Galactica* didn't call for heroics, in my mind he was always my protector.

A lush blanket of English ivy covers most of the remainder of the yard's top level. The plant's deep green leaves were once contained behind yet another stone boundary, established and maintained as a neat and tidy latrine for our Shetland sheepdog, whom we loved to play with for hours on end. If Chris was captain of our adventures, Buck—or as he was officially registered by Mom on his AKC papers, Lord Buckley of Naripa III—was his first lieutenant. A little soldier with a big attitude, Buck regularly defeated our mother's efforts to grow a thick lawn by tearing up tufts of grass while nipping at our heels, his herding instincts driving him to run circles around Chris and me.

Ready now to swap stories, Marian explains that she bought the house from my parents two decades ago, as a new beginning for herself and her young sons after their home had burned down. I was unaware that it had been that many years since my parents had sold it, and that the house had not changed owners since. Marian didn't give many details about the boys' father, but from what she did allow, about her long work hours and single income having made

it difficult to keep up with the house, I gathered that going it alone
was a tough but necessary decision she had accepted without hesitation. She speaks endearingly about her sons still coming by for visits,
helping with things around the house when they can, and the future
projects they have planned. Her face lights up when the subject turns
to travel. She tells me of her solo trips aboard her Harley on any given
day when nice weather coincides with a rare day off work. When I
respond with my own history of solo hikes in the Shenandoah and
my Kawasaki EX500, she is gracious enough to not knock me for
having owned a crotch rocket.

With a nudge and a yelp, Charlie informs Marian that he is done,
and I am surprised when she invites me to follow them inside.

———————

AS I STEP INTO MARIAN'S KITCHEN, the odor of spent nicotine
overwhelms me before the storm door closes. Fighting my allergy to
the smoke and my urge to retreat, I fail to cough discreetly.

"Oh! My goodness! Do you need some water?" Marian kindly
offers.

I glance at the eruption of glass and stoneware that flows from the
kitchen sink onto the countertop, clean but chaotic. "No—no, thank
you. I'm fine." I suppose the conditions outside the house should
have prepared me for what might lie within. Still, I am humbled that
Marian has invited me into her home. Her smile is comfortable and
enticing, and even Charlie yips and spins in his excitement to begin
the tour.

"Excuse the mess," she apologizes as she leans against the table.
"I've just been *so* incredibly busy!" The excessive piles of paper
and mail have been carefully organized, leading me to believe that
she has a specific identity for each stack. Ashtrays occupy every
horizontal surface. Almost everything around me, aside from the
clutter, appears just as it did when I stood here as a child: the layout,

the cabinets, the counters and backsplash, even the appliances are the same.

"I remember making drop cookies on this stove with my friend Denise," I reminisce.

Marian seems pleased as I travel back in time. I recall a photo of Buck and me sprawled on this floor, fast asleep, taken on the first day we brought him home. Nestled in my yellow sweatshirt, he was just a puppy. I was in pigtails.

Marian takes me across the main floor of the split-level house. The blue floral wallpaper I remember from childhood has been replaced with a coat of adobe beige and Navajo sandpaintings. We continue down two flights of stairs to the basement, where my parents kept their office. This is where Mom spent most of her time—often in pajamas, a down vest, and slippers—hard and fast to the day's work as soon as she was awake. She had traded her own career aspirations for the promise of a brighter future by helping Dad start User Systems, Incorporated, an aerospace engineering and consulting firm specializing in airborne and space-based radar design. The long hours they put in made them wealthy. But not happy.

Mom was constantly typing and editing documents, making copies, preparing and binding presentations. Before we left for school, she was on her fourth cup of coffee. In addition to her office work, she was obligated to do infinite loads of laundry, keep the house spotless, maintain a beautiful yard, and serve dinner punctually. By the time Chris and I returned home from sports practice and band rehearsals, she had replaced the pots of java with bottles of red wine, to begin numbing herself before Dad got home. During the workday he was meeting with prestigious scientists at NASA; acquiring contracts with companies like the Jet Propulsion Laboratory, Northrop Grumman, and Lockheed Martin; or giving lectures at the Naval Academy.

Sometimes, if Dad was away on an extended trip, we were blessed with a few days of calm. Most days, though, as soon as we heard his

Cadillac pull into the carport, Chris and I ran and hid. He yelled out names and barked orders as soon as he opened the front door. He often complained to our mother that she should be fully dressed for his arrival: short skirt, three-inch heels, hair and makeup immaculate.

Chris and I did plenty of chores and became more useful as we got older, but Mom's workload was copious and challenging. She eventually reined in her "I can do it all" determination and hired a part-time maid to help with the housework. This resulted in the boss telling her she was getting lazy and now had no excuse not to fulfill the sexy secretary role.

In actuality, she played an equally important role in their business. He never acknowledged how valuable she was to their company, but his awareness of it is likely why he constantly bullied her. "You're nothing without me, *woman*!" he would scream at any indication of her insurgence. "You have no college education! I'm a fucking genius! I put the first American spacecraft on the moon! You've never done anything important!"

If our mom had been willing to rely on her own resourcefulness, she could have accomplished just about anything—even mutiny. Regardless of his scientific degrees and expertise, our father stepped on her to attain each level of his success. I learned at a very young age how to identify a narcissistic, chauvinistic asshole and vowed that I would never put up with one. Just as soon as I was old enough to have a choice.

Mom always appeared beautiful and well composed on the evenings Dad brought home business associates for dinner. Chris and I were also expected to perform at our highest level. This usually included a piano, violin, or French horn recital, along with the touting of our most recent academic and athletic awards. I remember right before one such evening, when I was nine years old, lying at the foot of Mom's desk, writhing in pain. There was so much movement inside my gut I thought my intestines might explode at any moment.

"Shhhhh! Quiet!" Mom hissed. "I *have* to get this done before your father gets home!" She was half dressed, with curlers in her hair and dinner in the oven. When I expressed an opinion about the cause of my agony, she shouted, "I said be *quiet,* Carine! Go to your room and lie on your stomach! It's probably just gas!" Fortunately, she was right about the gas. Unfortunately, I learned to just lie down and keep quiet.

Marian leads me back up one flight into what was our family room, where Chris and I demonstrated our architectural prowess with elaborate fort making. We stripped our beds and emptied our shelves, stacked books onto table corners to secure sheets for ceilings and blankets for walls. There wasn't a pillow spared; we needed them all for hallways and doors. Sometimes Mom and Dad would let us sleep inside the fort overnight. Chris carefully removed one precarious anchor and read to me by the glow of his camping lamp. There was usually popcorn involved closer to bedtime, especially if the television was being utilized as an interior fixture.

Today, next to a large couch sits a pedestal antique smoking stand. Traces of ammonia linger with the ashes. The carpeting has been pulled up, no doubt from too many times ole Charlie didn't make it outside. The tack strips remain unattended along the edges of the baseboards.

"Watch your step," Marian warns. "I've got to replace the carpet soon." She dodges the rows of sharp nails as she leads me down the hallway to a bedroom and half bath. "I just use this room for storage now," she says as she opens the door, and I take a quick peek at what was my bedroom for a short stint as an emerging teenager.

"You still get camel crickets?" I ask.

"Whoa, do I!" exclaims Marian, and we exchange a wince of revulsion.

The fact that our house was always neat and clean did not keep these nasty insects from invading the half-sunken ground floor and basement below. What appeared to be the result of a demonic union between a spider and a common field cricket, these fearless creatures blended perfectly with the plush brown carpeting and attacked—rather than avoided—any larger moving target. Every morning I had to hunt and kill four to five of these disgusting bastards before I could safely get ready for school.

Marian and I continue to the sizable laundry room, which served as another avenue to flee outdoors. I am once more amazed by the muscle of seventies-era appliances when she points out the same washer and dryer that Mom taught me to use. A new fridge sits where our deep freezer held extra meats for Mom's dinners and extra bottles of Dad's gin.

As we walk back through the hall, we pass a closet that provided access to a crawl space beneath the stairs. *Chris and I used to hide in there,* I think, and I am completely unaware that I've said it out loud until I notice the disquieted expression on Marian's face.

Up the stairs and back on the kitchen level, Marian ascends another flight to the bedrooms. Suddenly my leather boots become lead. I look away as an excess of emotion quickly collects, then falls, smooth and fluid, down my cheek.

"Why did he hate them so much?" Marian asks gently. "I read the book about your brother, and I saw the movie. Why did he have to leave like that? Were your parents really so bad?"

I sigh at the innocence of her question, one that I have been asked too many times, by too many people—an ignorance based on a lie that I helped to sustain, a lie that I once believed to be necessary. "Honestly"—my voice cracks—"compared to our reality, the book and film were extremely kind to them."

ON THE DAYS WE DID NOT PICK UP on signals of slamming doors and elevated voices fast enough, Chris and I were damned to bear the brunt of our parents' latest battle. Their dispute would begin with a barrage of insults, then escalate to Dad chasing Mom up the stairs and throwing her around until she eventually landed on the vintage walnut-stained bed set in the guest room, where it appeared he planned to choke her to death.

"Kids! Kids! Help! Look what your father is doing to me!" she would scream out between breaths.

"Kids! Get in here *now*! Look what your mother is making me do!" was his pathetic defense.

I would scream at him to stop and try to push him off her. Chris— three years older and wiser from his own injuries—would quickly pull me back, until I learned to watch from the doorway. We were forced to witness, and then wait. We waited in fear of what would happen—not just to our mom but also to ourselves—if we left before being given permission. We learned early on that if you haven't managed to run before the bear smells you, the best course is to just stay really still. Eventually Dad would release Mom, without apology, and she would collapse into the doorway with us.

"I'm sorry, kids," Mom would shriek toward Dad as he walked away, "but when I got pregnant with Chris, I got stuck with your father!"

I remember Chris crying desperately, in anguish over being born, apologizing for causing such trouble.

Our parents' hatred of one another needed an additional outlet as their brawl dissipated. Undoubtedly, this would result in a recollection of Chris's and my most recent heinous crime of childhood: forgetting a chore or perhaps sticking our tongues out at each other while fighting over who got the last Oreo. We would then be instructed to choose the weapon for our punishment. Dad and Mom would wait down on the main level, just off the dining room at the bottom of the steps. Chris and I would take the customary walk down the hall and into our father's closet.

Hand in hand, we looked through his assortment of belts, trying to remember which ones hurt the least, which buckles lacked sharp edges. If we chose incorrectly, he would surely drag us back in here to select a much more suitable option himself.

"Hurry up, goddammit!" he roared while spilling his gin.

Having made our selection, we started back down the hall: me hyperventilating, Chris consoling, "Don't worry. It will be over soon." As we dragged our feet down the staircase, Dad seemed excited while he sat waiting on a dining room chair. He forced us down together, side by side across his lap, and then yanked down our pants and underwear, slamming his palm against Chris's bare ass and running his fingers across mine.

The snap of the leather was sharp and quick between our wails. I will never forget craning my neck in search of leniency, only to see the look of sadistic pleasure that lit up my father's eyes and his terrifying smile—like an addict in the climax of his high. Mom looked on, I imagined fearful to intervene yet also with a certain satisfaction, as if she were a victim observing a sentencing. We were getting what we deserved. We had ruined her life with the weight of our existence, trapping her in this hell.

When Dad was done—the length of the punishment varied depending on his level of inebriation—we usually retreated to Chris's room and hid under his bunk beds until we were called to dinner. As we passed the flank steak and mashed potatoes, the discussion circled around everything but the day's conflict: what we were learning in school, what big contracts they had recently acquired, how smart we were, how rich they were, the next renovation happening to the house, or the upcoming family vacation. The only acknowledgment of the events that had just occurred were veiled stories about how other children who overreacted and talked about such things were separated from each other and thrown into foster homes.

Dad was cunning enough not to leave marks on any of us that would be noticeable to outsiders. Both our parents seemed ignorant of the deeper emotional wounds they were inflicting. "Don't be overly dramatic," we were told. "If it's not visible, it isn't really abuse." We needed to be more grateful for all the advantages we had in life. We knew from watching the news that we were better off than lots of kids, and we assumed that most households were similar to ours. It was our normal, and we became acclimated to it.

"Hey, are you all right? Do you want to go up?" Marian snaps me back to today.

"I'm sorry. Yes, thank you, I'm fine," I answer, less than convincingly. "It's a lot to take in."

"I'm sure it is," Marian concurs, "but sometimes it helps to work back through some things, doesn't it?" I am touched by her willingness to walk me through this catharsis, and I follow her upstairs.

The first door she opens was my room. I point out where I had my bed and my vanity—my collection of stuffed animals as a kid, my collection of makeup and hair products as a teenager. The next door was Chris's room.

"Would you like a few minutes to yourself?" Marian offers sweetly.

"No, I think I'm okay, thanks." I know full well that I would be completely incapable of containing my emotions if left alone in this space.

I show Marian where Chris had his bunks and his play table, always set up with hundreds of army men. The little figures of green plastic seemed to come to life as he described the battles to me, and I convinced myself that he was a brilliant strategist. Ultimately, a full-size mattress and study desk took over the artificial war zone.

I am secretly relieved when Marian opts not to show me the guest room. "I've got all my ironing in there—too messy!" She laughs. And again with the master bedroom—there was no reason to drag the tour into Marian's private space. The only fond memory I have of that room was one classic day when our cat, after being kicked by our father, proceeded to steal into his closet and methodically piss in all his shoes. Chris and I gained a lot of respect that afternoon for the Russian blue we called Pug.

I thank Marian for her kindness as she walks me back out to the front yard. We exchange cell numbers and email addresses. I embrace her for giving me the chance to revisit this place, to remember the good with the bad.

Before I pull away from the curb, I envision Chris sprinting toward me on the street, Buck fast on his heels, me with stopwatch in hand cheering him on to beat his latest personal running record. One last look at the yard recalls the building of snow forts, storing our frozen ammunition in hidden bunkers in preparation for a surprise attack from the other neighborhood hoodlums out of school for the day.

What I initially saw as a property suffering from neglect now appears to just be a very relaxed home. Exhausted from the charade it hosted for the better part of two decades, it is no longer expected to uphold any impression, no longer required to hide any sins. It is what it is. It might not look as pretty, but it now lives with peace, and I find myself envious. I watch the house get smaller and smaller in the rearview mirror, until it finally disappears.

PART ONE

WORTH

> . . . I want to go up to them and say Stop,
> don't do it—she's the wrong woman,
> he's the wrong man, you are going to do things
> you cannot imagine you would ever do,
> you are going to do bad things to children,
> you are going to suffer in ways you have never heard of,
> you are going to want to die. I want to go
> up to them there in the late May sunlight and say it,
> . . . but I don't do it. I want to live. I
> take them up like the male and female
> paper dolls and bang them together
> at the hips like chips of flint as if to
> strike sparks from them, I say
> Do what you are going to do, and I will tell about it.

—Sharon Olds, excerpts from
"I Go Back to May 1937," *The Gold Cell*

CHAPTER 1

M Y PARENTS' BEDROOM was fairly large for a sixties-era upper-middle-class home in Annandale, Virginia. It was simply yet elegantly decorated in blue and white. The light carpet looked plush and warm yet felt prickly due to the Scotchgard that protected it from stains. The squared edges of the sturdy teak furniture were seamless and smooth. Not long after my seventh birthday, just a few days before entering the second grade, I sat on the white bed, legs crossed around the day's stuffed animal of choice, attempting to braid my shoulder-length hair while Mom folded laundry. As was often the routine, I became lost in thought, admiring a picture on my mother's dresser. This image seemed special to me, not just because there were very few pictures displayed in our home but also because it looked like something out of a fairy tale. My mother stood beaming in the rose-hued portrait, a beautiful smile on her flawless face, her bouffant beehive, dress, and pearls reminiscent of a Cinderella storybook. Beside her stood a handsome prince. His kind eyes welcomed you into the safety of his broad shoulders.

"Who's that, Mom?" I asked.

She looked up from the pile of clothing, and I couldn't tell if her puzzled expression was due to the tangles my fingers were creating or the sea of socks she was attempting to reunite. "What?"

"That man in the picture." I pointed. "Who is he?"

She dropped her hands to her sides, tilted her head, and gave me an answer I would never have expected. "Oh, Carine, don't be silly. That's your father!"

Although the mother I knew rarely smiled and had a different hairstyle, it was obviously her in the picture. But my father was completely unrecognizable. I was staring at a stranger, one who clearly loved my mother. I imagined his hands rested peacefully at her waist. His head leaned slightly toward hers, as if she might turn at any moment with something important to say.

Over a decade later Chris would tell me the true history behind that mystifying photograph. Through Chris, other family members, and my own recollections, in time I pieced together the entire story.

Back in the early 1960s, before I was born, my mother was a beautiful young dance student fresh out of high school. She left the small town of Iron Mountain, Michigan, for the dream life of affluence and prestige she believed awaited her in sunny Los Angeles. Her name was Wilhelmina Johnson. Friends called her Billie.

My mother was the third of six children born into a hardworking, low-income family. The siblings shared one bedroom in a tiny house built by their father and nestled in an expansive pine forest. I remember Grandpa Loren as an accomplished outdoorsman, with a body that seemed too thin, skin that seemed too thick, and a smoldering cigarette permanently attached to his right hand. He had great hair—a lush wave of deep brown and silver that flowed straight back until it disappeared behind his ears. His voice was gentle and kind when he spoke to me, to my brother, or to the wildlife around his home, but it grew harsh when he criticized my Grandma Willy—for being overweight, for the mess that accumulated indoors, or for being lazy. Grandma—a thoughtful woman who always had her hands busy crocheting, making crafts for her next church bazaar or gifts for her many grandchildren—barked back just enough to let him know that she had heard him and was choosing to ignore him.

I remember Mom often speaking about her difficult childhood. How they had very little money, how she had to endure the brunt of Grandma's aggression, which was not aimed back at the proper assailant. But she also spoke of the solace she found along the wooded trails where she led tourists on horseback as part of the family business and the comfort she found in the peaceful snowfalls of a long winter.

At eighteen, Billie was bright and eager but also naïve. She thought the dance lessons she'd taken in Iron Mountain could be parlayed into a career, but after several fruitless attempts to develop her talent in the bustling entertainment capital of California, she tagged along with her roommates one day to apply to be a stewardess. Although her slight figure fell within the strict requirements of the era's airline industry, her height did not measure up to her adventurous spirit. Unafraid of hard work and determined to succeed in her independence, she created a fallback plan with her excellent typing skills and landed a secretarial job at Hughes Aircraft. There she met her new boss, Walt McCandless.

Walt was a respected leader in his division and quickly climbing the ladder. In the decade after the Soviets launched Sputnik, the U.S. space program was well funded, and the Hughes operation in California was large—the epicenter of the effort to prove American dominance in space. Walt wore his lofty position well. He was well educated, a hard worker, and a talented jazz pianist with a voice that made ladies at after-hours socials swoon. He was also a married man with three children and another on the way. Billie was attracted to his success. Walt noticed.

I can imagine my father as my mother must have seen him. When he walked into a room, he commanded it, his magnetic hazel eyes daring you to look away. But when he laughed, his eyes watered, making him look far less dominant. He swept you up in his knowledge about books, world history, music, travel, and science. He knew how to make a perfect omelet and how to make his smooth singing voice heard over an entire congregation's. His fiery temper made you watch him as you would a volcano, awestruck by the intensity even as you wanted to get out of its way. You wanted to do everything you could to please him, and you drove yourself harder and harder to receive the nod that said he was impressed.

And I can imagine my mother as my father must have seen her. She was easy to fall in love with. She was a gifted homemaker who could resurrect a dining room table someone else had discarded on the street and serve up a delicious and healthy casserole concocted from a week's worth of leftovers. When she ice-skated, her dance background showed in every elegant move of her wrist or smooth turn across the ice. When my parents danced together, my father's movements became graceful, too, because she led him so well. She was refined, she was determined, and she was unfailingly loyal— though toward the wrong person.

I'd like to think they knew better. I'd like to think they tried to stop themselves. Eight years older and well aware of his influence, Walt took immediate advantage. Billie—old enough to know it was wrong yet youthful enough to let desire override her conscience— willingly pursued the affair. Walt convinced her that he was going to leave his wife, Marcia, as soon as the time was right. The problem, he told Billie, was that Marcia refused to grant him a divorce. He went so far as to keep a separate apartment for a while, to convince Billie he was trying to extricate himself from the marriage. But in truth, Walt had no intention of divorcing Marcia—or of letting Marcia ever divorce him.

Walt and Marcia's history was long, and she was a very different woman from Billie. Marcia was quiet in nature and inclined to avoid conflict. She came from a small family with strong-willed yet devoted, loving parents. She was a few months older than Walt and had grown up with him in the small town of Greeley, Colorado, about fifty miles from Denver. They began to date when Marcia was just seventeen. Though Walt showed signs of aggression during their courtship, Marcia told me he never hurt her until after they were married.

Marcia had been reared with the values of her community, which had been founded as a sort of utopia, a place where all who breathed its air would shun alcohol, worship together, and raise strong families. She had every reason to believe her childhood sweetheart wanted just what she did, so when her father asked her on her wedding day if she really wanted to go through with it, she said yes.

By the time Walt and Billie began their relationship, however, Marcia had grown weary of Walt's history of indiscretions. One day while tending to Walt's dry cleaning, she found Billie's ID in one of his jacket pockets. When she voiced her suspicions, she remembers they were met with a vile mix of aspersions, threats, and violence—all easily anticipated by Marcia and her three young children, Sam, Stacy, and Shawna. Another daughter, Shelly, had just been born. The family life Marcia envisioned had become a distant dream.

The affair continued into the following year, when Walt in his arrogance began to flaunt his relationship with Billie, not bothering to deny it and even orchestrating moments when Marcia would see it firsthand. Once when Marcia and Walt were out having dinner together, Billie came into the restaurant with some of her friends. She was eight years younger than Marcia, who recognized Billie from the ID in Walt's jacket. "Hi, Walt," Billie said coyly, smiling directly at Marcia as she passed by.

Soon after this incident, she told Walt for the first time she was going to leave him, and she tried to pursue a separation over the next several years. But Walt had an imperious drive when it came to the women in his life, and needed to make them feel trapped into staying under his control. Whenever Marcia showed her resolve to follow through with a divorce, his propensity for physical violence amplified. Marcia gave birth to another son, Shannon, just three months before Billie gave birth to my brother, Chris, in February 1968.

In a desperate attempt to protect her reputation, Billie scheduled a portrait sitting for her and Walt and sent the picture to the Iron Mountain newspaper as a post-wedding announcement. They appeared to be the perfect couple and Billie the epitome of success, a shining example of what was possible in a life outside the limitations of her small Michigan hometown. She went so far as to send pictures to her family of her and Walt on a trip together, claiming it had been their honeymoon. Of course the marriage could only exist in her mind, but she lied to herself enough until lying to others became second nature. She was learning from the master.

Walt acquired a home for his second family with Billie, a little beach-style bungalow on Walnut Avenue, and divided his time between the two residences. Marcia quietly struggled to find the means to follow through with a divorce, while Walt continued his oppressive reign over her life and her children. Shawna remembers being terrified of him during one such incident, when Shannon was just a year old. The tirade her dad unloaded onto her mom resulted in Marcia being left alone again to tend to her worried children and a new injury. A future visit to the doctor would confirm that Walt had fractured a vertebra in Marcia's back.

I WAS BORN THREE YEARS AFTER CHRIS, in July of 1971. The stress in Billie's life began to lift, with a progression of Walt's promises seeming less hollow. He spent more time with us and paid more attention to Billie. She was also busier than she'd been before, because she now tended to two young children and their father and had started selling Jafra Cosmetics.

My father continued to tell Marcia all about my mom; Marcia says when he left her for two weeks out of every month, she was made to understand that he was staying with his second family. He was proud of having produced so many offspring and saw no reason to hide his other children from her. In fact, he envisioned us all eventually living together under one roof, and by way of convincing Marcia, pointed out that my mother made a fantastic pot roast—Marcia's least successful culinary endeavor—but he said that Marcia's spaghetti sauce was much better. Marcia remembers that in response, she quipped, "I didn't know you were a Mormon fundamentalist, Walt."

The two families wouldn't come to live in the same house, but my father kept a special phone line in the office of his home with Marcia that no one was allowed to touch. All the older kids knew that phone line was for Billie.

Marcia wanted out and went back to teaching in order to save money. My dad showed up on payday and asked for her check. "It's already in the bank," Marcia explained as she continued making dinner for her children.

"In our account?" my father asked.

"No, in mine," Marcia said in her understated way. Dad punished her, but she won the day—her money remained in her account, in her name.

My mother's awareness of Marcia was much less clear, and it remains confusing to me how much she actually believed and how much she just chose to believe. I also don't know if my dad's violent and threatening behavior toward my mother began before or after Chris was born. My dad claimed to be working out of town for the two weeks out of every month he was living back with Marcia. But Dad's secretary, Cathy, tired of her role in the charade; when my mother called the office one day about an order Cathy had placed with Jafra and mentioned Walt's business trip, Cathy told her Walt was *not* out of town. When my mother told her she must be mistaken, Cathy replied that she was looking right at him. My father's excuse for his latest deception was yet another false claim—he concocted a ridiculous story to appeal to my mother's compassionate side, saying he couldn't desert Marcia because she had terminal cancer.

There were repeated encounters like this between my father and both women, some that led to angry confrontation, others that were just shrugged off out of fear, frustration, or convenience. But for anyone who cared to see the truth, it was obvious: Walt was not leaving Marcia.

In time, the women in my father's life reached a forced acceptance of the bigamous situation. Dad even dropped Chris off with Marcia while my mother was giving birth to me. Though the two women were rarely in the same place at the same time, all their children began to spend time together in varying combinations. Marcia occasionally took care of Chris, and Marcia's kids visited us on Walnut Avenue.

Then, on a balmy summer morning in 1972, a knock on the door began to weave yet another strand into this expanding fabrication. Mom remembered standing face-to-face with an officer of the court. Maybe my father would never leave Marcia, but Marcia had decided yet again to leave him—and this time she was determined to follow through. She had filed for divorce and had listed the Walnut Avenue address as the location for Walt to be served. As Mom looked through the petition of complaint, she came to the section where dependents were listed: Sam, Stacy, Shawna, Shelly, Shannon . . . and Quinn McCandless. Quinn's name was a surprise. Billie knew the others, of course, and had had the older ones over to her home on numerous occasions. But surely there couldn't have been another baby with Marcia, one Billie didn't know about. She would have known. Walt would have told her. Mom immediately loaded three-year-old Chris and me into the car and drove by Marcia's house. There she saw Marcia out in her yard, watching five of her children play and holding a sixth—a toddler—on her hip. According to the court petition, Quinn had been born just before Christmas, 1969.

The evidence of our father's continual dishonesty was too large to ignore, and my mother was infuriated. She even packed Chris and me up and sent us away, to her parents in Michigan. But in a pattern that would become all too familiar, she soon forgave Dad and retrieved us. Quinn wasn't his, Dad insisted.

Mom chose to believe him.

Shortly before Marcia had filed for divorce, Walt had beaten her so badly that Sam—who was thirteen years old—called the police. When they got to the house, they'd simply asked Dad to leave and not come back. But Marcia was no longer concerned about the lack of protection from police or Walt's next menacing act. It didn't matter, because *she* was leaving. She sold the house, packed up their six kids, and moved back home to Colorado. Then Dad got a job that moved Mom, Chris, and me to Virginia. Distance now separated the two families, but we were intertwined and always would be.

———————

THEN AND FOR THE YEARS TO COME, I knew my half siblings only as fun, cool playmates who would pick me up, play with me and Chris, and then leave until next time. As a little girl sitting on Mom's bed, my hands playing in my sun-bleached curls, I knew none of this puzzling history.

Instead, I knew sometimes we had a large family, and sometimes we didn't. When we didn't, it was Chris and me, partners against the evil forces of the world. When our family was larger, it felt like the Brady Bunch, but with a lot more yelling. There were group outings with Dad and Mom; there were visits with family and friends. On one occasion, my mom had made all the girls identical green dresses to match her own for a party we attended, and we all wore our hair in matching fancy updos. Shawna recalls feeling special, finally included by way of these thoughtful gifts from Billie, and beautiful. To partygoers, we were the darling and closely blended family. But what Shawna remembers most about the day is the way her stepmom required the dresses back when the party was over and the pictures had been taken.

When friends asked what grade Shannon was in, Mom would tell them he'd been held back as a way of explaining why he and Chris were in the same grade. Sometimes our parents would claim that one or more of us did not biologically belong to the family—usually that was to explain Quinn. As the child born between Chris and me, he was incriminating evidence. The level of pain and confusion for me and my siblings was determined by our ages and ability to understand.

Somewhere along the line, Mom had become Dad's accomplice. "Your father is so good to provide for Quinn," she would say to me. "Since he doesn't have to." Anyone could see, she elaborated, how much like Marcia's "good friend" Quinn looked. In truth, it was obvious Quinn had Dad's jawline, laugh, and gift for working a room.

The summer I turned seven, Dad rented a house from his friend and colleague, Ted Pounder, in Altadena, California. He was working as project manager on the Seasat 1 launch program—the first satellite designed for remote sensing of the earth's oceans with synthetic aperture radar—and the house allowed all the kids to spend time together while he did so.

It was a wondrous experience for me to have all my brothers and sisters in the same place at the same time. On my parents' bad days, Sam, the oldest at nineteen, analytical and responsible, substituted as something of a father figure, leading us all outside to the pool; Stacy, eighteen, creative and nurturing, became the mother. Shawna, fifteen, was sweet, accommodating, and unashamedly girlie—always more content painting her fingernails than getting dirt beneath them with the rest of us. Brash Shelly, fourteen and gorgeous, was Walt's daughter in so many ways and yet always able to channel her intensity toward loving and protecting those who mattered most to her. Shannon, ten, was strong and fun, but then quick to become withdrawn and angry, and also highly sensitive. Chris, also ten, was always leading the gang in one adventurous endeavor after another.

Quinn, eight, was easygoing and gentle, boyish to his core, and incredibly cute.

At seven years old, and befuddled by the number of times I had heard that Quinn was not really my brother, I had a misplaced crush on him—one that was easily noticed by the oldest children. One night we had a dance party in the house, and Shelly teased me relentlessly every time I blushed when Quinn grabbed my hands to swing me around.

We swam almost every day that summer in the large pool in the backyard. We took sailing trips to Catalina Island on Mr. Pounder's boat. We went to Disneyland, where we reveled in the freedom of our parents' distraction, and on days we didn't have anything planned, we set off on long treks around the neighborhood. Sam and Stacy had jobs and were only able to spend a couple of weeks at the summer home. Shawna's visit was also shortened, because she developed mono and was sent back to Marcia. So, it was Shelly we looked up to for the rest of the summer. She had a tough interior underneath her long red hair and perfectly freckled cheeks. Having inherited Dad's green eyes and his forceful disposition, she was not one to accept the poor behavior of our father and her stepmother without commenting within earshot of them both. "I guess I'll take everyone outside . . . *again*," she'd say pointedly when things heated up. When we went out for dinner and Dad told everyone what they would order, Shelly spoke up. "No, I don't want a Greek salad. I'm having a Caesar salad." Dad wouldn't argue with her.

Of all his children, Shelly seemed to revere our father the most—though that reverence could quickly turn to fury. Outside, near the Pounders' flower garden, I overheard her telling Chris about how she used to sit in an open window at their Colorado home for hours on end, looking out at a flower bed of marigolds and waiting for Dad to visit on a day he'd promised he would. Dad wouldn't show up, so she came to hate the sight of marigolds. She demonstrated her dislike of the flowers by picking one from the soil, plucking off its head, and grinding it into the patio, the orange and red petals staining the concrete in a fiery display. Chris made his own pattern with another bloom, for good measure.

The casting was complete. Everyone knew their place; everyone had been given their lines. Eight children were extras in the show, with limited access to the script. We would all have to unravel the mystery in our own time. The foundation was set for a lengthy spectacle that sharply contradicted the truth.

CHAPTER 2

Saint matthew's United Methodist Church was just three miles from Willet Drive. A quick drive on a rushed Sunday morning, but a long walk for a nine-year-old and a twelve-year-old.

"Look at this, Carine!" Chris exclaimed with outstretched arms. "If we were in the car, we'd pass by all these colorful leaves too fast, and all we'd smell would be Dad's cigarettes!"

I was well aware that the change of season made Chris's allergies unbearable, and I appreciated him putting a positive spin on the situation for me. Though it was only nine A.M., it had already been a long day.

Chris had been the first to hear the yelling that morning and had come into my room to rouse me.

"Carine, wake up, quick!" he whispered, pulling the covers off me.

"What? What time is it?" I asked, still half asleep.

"Hurry. Come into my room."

He led me by the hand as I stumbled out of bed, several stuffed animals falling to the floor, along with my comforter. As we snuck from my bedroom door to his, the shouting from below electrified the air in the hallway and stung my still groggy senses.

"We're supposed to leave for church in an hour. I don't think they're going," Chris said. "You stay here." He nodded toward his bed. "I'll grab us some breakfast."

"No, don't go down there," I warned. "I'm not that hungry."

"It's okay," he assured me. "They're working on something. They'll stay in the basement. I'll be right back." He returned shortly with two peanut butter and jelly sandwiches and a couple of Cokes. As we sat on his bed and ate, we tried to determine the subject of today's clash. Something about Dad not respecting Mom's contribution to some proposal that was due the next day. They were working against a deadline, and that meant today's fighting would remain contained, at least until the work was finished.

"Fuck you!" Mom yelled as she slammed the office door shut and stomped up to the laundry room. As we heard the washing machine begin to assault another load, she returned to the basement, and on it went.

This Sunday morning was slightly unusual in that conflicts were typically suppressed until the hostility boiled over onto the breakfast table. Then a temporary ceasefire would be called in time for us to trade pajamas for church clothes and march out into the backyard for pictures in our prim costumes. "Smile! *Now!*"

Chris and I always dutifully donned our disguises as the perfect little kids in the perfect family. In these childhood photographs, Chris looked like a tiny gentleman. His suit was ironed and starched, his hair neatly combed. Only his defiant stare threatened to expose the truth. I, on the other hand, in frilly dresses and bows, wore the smile my father demanded.

"Go get dressed and meet me at the front door," Chris instructed. I knew without asking him that my brother and I were still going to church.

When I came down the steps, I saw him waiting for me, holding my jacket. "Here, it's cold," he said, tossing it to me.

We knew the route well. As we went past our neighbors' peaceful homes on Willet, all we saw were people walking their dogs or raking leaves. But as we neared the church, we saw other families that were also headed to Saint Matthew's.

We sat in the Sunday school classes our parents used to teach, listening to the new teacher talk about God. Then we made our way into the church, greeting Reverend Smith on the way in. After he shook our hands, he looked around expectantly for our parents. But before he was able to quiz us on where they were, the next person in line shook his hand and Chris and I rushed in to take our seats.

We felt safe standing amongst the congregation. It was familiar and right. We sang "The Old Rugged Cross" and "Rock of Ages," the warmth of the lyrics wrapping around us as we watched our fellow acolytes light the candles on the altar. The room smelled like Pine-Sol and flowers, but mostly like the perfume of all the women who wore too much. We sat quietly and listened to Reverend Smith sermonize about the will of God and the truth and peaceful beauty realized in a life that served Him.

Reverend Smith always looked to me like he was surrounded by a holy glow. I thought a lot about his description of God and what that God had to do with me. It was always an odd concept. Was God like the reverend described? I imagined an ethereal being with a long beard, a white light, a warm presence. Or was God like the Wizard of Oz, all-powerful and good, so long as you didn't cross him? Or was I supposed to fear God? Was he like my dad, who liked to invoke His name when he wanted me, Chris, and Mom to never question him? "I am God!" he would shout. "Nothing I say or do can be wrong!"

I looked over at Chris, who looked as serious as he always did in church. I knew that, like me, he was enchanted by the idea of a Father's pure and unconditional love existing somewhere outside of our reality. We talked broadly about what we believed in, and sometimes spirituality hit home in a more personal way. There was the night Mom had told us that Uncle Phil had died. Uncle Phil wasn't technically our uncle but the husband of Ewie, a woman who'd been like a grandma to us. Uncle Phil was kind and sweet, and always showed us funny magic tricks. His was my first experience with death. The night we learned about Uncle Phil, Chris saw I was sad and let me curl up with him. We lay in his bed and compared our visions of heaven and the angels, wondering what Uncle Phil might be doing up there with God and if God liked quarters being pulled out of his ears or cards that somehow appeared and disappeared. I held a pint-size bucket of green slime in my hands, and I turned the rigid container around, trying to look introspective.

"What are you doing with that?" Chris had asked.

"Uncle Phil gave this to me," I said.

"It's not about the *things* he gave us, Carine," he said softly. "It's about the memories. You can't touch those with your hands. Everything you can touch with your hands is just *stuff*."

Sitting on the wooden pew with Chris in church, I wondered if he was right. We accepted Communion when it was passed around, and as the dry bite of bread and the sweet grape juice touched my tongue, I thought, *Well, these are also* things, *but they have great meaning*.

After services were complete, we made our way down to the social hall. As we passed by the membership portraits lining the hallway, I saw my family as other members must have seen us in our Olan Mills special: cute and smiling kids, happy parents, the perfect Christmas-card family.

We looked, I thought, like Denise Barker's family. Denise was my best friend and lived just down the street from us. It was during after-school playtime and sleepovers at her house that I realized what was happening at mine perhaps wasn't that normal and probably not okay. Her house was always immaculate, like mine, but quiet. I didn't really comprehend how boisterous my personality was until Denise's very sweet and reserved mother had to warn me on several occasions that if I did not lower my volume, she would have no choice but to send me back home. Denise and I would retreat to her room, doing our best to refrain from giggling. She had two older brothers who played a lot of soccer, and Denise took piano lessons. They went to church every Sunday as a family and they prayed before every meal, even if it was McDonald's Mondays. Denise's dad was a highly educated engineer who worked in a similar field as my dad, and they crossed professional paths from time to time. I wondered what Denise's dad thought of mine—if he assumed my dad was as stellar a husband and father as he was a scientist. Whenever I saw Mr. Barker disciplining his children, I was struck by how rational and even-tempered he was. His face changed from its amiable norm to something stern yet not threatening. He actually had a conversation with his children and listened when they replied. And they weren't afraid to reply. It was completely foreign to me. I reeled in my gregarious behavior and spent as much time as possible at Denise's house. I'm sure her parents didn't have a perfect marriage. But I never heard them say a cross word to each other, nor about the other to any of their children. Most noticeable to me was the way her parents looked at each other; I realized what genuine admiration, respect, and kindness were supposed to look like. They had a perceptible pride in what they were fostering within their family and accomplishing together through their children.

Chris and I finally arrived in the social hall to the smell of Krispy Kreme donuts—my favorite part of church. Chris handed me two dimes, as my mother usually did. I plunked them into the green plastic basket and retrieved one cinnamon and one powdered from the boxes of sweet deliciousness. As I alternated a bite of one donut with a bite of the other, to achieve the perfect combination, I heard other parents asking Chris where ours were.

"Oh, we came with friends today," he answered to one. "They're out of town; we're here with neighbors," he told another. They smiled at us and said, "Well, give your parents our love."

We put on our coats and began to make our way home.

"Do you want to cut through the woods?" Chris asked. I did. Taking the detour on the way home would keep us away a bit longer. Plus, Chris always cheered up when we were in the woods; he loved nothing more than when our family hiked in the Shenandoah, and he often provided captions to the scenery, as if he were preparing an image for *National Geographic* magazine. Chris loved to look at every type of plant, animal, and bug he hadn't seen before on the trail and point out those he did recognize. He enjoyed walking along small streams, listening to the water as it traveled, and searching for eddies where we could watch the minnows scurry amongst the rocks. On one Shenandoah trip, while we were resting at a waterfall, eating our chocolate-covered granola bars and watching the water pummel the rocks below, he said, "See, Carine? That's the purity of nature. It may be harsh in its honesty, but it never lies to you."

Chris seemed to be most comfortable outdoors, and the farther away from the typical surroundings and pace of our everyday lives the better. While it was unusual for a solid week to pass without my parents having an argument that sent them into a negative tailspin of destruction and despair, they never got into a fight of any consequence when we were on an extended family hike or camping trip. It seemed like everything became centered and peaceful when there was no choice but to make nature the focus. Our parents' attention went to watching for blaze marks on trees; staying on the correct trail; doling out bug spray, granola bars, sandwiches, and candy bars at proper intervals; and finding the best place to pitch the tent before nightfall. They taught us how to properly lace up our hiking boots and wear the right socks to keep our feet healthy and reliable. They showed us which leaves were safe to use as toilet paper and which would surely make us miserable downtrail. We learned how to purify water for our canteens if we hadn't found a safe spring and to be smart about conserving what clean water we had left.

At night we would collect rocks to make a fire ring, dry wood to burn, and long twigs for roasting marshmallows for the s'more fixings Mom always carried in her pack. Dad would sing silly, nonsensical songs that made us laugh and tell about the stars. "Come on, Dad," I'd say. "With all you know about space, you have to know if there are aliens. Are there? Tell me, please!" Dad would grin mysteriously and dodge the question. "Space is vast, Carine. We've only been able to explore a tiny part of it. Maybe they do exist; maybe they don't. Maybe they live among us and we don't even know it!"

Later, in our tent, Chris and I would curl up in our hunter-green and navy-blue sleeping bags, the soft linings covered with pictures of mallard ducks. On particularly cold nights we'd zip them together, and Chris would whisper, "Carine! Shhh. Listen . . . I'm pretty sure there's an alien outside our tent." Depending on my mood, and on the level of noise in the forest, I would either panic or laugh.

Though the wooded grove shortcut from church was nothing like the Shenandoah, Chris made the most of it. He told me about all the different trees, and we collected leaves that had fallen from each. We looked for the empty shells of the cicadas that had sung to us all summer. The bugs always climbed up the trees before shedding their skin for a new life. We loved to spot their old armor piled up on the ground, no sign of the cicadas in sight.

———

A FEW WEEKS LATER, Dad went away on business. He was gone for several days and it was like the house's vibrato changed frequency, lowering until it could barely be felt at all. We made chocolate chip cookies with Mom, and I snuck bites of the dough even though she warned me I'd get worms.

"After the cookies are done baking," Mom announced, "we're going to go on a drive and do a little house hunting."

"What's house hunting?" I asked.

"We're going to find a place for the three of us to live."

"Not Dad?" Chris asked.

"No, not Dad. Just the three of us. I'm going to get us out of here. We shouldn't have to live like this anymore."

Chris and I exchanged a wide-eyed look. *Finally!* we thought, but neither of us dared say it.

"I've been to see an attorney," Mom continued. "I'm going to leave your father."

Warm cookies in hand, we climbed into the Suburban and drove around town, eager to spot FOR RENT signs in front of smaller houses on streets that were just far enough away. Chris sat in the front, wrote down the phone numbers, and talked about his friends who lived near one place or the other.

"Look, Mom, that one has a swing set!" I pointed.

"That one has a basketball hoop!" Chris said when we passed another.

"Look at that flower bed," Mom said, shaking her head. "What a travesty. I could put some petunias in there and brighten it right up." In front of the next house, she said, "I know this one doesn't look like much, but imagine the potential! All it needs is a fresh coat of paint on the windows, doors, maybe the shutters. It'll come to life and we'll have gotten it for a bargain."

She looked stronger with every mile we traveled. Her eyes and shoulders lifted and her voice had an exhilaration to it as she told us about her meeting with her attorney, Doreen Jones.

When we got home, Chris organized his army men so they'd be easy to pack up, and I organized my stuffed animals. The notepad of rental phone numbers sat next to the phone, with Mom's notations about whom she'd left a message for. When Dad returned, Mom told him she was divorcing him, that the three of us were moving out. A massive fight ensued, one in which Dad beat Mom down even more with his words than with his hands: "You're stupid, Billie! You don't even have a college degree. I can see to it that you can't get a good job, and there's no way you can take care of those kids on your own!" He peeled away her strengths until all her insecurities were exposed. Then came the salt in the sugar jar. He gave Mom an expensive token from his trip, and all was forgotten.

The next time Dad left, we went house hunting again. And the time after that. *Doreen says* this and *Doreen says* that—Mom would chirp about her most recent meeting with the attorney. With each trip, Chris took less interest in writing down the phone numbers of rentals, until he stopped bringing a notepad altogether.

Occasionally I lost patience with my mom's unwillingness to leave Dad. I'd pack my little red vinyl suitcase with essentials, like my favorite pajamas and stuffed animals, throw in a couple of Pop-Tarts, and announce *I* was leaving. I'd get as far as the end of the street before realizing that no one was coming after me. I'd return to the house, but instead of going inside, I would climb into the Suburban and lie down until someone came out to retrieve me. "If I could drive," I contended, "I'd be out of here."

Sometimes Mom kept her resolve to divorce Dad longer, and Chris and I were summoned for a sit-down with both parents to discuss important matters. "You each need to say who you want to live with. And we need to know that right now," they'd say. To answer correctly was impossible. The chosen parent would look smugly at the other in victory, while the odd one out would scream at Chris and me for being so cruel and unappreciative of all that they had sacrificed on our behalf. This summons to appear and decide came frequently, always with the same outcome.

But when we were older and the divorce bomb was launched into the air, we caught it and kept it alive, tossing it around and examining aloud with our parents what a great idea we thought it was, daring them to finally follow through with it and bring the relief of an explosion. All the while, the house hunting continued. In time, Chris and I viewed the drives around town as just that: drives. And when we were old enough to stay home alone, we declined to get in the Suburban at all.

"Okay, kids, I'll be back soon. I've seen some great options over in Mantua. You'll see!" Mom enthused, though we didn't really listen.

MY OLDEST SISTER, STACY, always said her life began the day Marcia took her and her siblings away from Walt. They didn't have much money, and Walt's child support payments were sometimes inconsistent; with the distance Marcia had gained for herself and her children, Walt could no longer control them, and money was the one weapon he had left against his ex-wife. Marcia contacted authorities three separate times to collect back pay from Walt.

In addition to income from Marcia's jobs, they relied on church friends and family to help them get by. "Do what you can, with what you have, where you are," wrote Theodore Roosevelt, and the quote inspired Marcia through the most difficult years. Walt's parents sent birthday and Christmas presents and back-to-school clothes. Walt and his siblings had come from a volatile home, but with Walt's musical and academic talents he was regarded as flawless, especially by his mother, Margaret, who reportedly doted on him. But as loyal as she remained to Walt, even she could see that her son had not done right by his first wife.

Marcia's parents were immensely reliable with their support, helping their daughter and grandchildren both monetarily and beyond. They watched the kids when they weren't in school while Marcia worked, and they helped care for them when they were sick. It wasn't an especially easy life, but it was peaceful and loving.

It was sometimes a little uncomfortable when Marcia's kids would visit us in Virginia, because Chris and I had a lot more material things than they did. We had new skis, new bikes, the latest styles in clothes and shoes, newer models of everything electronic that Marcia's kids didn't even have older versions of. We were the ones Dad always provided for. Yet they never complained when it was time to go back home.

Our siblings came in different groups, usually, for several weeks at a time, but then Shelly came to live with us for her last two years of high school. I was ten and Chris was thirteen.

Soon after arriving, Shelly realized she'd underestimated how bad things were. For much of her life she'd witnessed Dad beating her mom, but now she was witness to Dad and Billie violently assaulting *each other*—sometimes physically, always verbally. Mom often ignored Shelly, and Dad traveled so much he was barely around. When Mom did acknowledge Shelly's existence, it was usually to bark an order at her or chastise her for some wrongdoing. But Shelly was committed to staying in Virginia. Hardened from past experience, she proved to be even tougher than Chris was. We learned from her what it looked like to stand up for yourself.

When Dad next traveled to Europe, he took all three of us kids with him, as well as Mom. When Chris ducked into nudie magazine stores in Amsterdam, Shelly told Mom he was checking out tennis shoes a block over. Though she had his back, Shelly and Chris bickered like crazy on that trip, once even to the point that Chris screamed that Shelly was going to kill him after he'd teased her too much. When we were all in the car one afternoon, Dad reached his limit with them. "I'm going to pull this car over and spank both of you!" he said. Shelly laughed at him. She was seventeen, much too old to be spanked, plus she had our father's number: he'd never laid a hand on her before.

Perhaps because they were so similar, Dad had a soft spot for Shelly. When he'd spent time with Marcia's kids in California, he'd made them all line up outside his office door, to come in and be smacked one by one for whatever the baseless infraction of the day was, his sturdy frat-house paddle firmly in hand. When it was Shelly's turn, though, he told her he wasn't going to hit her. She should scream out loud anyway, he explained, so the others wouldn't know. She felt the special treatment was because she saw him for what he was, and he knew it.

One night while Shelly was living with us, I was taking care of my daily chores in the basement—organizing some office files; Windexing the glass-fronted cabinets and tabletops; ensuring that Dad had one pen in each color of blue, black, red, and green, in soldier formation, awaiting him on his desk alongside one yellow and one white lined pad of paper stacked beneath one green steno notepad. Upstairs, Mom was making dinner. I could smell the ground beef and cumin as they sizzled together on the stovetop—taco night. Dad was working on his own creation on the piano, concocting a rendition of a Bill Evans song. Evans was just one of the many jazz greats Dad taught Chris and me to appreciate; Miles, Ella, and Duke were also favorites. The soft thump of the piano pedals began to form a repetitive pattern on the wood floor above me as he delicately worked a decrescendo into a specific chord progression again and again.

"Jesus Christ, Walt!" I heard Mom implore from the kitchen. "Do you have to keep playing that same line over and over like that?"

"Yes, Billie!" he yelled back to her. "And if you knew anything about music, you would understand why!"

I had already finished all my less-than-challenging sixth-grade homework and knew Chris was doing his in his bedroom. I trotted up the steps from the basement and saw Shelly lying back on an array of pillows on the family room couch, studying for a world history test. Her long red curls fell softly around the headphones that covered her ears. She had her bare feet and polished toes up on the coffee table, textbook on her knees. Her Walkman was turned up so loudly I could hear every word of Supertramp's "Take the Long Way Home."

She turned off the music when she saw me.

"Now, Carine," she mimicked, "you'd better make sure that I have one blue pen, one black, one red, and one green all lined up next to my notepads. And they better be set up parallel to the lines of the wood grain on the desk. Do you understand me?"

"It's impossible to line up a straight edge with walnut wood grains," I mused. "The grain isn't straight."

"Oh, whatever, little Miss Smarty Pants!" she teased back.

"What are you reading about?" I asked.

"Wars," she answered flatly. "As if I don't know enough about that already."

"*Totally,*" I answered, trying to sound like a high schooler. It didn't work; Shelly gave me a small smile and reached for the buttons on her Walkman. Desperate not to lose her attention, I thought quickly of another subject. "So," I began.

"So?"

"So . . . we're doing a sex ed unit in school."

"Okaaayyyy." Shelly looked at me quizzically. She probably thought I wanted her to explain the birds and the bees or something, which I didn't. Not really. Mainly I wanted to ask her—had wanted to ask her for a while, actually—to explain what the deal was with Quinn. When Quinn and Shannon had last visited, I'd heard them whispering with Chris about something, and I had a pretty good idea what it was. But the boys shut down as soon as they saw me. Maybe my big sister would answer, girl to girl.

"So . . . how is it that Quinn's older than me and younger than Chris?" I ventured. "I mean, how is that even possible?" The pieces of my parents' history were starting to become clearer, but the edges were still blurred and I had yet to grasp how they all fit together.

"You're just figuring that out now?" Shelly's eyes widened as she paused and waited for me to solve the puzzle. After a minute, she looked at me intently. "What about Shannon?" she pressed. "Haven't you ever noticed that Shannon's birthday is only three months before Chris's? They're the same age, Carine. Did you ever think about that one?" She waited again as I tried to comprehend how the multiple explanations I had heard could still make any sense. "Never mind," she finally sighed. "Tell you what. We'll talk about it when you're older."

Feeling thwarted by my youth, I sniped at her, "Don't you think you might do better in school if you didn't study with that music blaring in your ears?" I'd gone for a sore point, and I'd hit it. Shelly was undoubtedly smart, but she struggled to meet expectations, while I easily brought home the mandatory straight As.

Shelly's striking green eyes flared, then narrowed. Then her freckles melded as her nose crinkled up and her lips curled. "Shut up, you little shit!" I successfully dodged the large white pillow she threw toward my head. But as I walked up to my room, I was only mad at myself. I really wished I'd pressed harder instead of teasing her. I still wanted to know the truth.

SHELLY WAS A GOOD STUDENT but not a great one. As long as she brought home Bs and Cs, my parents would not allow her to join any extra-curricular activities or student-organized outings. When the senior ski trip plans began and again they told her she couldn't go, she decided she'd had enough and went on the trip anyway. But she had an accident on the mountain and had to return to our house with injured pride and a blown-out knee, wearing a full cast up to her hip. Dad was doing extended work in Germany and Mom grudgingly helped her recover.

On the night Dad got back, a vicious fight started up between Mom and Dad. Shelly immediately took Chris and me out to dinner to keep us all out of the way. By the time we returned, the house was silent. When Shelly got home from school the next day, Mom greeted her. "You need to leave tonight," she said. "And you are not welcome back in this house." Mom then left for the evening.

Though Dad might have favored Shelly, he did not stand up for her against the woman he'd begun an affair with before Shelly had even been born. When he got home that evening, he helped Shelly pack.

Shelly moved in with her friend Kathy's family for a short while before finding an apartment to share with some college kids, where she slept on the floor of their walk-in closet. She worked nights as a cocktail waitress to get by until she would graduate. I didn't see Shelly again until she was invited by Mom and Dad to stop by to say hello and take pictures on her way to prom. When I asked Shelly why she had come back for such a farce, she replied, "I guess I was just wanting to feel some sense of normalcy." She'd see Chris in the hallways at Woodson High, and he'd tell her that Mom sometimes checked with the high school to make sure Shelly was there and not cutting. He let her know he had her back.

Although my father did nothing to stop Mom from kicking Shelly out, late on that evening Shelly left I heard him cry for the first and only time. I was upstairs and heard a howl like an animal caught in a trap. I followed the wailing down to the basement and was shocked to see my father sitting at his desk, his face completely covered by his hands, his fingers stretched from ear to ear. It looked like he was trying to disappear.

———————————

CHRIS AND I, INSPIRED BY SHELLY'S DEFIANCE, took on the role of detectives when it came to the reasons for our mom and dad's arguments. We stayed aware, listened carefully, gathered evidence, and met to discuss whatever was the case at hand. Our investigative skills improved with age and experience.

In school, we were both learning about the negative effects of drugs and alcohol and the signs of substance abuse. Our parents reinforced the lessons with their own threats of what would happen to us if we were ever caught using. We were conscious of the Jekyll and Hyde effect we witnessed on a regular basis within our own parents, relative to the daily intake of his gin or her wine. Then one day we found a questionable plastic bag in one of Dad's coat pockets. We took it down to the basement office in search of a confession.

"What is this?" Chris inquired with eyebrows raised, his right hand holding the evidence in the air, the other resting confidently on his belt, feet at the ready.

"What?" Dad looked up, annoyed with the interruption. The surprise in his eyes turned into a scowl. "That's tobacco."

"Doesn't look like tobacco" was Chris's retort.

"It just looks different. Give it to me!"

"*Why* does it look different?" Chris didn't back down as Dad snatched the proof out of his hand.

"I bought it on my last business trip to Europe, and it's none of your goddamned business! Why are you two going through my things anyway!" he yelled. "Tell them it's tobacco, Billie!"

"It's tobacco," she obeyed, but the daggers she shot at him with her eyes said something else. A titanic fight ensued, up through every level of the house until we were all in their master bedroom.

"Fine! It's marijuana!" Dad finally admitted after pushing us away and throwing Mom around the room a few more times. "It's for my glaucoma!"

"I'm calling the police!" Mom screamed and moved toward the phone.

Dad rushed through the room again; we all flinched, but he passed by us and ran into his closet, screaming the usual threats. "Go ahead, Billie! You'll see where that gets you and the kids!"

I gasped at the size of the marijuana bag he resurfaced with. He held it high in the air and announced, "I've done nothing wrong! My doctor gave me this for my eyes! It's perfectly legal!" He continued his rant as he stomped into the bathroom, red-faced and furious, and began to flush the contents of the bag down the toilet. "Fuck all of you!" he shouted between flushes. "I'll just go blind and you will all be left out on the street to starve to death!"

"If it was really from your doctor then you wouldn't care if Mom called the cops!" Chris insisted as he looked back at Mom. She wasn't dialing the police, or anyone else for that matter. She never did.

Chris walked out of the room and I followed, satisfied we had made our point. The fight died down after that.

When we told Shelly about it a while later, she laughed hysterically at the ridiculousness of the entire incident. For my part, I focused on my mortification that my dad was a drug abuser, destined for prison one day, I was sure. Chris's reaction was different. He was incensed by our parents' hypocrisy, and that never went away.

CHAPTER 3

A T THE END OF MY FRESHMAN YEAR of high school, I sat on the driveway brushing out Buck's thick coat—a task Mom had deemed critical to save our vacuum from an early demise.

"Hey, Carine!" our next-door neighbor Laura called out, walking across the yard.

Laura was in the same class as Chris, another cool senior. She was a bit heavyset, eternally tan, and very pretty. Her thick blue eyeliner was always perfect, and she'd recently cut her long blond feathered locks into a shorter style. Though most girls were trying to duplicate Farrah Fawcett's look, Laura was not one to conform to the masses at Woodson. I respected her.

"So"—she sat down next to me and welcomed Buck's request for attention—"I drove your brother to school today. His car wouldn't start."

"Oh! I was wondering what the Datsun was still doing here. How's he getting home from track practice?" I asked, as if she were his secretary.

"How would I know? Andy, probably," she said. Andy Horwitz was Chris's best friend and constant companion on the track.

"So . . . listen," Laura continued cautiously. "So . . . we're driving to school and talking about graduation, summer plans. I'm telling him how much I'm going to miss my boyfriend and about all this stuff we want to do before I leave for college." She took the brush from me and started in on Buck's stomach as he rolled over in delight. "And Chris is all quiet," she said, finally. "Weird. Because all he's ever talking about is how much he wants to travel. So, I ask him where he's going to go before heading to Emory. And he's still quiet and looking out the window."

"Okay?" I wondered where she was going with this.

"Well, he finally looks back at me, and he's crying! And all he can say is that he feels guilty about leaving you behind . . . leaving you alone with *them*. What's that all about? Who's 'them'?" She stopped brushing Buck and waited for my reply.

"I don't know," I answered softly.

"He was crying," she repeated.

"Well, you know how much he loves that car," I offered. "Maybe he was just extra emotional because it broke down? Or maybe he and Julie had a fight?"

Laura's eyes narrowed. "Julie? As in his girlfriend? Are you kidding? They never fight. That's not it."

I gathered up Buck's leash and collar. "I've got to get inside and study for finals," I said and retreated from the inquisition.

CHRIS DIDN'T SHARE HIS CONCERNS about leaving with me. But he also didn't need to—the thing about me and Chris was that we could give each other a look or a squeeze on the shoulder and know exactly what the other was thinking.

The awareness that he'd be leaving soon was all around us. The family buzzed around him. With the end of the school year came a steady flow of carbohydrates across the dinner table to prepare Chris for his final cross-country track meets. He was determined to perform well at districts and move on to the regional championship.

To keep things interesting, our mom pulled *The Joy of Cooking* from the shelf to improvise on her standards, inventing tasty new versions of lasagna, manicotti, ravioli—she was never one to shortcut in the kitchen with Hamburger Helper. During the meets themselves, Mom and I would rush to stand along different parts of the route to hand Chris cups of water while Dad stood, stopwatch in hand, calling out his times to him. To onlookers, we were a close, supportive family. And on those days, we were.

These track-meet weekends had replaced family hiking trips to the Shenandoah. But as Chris ran past me, flush faced and sweat soaked, I saw the same mix of determination and peace come over him that I'd often seen when we'd walked together on the trail. "Everything in my head gets organized when I run," Chris told me. "I think about all the stuff that gets me so angry, and it drives me to keep on pushing forward. I don't get tired. I always need more time to figure it all out. Even at the end of a long race, I just want to keep on running."

I joined the track team, too, only I wasn't a distance runner. I wasn't much of a runner at all, actually. The coaches had been wide-eyed and hopeful when the name of Chris McCandless's little sister had appeared on the sign-up sheet. It quickly became apparent that I did not share his speed or his endurance, and track was not going to be added to the list of school activities in which I made a reputable name for myself. The coaches remained polite in their disenchantment. For my part, honors in track didn't matter. It was another activity to keep me away from home. I never felt the need to compete with Chris. I just wanted to be like him.

Although we really had no sibling rivalry, I couldn't help but tease Chris a bit when I surpassed him in the one and only skill of playing the French horn, akin to the mellophone in my favorite musical division, marching band. Chris had rejected the band's regimented, militarized culture even before I came to Woodson to compete. The environment rankled him, whereas I excelled in both the instrument and the ethos. I liked how structured and predictable it was: march here, then move three steps there, then play these three measures. I loved to see the successful communication between us play out in patterns on the field. It took discipline and hard work, and I thrived, making section leader in short order, then first chair when we traded the field for the stage in symphonic band. I reveled in bringing trophies and accolades home—they were proof of my success, proof that my parents should be proud.

Chris couldn't have cared less about trophies or honors, and yet he was still so good at everything. He set high goals for himself and achieved them all without the pressure of knowing that others were depending on him. Whereas I didn't want to disappoint anyone else, his concern was to not disappoint himself. He was more of a solo act, while I enjoyed being part of a team. He was an improviser, while I was a rule follower. He would tease me about my conformity, telling me I was band teacher Mr. Casagrande's favorite, but he would quickly follow it up with a wink. "But I'm proud of you, Carine," he would say. "You really did a good job."

Our different approaches played out at home, too. Chris would say he wished he could see my parents more like I did—like they were a problem that could be solved if everyone just sat down and talked rationally. Now that we were both in high school, the physical violence had slowed—we were too big to be forced over Dad's knee, too fast for him to catch, and more willing to defend ourselves. Likewise, because we could now come to Mom's aid, Dad's hands-on approach to bullying her took a backseat to his constant verbal abuse, which she still accepted.

Now every time Mom and Dad fought, Chris would listen only long enough to confirm it was the same old scene, just with new dialogue. Then he'd throw up his arms, tell them they were both idiots, and take his exit. I, on the other hand, would encourage my parents to calm down, have a seat, and discuss things rationally, to try to get to the basis of the argument and solve it. If Dad's bullying included any physical threats, I would demand to know what he expected that to accomplish. I was the marriage counselor. Chris was the divorce attorney.

Dad's need for control still resulted in violence on occasion, though, as it did one day when he sensed he was losing an argument to Chris. Summer was drawing near, as was the end of Chris's high school years. I was sitting on the living room couch, looking through the yearbooks we had received in school that day. Mom was ironing Dad's dress shirts. My trip down memory lane of the 1985–86 school year was interrupted as the most recent cause of dispute surfaced once again: Chris's summer plans. Chris was eager to hit the road with the Datsun immediately after graduation, and Dad was incensed that he didn't see the logic in having a predetermined travel plan to submit for our parents' approval.

"Why can't you just understand that not having a plan *is* my plan?" Chris implored. "I don't know exactly where I'll be. That's the whole point, the freedom of it. I've been so structured with school and sports and work—everything has been scheduled and laid out for me. I just want to get out of that mundane existence and purely enjoy life for a while. I'll decide on the fly where I want to go next."

"You will not leave this house without giving us an itinerary for where you'll be, week by week!" Dad demanded. "You're being completely irresponsible! How do we even know you'll return for college?"

"What? How can you call me irresponsible?" Chris challenged. "Was it irresponsible of me to study hard and get good grades? Was I being irresponsible to work two jobs to make money for college and save up for this trip? How about how hard I trained for these last cross-country meets? And of course I'm going to Emory. Why would I go through all of that if I had no intention of going? What

I have no intention of doing is laying out my entire summer on paper, making everything predictable and destroying my chance for adventure." He continued, "If I'd made you a list, it would've been a fake one just to appease you, and you wouldn't have known any better. I'd simply throw it out the minute I walked out the door."

It was hard to deny Chris's logic. He waited patiently for a response. Dad stood there staring at him, at a loss for words, his eyes and nostrils flared. The red on his face spread until even his bald spot was completely flushed. Knowing he had won the debate, Chris turned his back to Dad and began to walk away. Dad's reaction to the defeat was so swift that I couldn't even bark out a warning as I saw him wind up his right arm like a baseball pitcher preparing to unleash the final strike of a perfect game. He lurched forward and slammed his fist into the center of Chris's spine, as if he were expecting to level Chris to the ground immediately.

Chris, not at all diminished, simply stopped moving away. Though shorter and slimmer, he was in impressive shape. His superior strength was more than physical. He saw the panic in Dad's expression as he slowly turned to face him. But Chris just looked at him with little emotion. A single puff of disgust passed over his lips and then he turned again and slowly walked upstairs. I understood. To Chris, Dad and Mom weren't worth the effort of rebellion anymore. Rather than feed the beast of turmoil, Chris just separated himself from it.

I sat to the side, wide-eyed as he walked off. I had to tell myself to start breathing again. His reaction—or lack thereof—to Dad's behavior was a victory for both of us that day. Dad looked over at me and then narrowed his eyes, a silent warning that I'd best not ever repeat my brother's mistake of being bold. I rolled my eyes back at him and returned my attention to the pages of the yearbook. I don't know why I didn't jump up to defend Chris. I guess I didn't feel that he needed my help, even though I often needed his. If it had been me in the argument, he would never have allowed it to escalate.

CHRIS'S PRESENCE IN MY LIFE felt enormous. I was surrounded by the powerful perfect pitch of his singing voice as he belted out lyrics and played the piano, by him debating politics eloquently with his friends, and by him fighting battles for the both of us when it came to my parents. I knew he wanted to protect me while also giving me enough space to learn to do that for myself. But he was a constant that I couldn't imagine life at home without. Chris was not only my buffer and my co-conspirator. He was my best friend.

My parents never seemed to read Chris accurately, the way others could. It was clear to all who knew my big brother that there was nothing typical about him. His intensity was legendary. Of the handful of Chris's closest friends, perhaps no one besides Andy understood the delicate balance between Chris's serious side and his sense of humor well enough to feel comfortable testing the boundary. Once when he was driving Andy and a bunch of others back from cross-country practice, Andy teased him about how as soon as Chris left for Emory, he was going to pursue me. At first Chris simply smiled and tried to shrug off the ribbing. Whenever Andy was at our house, he was quick to chat me up just to get a rise out of Chris, but now Andy persisted with a few renditions of how the chase would unfold. This time, even to Andy's surprise, he pushed a little too far. Chris slammed on the brakes and kicked him out of the truck. "Don't talk about my sister like that!" were his parting words. It took several minutes for the others in the car to convince Chris that it was all in good fun and to return to pick up Andy as he strolled down the street, his smirk now well under control.

People would tell me "Your brother is intense," but they would never say anything like "He's weird." They knew that just as he was protective of me, I was protective of him. But the plain truth was that he didn't react softly to things. Whenever we went bowling, he'd get so pissed off if he rolled a gutter ball, he'd stomp his way back from the lane, then throw himself down on the plastic booth so hard I expected to hear it crack beneath his slim build. I would laugh at him and say, "Geez, bro. It's just a *game*! Don't punish the booth!" He used to say, "I don't take my frustrations out on people, so I get angry at things instead." He was harder on himself than anyone else. He intensified the air around him, and people picked up on that, even if they didn't understand it.

He was the same way in his romantic life. He didn't discuss these things openly with anyone but Julie, but his feelings for her grew to be years ahead of most of his friends' feelings for their girlfriends. His emotions were years ahead of where they should have been, probably.

Julie Carnes was a year younger than Chris, petite, and remarkably pretty. Her identical twin sister, Carrie, had dated my boyfriend Jimmy before me, and they had all remained good friends. Still the immature freshman, I sometimes failed to contain my jealousy about Carrie, and Julie was polite but firm whenever she needed to remind me not to engage in juvenile chitchat. I liked her a lot. She was very smart, had beautiful blue eyes and an amazing figure—everything a girl wanted to emulate.

Chris was shy and reluctant to ask Julie out, but she could tell he liked her. Julie was attracted to Chris's intellect and the depth she saw behind his eyes. She told a mutual friend that she thought he was cute, knowing he would be informed shortly thereafter. But their palpable crush just lingered until he finally made his move. Saying nothing at all, he simply took her hand into his one day as their group of friends sat talking on the bleachers. And they were officially an item.

On their first date, they skipped over the typical movie-and-mini-golf ritual, and instead Chris took her on a long bike ride through the state park trails and into downtown D.C., where he led her to the grassy carpet of the Mall. Overlooking the Washington Monument and surrounded by fragrant cherry blossom trees in full bloom, he removed from his backpack a full-on picnic. They dined on cheeses, fruit, and sandwiches. He brought her a cookie for dessert. He didn't try to kiss her that day, but later she told me she could tell he wanted to. They talked—about transcendentalism, existentialism, the concept of nonlinear time, which he discussed incessantly. They didn't talk about movies or sports or who was dating whom at school.

They also didn't talk about our parents, nor would they. Chris never talked to Julie about our family life, and he never invited her over for dinner. The only time she met our parents was when my mom insisted on taking pictures of the two of them before prom. If Julie pressed him at all about our parents, he became aloof and sullen. So, she stopped asking about them.

With Julie, Chris let in our parents' influence only once. On prom night, he picked her up in our father's "fancy boat" Cadillac, labeled as such because Chris hated it. He also bought her a much-too-expensive, gorgeous orchid corsage and almost broke the petals off as he fumbled to put it on her arm. He took her to The Black Orchid, one of the area's nicest restaurants, gently held her hand throughout the night, and ordered veal for them both. He had worked hard to earn money to cover the dinner and flowers. But it was the first time he, wearing an expensive suit and arriving in the Cadillac, had been willing to acknowledge to Julie that our family was well off.

Shortly after prom, Chris's attachment to Julie was even stronger. He started talking seriously with her about the future, about all the things he wanted to share with her, including traveling to Alaska—a fascination of his ever since he'd read Jack London's books as a kid. He encouraged her to read *Call of the Wild* and described the adventures he wanted them to embark on together. He told her he loved her and missed her whenever they were apart.

It turned out to be too much, too soon, and Julie broke things off. Sitting in Chris's yellow Datsun outside her parents' house, she told him that she wanted to date other people, that she just wasn't ready to be as serious as he was. He flew off the handle at her. "You really *are* just like all the other girls, Julie!" he told her angrily. "I can't believe I thought you were different!"

But as soon as his rant subsided, he pulled her close and held on in an intense hug. For as long as five minutes he kept her wrapped in his arms. Then he let her go and never talked to her again.

I didn't find out about this until years later, when Julie told me the whole story. I never asked Chris questions about their relationship—it would have been too weird. But I did notice that he was different with her than most guys were with their girlfriends. He had no strut in his step when he walked around with her; he just looked confident and content.

So, I found out that Chris and Julie had broken up the same way everyone else did—through the grapevine. It never occurred to me to ask him if he was upset. He was my big brother, my strength, and of course he was okay. He was always okay. The only time I ever saw frailty in him was when we were kids after a long day on the beach. He was maybe ten years old and had just finished a long run. Racing now against the sunset, he was so determined to finish a sand mountain by himself—sandcastles were far too formal for his taste—that even though he was getting cold, he stayed there, shivering, piling the sand higher and higher until he was satisfied with its stature. The image of him shaking remains so vivid: He wore a navy-blue bathing suit with white trim and a puka shell necklace. He didn't complain about being cold, but I saw his teeth chattering and the ache in his eyes. It made me uneasy to see any weakness in him. I hated it. I hated knowing that he was uncomfortable, and that I couldn't fix it for him.

———————————

I'D STARTED A COUNTDOWN. Three more weeks of Chris, then two, then graduation and a final family trip to Colorado, this time for Stacy's wedding.

When our siblings were older and stopped coming to Virginia as often, my parents would take Chris and me out to Colorado for visits and often took several of us to the mountains for weeklong stays at upscale ski resorts. For a couple of seasons, Shawna and Shelly lived and worked in a ski town called Keystone, cleaning condos and time-shares in between guests. Shawna was dating a minister's son named Jim, whom I thought was cute with his short sun-bleached blond hair and dark mustache. One day Shannon, Chris, Quinn, and I hit the slopes with Jim. My brothers and I had all learned to ski at an early age and had spent enough time on these particular slopes to let our overconfidence get us into trouble, and Chris liked having brothers around to be rowdy with for a change. The boys loved to find fresh powder by cutting through the wider expanses of trees from one trail to another, and although it felt like my heart jumped into my throat when I tried to keep up with them, I wanted to hang tough, so I followed behind, always holding my breath until I popped out to find them waiting for me on the other side of a tall line of pine and aspen. Jim came up behind after making sure we had all made it through okay. He moved like an expert skier, and I loved to watch the rhythm of his effortless movements carving the snow. At one point when we were all stopped and discussing where to go next, Jim noticed a new rise in the slope at a steep edge where we all knew the trail wound back around beneath it. There weren't a lot of people on the mountain, and Jim bet us that he could make the jump.

He told the boys to continue downhill to check things out and make sure the trail was clear. When they motioned for Jim to come on, he dug in his poles and hopped away, then shoved his skis side to side a few times to gain momentum and flew down the slope. He hit the jump at top speed and soared through the air with an impressive hang time, but then I heard a horrendous scream that didn't sound anything to me like excitement. I couldn't see where Jim had landed, and I also didn't see him continuing down the hill. Quinn and Chris both yelled out, "Oh shit!"

Shannon looked over at Quinn and Chris, then up the mountain to me and announced in the quite matter-of-fact way that boys handle such situations, "He's not moving. I think he's dead." I couldn't see Shannon's eyes through his goggles to tell if he was serious or not, but Chris and Quinn quickly aimed their skis downhill and raced to where Jim was. "Oh crap! We've killed Shawna's boyfriend!" came out of my mouth as I started down the mountain.

By the time we got to him, Jim was sitting up and laughing, although through accusations that we were trying to kill him to keep him away from our sister. We all agreed that it had been a very notable jump, probably some kind of a record. A few years later at Jim and Shawna's wedding, we all concurred that we were glad Jim had survived.

ON STACY'S BIG DAY, Marcia's father invited Mom and Dad out for a drink before the ceremony. His invitation seemed innocent, but once they were all seated, he led Dad on a scornful trip down memory lane. The reminders of Dad's history with Marcia infuriated Mom, and by the time they arrived at the church, Mom and Dad were in a huge fight.

Stacy was beaming and beautiful as she faced her bridegroom, Rob, at the altar. He was a very smart college student and seemed a bit geeky to me as a fifteen-year-old, but I could see that he would be strong and steady. His full and gentle heart was a good match for Stacy's wounded one. He was always sweet and attentive to her, and he noticed the subtleties that could dim her otherwise prolific smile.

With such a large and complex brood hovering in the aisle, Rob held Stacy's hand and kept looking into her eyes as the perplexed photographer asked her questions about who goes where during the progression of family photographs. Rob's hand lifted to her waist and pulled her close as the traditional photograph with the parents was attempted.

Tension pressed at the seams of the wedding, but Stacy rose above it all and didn't let it ruin her day. Dad yelled at Chris to sing for the guests, but Chris had no interest in performing for our parents that day. Mom sulked, still angry about the meeting with Marcia's dad.

These types of full-on family events were predictably poised for discomfort. Wanting to keep the mood light, Sam snuck a bottle of tequila into the reception, which my older siblings passed back and forth between jaunts to the dance floor to do the polka. I loved to see Marcia's kids all having fun and laughing together. As I watched them tease each other, I wondered a lot about what they thought of me. With Chris, I was less self-conscious. I could be wholly and completely myself with him. As the reception wound down and I watched Stacy and Rob say good-bye to their guests, all I could think about was my brother's looming departure.

As soon as we returned from Colorado, Chris headed out of town for his summer adventure in the Datsun. He said he would be back just in time to repack and get to college at Emory. When we said good-bye, he hugged me for a long time before looking me in the eyes.

"Be careful," he said. Then he drove away.

CHRIS'S ABSENCE WAS SURREAL AT FIRST. When I walked in the front door after he'd left, everything looked just the same. The couch pillows were still set up just so, and Buck still dozed in the same corner. But everything felt different. A dynamic had shifted between me and my parents, and the change was as palpable to me as if all the walls and furniture had been painted red. But at least I had Jimmy—and I didn't have to worry about Chris's annoying jokes about how I'd fallen in love too fast or his skepticism about what Jimmy wanted to gain out of the relationship.

Jimmy was a motorhead. A smart one. He drove a black 1972 Chevy Monte Carlo that he had been restoring himself. My dad—who had a love of cars himself, having owned an old GTO convertible when we were younger—appreciated Jimmy's industriousness as a mechanic. But he warned me repeatedly that I would never have a successful life if I did not marry a man of a proper profession that earned him a large paycheck. During one of his cool-dad moments, though, my father helped Jimmy and me finance a project that we all took on together.

Jimmy had found a 1969 Stingray convertible suffering inside a ramshackle shed, and we came together as its savior. It was cheap to obtain the Corvette because it didn't run and needed excessive body- and paintwork. Jimmy and I worked on the car every day during the summer, in the garage at his house, disassembling and rejuvenating her 350 engine, rebuilding her 411 rear end and four-speed transmission. He tested me on the parts, taught me how they went together, and thought I was a cool chick for wanting to get my hands dirty. While my interest in cars began as a way to spend time with him, as we got further into restoring the 'vette, I fell in love with the process of taking something that had been broken and abused and making it come to life again. And the actual mechanics of it just seemed to click for me. Watching a machine be put together was like my two favorite subjects in school—math and music—joining together in tangible form.

One day late in the summer I stayed at Jimmy's house into the early evening, tinkering with a rear differential. It was almost dark when Jimmy drove me home, but as soon as we came over the hill on Willet Drive, I saw the old yellow Datsun sitting in the driveway.

"Oh my God! Chris is home!" Jimmy had barely come to a stop before I hopped out of the car. I ran inside and up the stairs to Chris's room and busted through his bedroom door. There he was—and in such a deep sleep that he didn't even flinch. I walked over to his bed quietly. He was so extremely thin, with a full beard and haggard appearance. It made me wonder if this was what Jesus might have looked like after hanging on the cross.

Later that night, he told me about his adventures as he unpacked his backpack. He placed cans with generic black and white labels onto the table as he told me about his long drive out west, his hikes along the Pacific coast, his final trek through the Mojave Desert, taking food to people who didn't have enough to eat—exactly who these people were or how he came to feed them, I didn't know and was too preoccupied by the cans to ask. I had never seen anything like them before. There was nothing commercial about the containers, no catchy sales pitches or luring pictures. It was just . . . food.

The trip was not one I would have taken or any of his friends would have wanted to go on—drinking margaritas on a beach in Florida was more the graduation trip ideal. But I didn't think it was strange at all for Chris to trek alone across the Mojave bringing food to people who needed it. That was just Chris. Our parents didn't get it. Though Mom immediately took to the kitchen to cook everything she could think of to fatten up her son, I didn't hear "We were so worried." Instead, Chris had to listen to a lecture rehashing the argument he and Dad had had before he left: "Who do you think you are to leave without telling us exactly where you were going? You said you would call and you didn't. You said you would be back on this day and you weren't."

I knew Chris was irritated with them, but I also knew there was something else bothering him. The toll on his mind was as visible to me as the weight that had fallen from his frame. I didn't push him on what it was, though. He'd tell me when and if he wanted to.

"Are you okay?" he asked. "How did it go over the summer?"

"It was good," I said, and I meant it. "You don't need to worry about me. I've figured them out. I'll just spend most of my time with

Jimmy until band camp starts. When I'm home, it's pretty easy to just stay out of the way these days." He looked relieved.

I didn't get his usual intense hug when he left with our parents for Emory. It was an unfulfilling good-bye in their presence, but as always, we understood each other. The summer alone with my parents *had* gone well. Yet both Chris and I also knew that I was their last chance to either succeed or fail as parents, and the pressure was on.

CHAPTER 4

OVER THE NEXT THREE YEARS, strange periods of tranquility among the usual dysfunction lulled me into believing I was finally earning my parents' approval. I didn't know at the time that the reprieves were simply because I was playing my part right. I was selected for gifted programs and my grades were good. I excelled in music and marching band, becoming drum major my senior year, and won lots of awards. I had no partners to strategize with, no detectives to investigate with who might make my parents feel insecure or equally matched.

Chris was mostly absent from our daily lives. After his first year at Emory, he'd opted for a monkish existence focused on study and a definite exit date from college. His apartment had no phone to call. Letters were infrequent. I missed him, but I understood why he wasn't in touch. Then, when I did get a letter, he would say everything that was just right to say, and it usually arrived on a day when I needed to hear it. There was one letter that I would reread whenever I was feeling particularly lost:

> I don't know why it is, but our parents have two-sided split personalities, and for some reason they have reserved [the very worst part of themselves] solely for you and I alone. You are the only one who

I could ever truly communicate with on this subject, because like me you have seen that other side and experienced the trauma, frustration, and pain of having to be subservient to such oppressive personalities for so many years of our lives. The events that we suffered are so outlandish in their proportion that it is useless to try to explain them to anybody, because they will never believe you. They will think you are some kind of freak, some kind of outrageous liar and exaggerator. They [will] think that you simply couldn't handle the normal conflicts which all teenagers and their parents go through.

I agreed with Chris in that it was hard to talk to anybody except him about our parents. But I did confide in one of my best friends, a boy named Giti Khalsa. Although Jimmy and I were very close, I was more insecure around him and thus hesitated to share too much about my home life that might drive him away. But Giti was different; I always felt confident that his friendship was unconditional and without ulterior motive. Somehow he saw past my always-animated demeanor and sensed there was something brewing underneath. Giti would sit and have long discussions with me about what drove irrational behavior in people. We would try to wrap our minds around how to exist with it while not allowing it to negatively influence who we wanted to be. When I finally opened up and began telling him—although still to a limited extent—about my troubles at home, I knew I could trust him not to tell anyone else. His summation of my parents existed somewhere between Chris's view that they were completely hopeless and my view that they couldn't possibly be beyond hope.

I sensed Giti's optimistic side came from his own home life. Whenever I walked into Giti's house, his parents were incredibly welcoming and I felt what I can only describe as a peaceful balance of energy. His family was from India, and in the early years of our friendship I thought it was just a cultural thing—as tangible as the turban Giti was required to wear, the indigenous décor on their walls, or the aromas of his mother's cooking emanating from their kitchen. At that time, there wasn't a lot of cultural diversity in the neighborhoods around Woodson High, but Giti was quite social and had a lot of friends. He was an excellent student and a talented musician—a good rule follower like me, for the most part. But he had experienced his own resistance to playing an expected part. He informed his parents, after much consideration, that he wanted to break from Sikh tradition and choose his own wife when the time was right for him to marry. Then one day he came to school clean-shaven and without his turban on. Even I had never seen his hair before. It was a lustrous wavy black mane that fell down well below the waistline of his blue jeans. About a year later, he had his hair cut short. Some members of his extended family thought his parents should disown him. While his parents' beliefs in following the traditions of their heritage remained strong, perhaps the deep-rooted spiritual meaning of those same beliefs, combined with their unconditional love for Giti, simply proved to be stronger. The development of their family dynamic was beautiful to watch. I suppose I must have been envious. It was hard to find the right balance with my own parents, especially when their actions were often so confusing.

Noticing that Jimmy and I had become inseparable, Mom and Dad had several, surprisingly rational conversations with me about sex, both together and separately. They said they remembered being our age. They assumed that Jimmy was pressuring me to do it, and they doubted that I was against the idea, considering we had already been together for so long and how often I attested to being head over heels in love with him. I was absolutely positive that we were going to marry, and Jimmy had sealed the deal with a promise ring. My parents assured me that while they wanted me to wait to have sex, they accepted it was probably unrealistic. They requested that I come to them if it did happen and implored me to have faith that they wouldn't get mad. They just wanted to ensure I could take the necessary precautions to protect myself from getting pregnant. I felt grateful for their sincerity, proud of their approach.

I lost my virginity to Jimmy three years into our relationship, when I was sixteen.

Still so hopeful and bargaining that my parents would be true to their word, I went to my mother after my special night. I lied about where it happened (their sailboat) but was honest about everything else, including that we had used a condom for protection.

I had expected her to say "Thank you for coming to me." I thought she'd hug me, I would likely cry a little, and we'd have this bonding moment.

"You did *what*? How *could* you!" she screeched.

I looked at her, confused. "You told me to trust you," I said. "You said you'd be cool with it."

She stormed up the stairs to her bedroom and presumably told my father, because he boomed at me to come upstairs. As I walked up the staircase, my legs felt leaden, like I was going to have to pick out my belt of choice, but this time I was all alone. When I walked into their room, I saw my mom sitting on the toilet in their en suite bathroom—not using it but slouching on it with her head tucked down to her knees, her hands covering her eyes. She looked like she'd just been told about a tragic car accident. She looked up at me, face flushed, with this expression of utter devastation.

Dad stood next to her, his eyes flashing. "You've completely disgraced this family," he said. "You're a whore. Who do you think you are? You think you're so pretty. You think you're a woman? You're not a woman. You look like a hooker with your makeup and long hair." His eyes narrowed. "I'm going to cut your hair off while you sleep."

I sat on their bed, dumbfounded, and said, "But you guys said to come to you. You said it would all be okay. That the only thing that mattered was that I be honest with you."

"We can't even look at you anymore," said my dad.

"Just go away," cried Mom.

I walked numbly to my room and called Jimmy.

"You told them *what*?" Jimmy shrieked through the phone. "Carine, why in the world would you do that?"

"But they said it would be okay! They said they wouldn't get mad!" I tried to explain it to him through the tears that were now coming on strong. I also broke the news that it was extremely likely I'd never be let out of the house again.

"Oh geez!" Jimmy cringed on the other end of the line. "What were you thinking?"

"I'm sorry! I'm so sorry!" I cried, then I heard my parents' footsteps approaching. "I've got to hang up. They're coming! At least we can still hang out at school."

I didn't get out much after that. I stayed home while friends spent sunny days at Burke Lake, and I was rarely allowed to join them for nights at the movies. But, thankfully and surprisingly, my parents still let me date Jimmy. Perhaps they feared losing credibility in the face of my inevitable rebellion from such an edict. Or perhaps Chris had worn them down by his withdrawal from their lives and there was a twinge of fear that if they pushed too far, they'd lose me. Or perhaps they just thought it more suitable that if I had done the most abominable thing by having premarital sex, at least I was still seeing the guy. They made the whole situation as uncomfortable as possible, though, with my dad taking me to the gynecologist to get a prescription for the pill (my mom was the one who took me to every other doctor appointment in memory) and then to the pharmacy to pick it up. He asked the pharmacist detailed questions about side effects as I stood beside him, grateful yet mortified.

Jimmy and I spent most of our time at his house after that. His mother was "cool," which meant he could tell her not to disturb us in their basement and she would comply. I went to church with his family. We went to the school dances. Mom bought me nice dresses for the events and tried to convince me, unsuccessfully, to tone down my excess makeup and over-teased hair. Dad documented our automotive endeavors by taking pictures as we swapped the 454 in our 1973 Suburban with the 402 in Jimmy's 1972 Monte Carlo. It was a pure example of blind love when I willingly parted with that monster big block. But we could still get the Suburban, even with the smaller engine, to chirp second gear with its automatic trans, so it wasn't a total loss.

Meanwhile, the Stingray's exterior had evolved from a three-tone flat primer to a beautiful Chevy Autumn Maple with gold metallic that sparkled in the sunlight. To my dismay, the classic restoration outlived our romance. Jimmy and I broke up. I was in love with him, but I was feeling confused and perhaps a bit like Julie had with Chris. Then I found out Jimmy had lied to me and had kissed another girl while we were together. Still immature in matters of love, and seeing an out, I refused to forgive him. So much of me wanted—badly—to still be with him, but I felt like I had been made a fool of, so I decided not to make reconciliation an option.

I immediately started hanging out with a guy from another school. Jimmy lost interest in me and in the Corvette, which was now almost in complete working order. My dad and I finished it together.

——————————

IN THE SUMMER OF 1988, my parents completed a custom-built waterfront vacation townhome in the Windward Key community in Chesapeake Beach, Maryland. Mom's youngest brother, Travis—a drunk who was often in debt to Mom and Dad for one bailout after another—was in town, paying off his debt in trade labor, as was the customary resolution. He was adding a sauna room in the lower level. If Uncle Travis didn't have a beer in his hand, his hand was shaking. His words were always slurred, his eyes lazy. But he was a good carpenter and handyman, and Mom's brother, so they always let him stay.

My room at the beach house was a top-floor loft with a foldout couch, a deck, and a full bath. When I was just one month shy of seventeen, I woke up to Uncle Travis in my bed with his hands up my nightshirt and his beer tongue in my mouth. I'd worn a long thermal oversize nightshirt to bed with nothing underneath.

Travis was very drunk, and his movements were loose and clumsy, so it wasn't difficult to get him off me. "What the hell do you think you're doing?" I yelled, scrambling out of bed.

"I jus' thought ya might wanna 'ave sex wimme," he slurred, not meanly but confused.

I ran down to my parents' room, where they were sound asleep. I woke them up and tried to keep my voice calm as I told them what had happened, but I was shaking. Mom got Travis back downstairs. Dad stayed in bed.

The next morning I came down from the loft and heard Travis working away on the relaxation room. "What's going on?" I asked my mom. "Why is he still here?"

She looked at me with a puzzled expression. "What do you mean? He owes us money, and the sauna's not done." She suggested that I ward off future advances by not wearing my bikini in from the beach. Later, I saw my dad bringing more beer down to Travis to keep his hands steady while he worked.

I missed Chris more than ever. If he had been there, I would have gone to him and not my parents. He would have never, ever let Travis get away with this. And if Travis hadn't been forced to leave, Chris would have taken me out of there instead. But since Chris wasn't there, I spent my summer nights sleeping on the bathroom floor behind the only lockable door in the loft, until the sauna room was complete and Travis returned to Illinois.

DESPITE TRAVIS'S PRESENCE over the summer, the Windward Key house was a blessing because it gave my parents space from one another. During most of my senior year, they alternated between the beach house and the Annandale house on Willet Drive, living and working separately. Though I didn't know who, I knew only one of them would be there when I came home from school each day. Without my dad, Mom looked more like the woman she had been on those apartment-hunting drives: lighter, stronger, more content. Without my mom present, my dad was more rational, kinder. I told him I was proud that he was controlling his drinking and his temper.

The calm ended, however, when my grades started to slip. I had a tough schedule of advanced classes. For the first time in my life the answers didn't come easily to me, and I brought home a failing grade in calculus. My parents bore down hard on my lack of performance, and the more they scrutinized me, the worse I functioned. To make matters worse, whether it was from hormones or stress, my face broke out terribly, also for the first time in my life. My perfect complexion and my high GPA were both lost, and my parents accused me of being on drugs.

Giti was still the only friend I talked to about my home life, and the only teacher I spoke with about it was the band teacher, Mr. Casagrande. One day I skipped school, lied to Mr. Casagrande about it, and got caught. He was extremely disappointed in me and quick to explain just how much I'd let him down. When he confronted me about the lie, he pointed to a blue stripe painted on the wall. "Do you see this?" he asked. "If you told me this stripe was green, I'd believe you. I would doubt my own perception because of the faith I have in you."

Mr. C. and I had grown very close over the past four years. Until now, I could not remember having disappointed someone I respected. I felt a trust from him that I had never felt from my parents. It was too much for me to take. Ashamed, I broke down. "I'm so sorry," I cried. "I'm just not thinking straight." I accepted responsibility for what I had done. I also told him about some of the stress I was feeling at home, but I only touched the surface. And, remarkably, he forgave me—another first for me. His attitude was *You're a good kid. You're a teenager and you've done something stupid. Wise up. Don't lie to me again.* But what I heard through his reprimand, which I was most grateful for, was the sentiment: *And of course I love you anyway.*

Several months later, I teared up when I saw what he wrote in a letter of recommendation for me to his alma mater, Ithaca College: *One of the biggest compliments I can give Carine is that she's someone you would want your own daughter to emulate.*

The contrast between Mr. Casagrande and my parents was hard not to see. I returned home from school one day, and when I opened the door to my room, it was trashed. My closet and all my drawers had been emptied, the contents piled high in the center of my room. Atop the pile were all my prized music accolades and drum major trophies, broken into pieces. I was devastated. Mom said she'd had to go through my room like that in order to find where I was hiding my drugs. Of course she found nothing.

One week after my high school graduation, I returned home from a date with not a minute to spare before my eleven P.M. curfew. I knew my father was sleeping in Annandale that night, and I unlocked the door quietly, hoping to delay until morning the questions about where I'd been and what I'd been doing.

Before I finished turning the key, the knob suddenly lurched out of my hand, jerking me forward as the door swung open. My father, angry eyes on fire, reeked of gin. I recognized his contempt, aimed as much at himself as at me. He had been needing this release. At that moment, he saw me as just my mother's daughter.

My feet crossed over the threshold without touching it, my sandals falling to the floor as he lifted me by the neck and shoulders, repeatedly slamming me against the wall. A deep, fierce roar escaped him as he threw me onto the couch and trapped me under his weight.

"You don't do this anymore, Dad, remember? Stop!" I pleaded. "You don't want to do this. You were doing so well. Stop!"

He closed his hands around my throat to silence me. "This is your fault!" he accused. "Look at what you're making me do!"

"No! Don't!" I begged between breaths. "Please stop this, Dad!" I wrestled one arm from under his knee and began to strike him in the face. But it didn't faze him. He just stared straight at me and tightened his grip. I saw the coldness in his eyes and a panic over his loss of control, and it terrified me. He brought his face down close to mine. I could feel his heated breath and taste the foulness of the alcohol.

"You think you're all grown up now?" he seethed. "You think you're in control now?"

I jerked and freed one knee to kick him in the groin.

"You fucking bitch!" he screamed.

As his grip released, I placed both my feet onto his chest and launched him to the other end of the couch. I ran up the steps to my room and barricaded the door with every piece of furniture I could muster. Then I grabbed the phone and retreated into my closet, slamming the door on the cord trailing behind me. It did not even occur to me to call the police. I wish it had. Instead, I called my mom at the Maryland beach house.

"Hello?"

"Mom! Help me!" It was hard to talk through my syncopated breathing as I told her what had happened. As soon as my father picked up another receiver, I knew my words were unnecessary. She could easily recognize the tone of his defenses after a drunken rage.

"She's lying, Billie!" he claimed. "It was all her fault! She came home late! I didn't do anything wrong!"

I exhaled and waited for her to reply to his intoxicated nonsense.

"You know what, Carine? I think you're a lying bitch" was all she said before hanging up.

I stared at the phone in disbelief until the dial tone became rhythmic and snapped me into understanding. Admitting he had done that to me meant accepting he would do that again to her. She couldn't allow that reality.

I threw the worthless phone onto the floor and wept for a few minutes. Then I took several deep breaths, picked myself up, and walked to my bed to look out the window. Too far to jump down. I walked into the center of my room, stared at the blockade mess at my door, and screamed through it, "You stay the fuck away from me!"

The house was silent the rest of the night. I awoke in the morning to a knock at my bedroom door and my mother's voice. "Carine. Get yourself cleaned up and come downstairs." I walked down the steps to see my mother and father sitting at the dining room table. Her expression was void of any emotion. Dad played the wounded innocent, a pattern long ago established as guilt.

Mom instructed me to pack my things. "You'll need to quit your job," she said, "because you're moving to Windward Key to stay with me. Your father will not be allowed over."

I turned to him and said, "I will never forgive you for this. As far as I'm concerned, you are no longer my father." He looked back at me, his eyes wide with hurt as if I were being cruel.

As soon as I arrived in Windward Key, my mom took away my driver's license and removed the phone from my room. In less than a week, my dad was coming and going from the beach house freely. My parents told me never to speak about what had happened. They continued to live, work, and act as if nothing had. Clearly they were not the problem, so the problem must have been me.

In a last-ditch effort to "set me straight," my parents took me to see a psychiatrist. I sat in the backseat of our deluxe Fleetwood, staring at kids in other cars on the highway and wondering about the better places they were headed to with their parents as mine droned on about how this doctor was of an elite status, brilliant, recommended by one of their most affluent business associates. This doctor was very expensive, and I had better appreciate what they were sacrificing, both monetarily and in social status, to get me this appointment. I had disgraced the family yet again.

Dr. Ray's first approach was to seat us all in his office together. I sat quietly and listened to my parents tell their tales of family dysfunction, brought on by the reckless behavior of some wild, drug-addled teenage girl who had my same name but whom I had never met. I stared at my parents blankly as I listened to their charges.

Then Dr. Ray spoke to each of us privately for about fifteen minutes. I was first. As I wasn't the one writing the big check, I assumed he wouldn't believe anything I said in my own defense. His questions were prudent and tactical. I didn't concede to his careful query about any violence in the house. He asked me about my parents' accusations of drug use.

I'd known my turn would come one day. Anytime one of the kids rebelled against Walt and Billie's behavior, my parents first defaulted to "It's drugs! You're doing drugs. That's why you're acting like this!" Now it was my turn—I was the one sitting in the crazy seat.

"I've never used drugs," I told Dr. Ray. "I've never smoked pot or even a cigarette. Hell, I've never had a cup of coffee. Lots of Pepsi, though. And I did get pretty tipsy on grain punch, twice."

He wasn't amused. "Tell me, why do you think your parents brought you here?"

I shrugged, then launched into the first thing to come into my head. "My mother used to brag about my beautiful *peaches and cream* complexion," I began, "and as you can see, it's not an accurate description lately. She's completely embarrassed that my face is like this. Did you happen to notice what *hers* looks like?"

He raised his brows and nodded for me to continue.

"So she takes me to the doctor to take a drug test. Dr. Hanfling tells my mom that he doesn't think I'm using drugs. And he would know—I have to see him for sports physicals all the time. 'Billie, she's a teenager,' he says. 'Sometimes teenagers get acne. It's a terrible thing for them to go through, especially the girls. We can try some medicated lotions, or . . .' 'But look at her face!' she cuts him off. She wasn't interested in any explanation other than her own. He looks back at her like she's nuts and then, real carefully, he says, 'It can also be an inherited condition.' Well, that really pissed her off. I thought her head was going to pop right then and there and land beside me on the examination table! So, I jump right up and say, 'Just give me a cup to pee in. I've got nothing to hide.'"

"And?" Dr. Ray prompted.

"And a week later I'm putting on my makeup, trying to cover this up." I made a circle in the air around my face. "And just like one of those freakish clown scenes in the movies, her face appears in the mirror, and I jump up and around to see her standing there with a sheet of paper held up high in her left hand, and she's breathing like a bull in the ring, looking like she wants to kill me. 'How'd you do it?' she shrieks at me. 'Do what?' 'How'd you pass the drug test? I know you're using! Your face is swollen!' I just rolled my eyes and told her I thought she was crazy. That didn't really help the situation, but lately I don't know what else to do but laugh about it."

Dr. Ray dismissed me to the waiting room and brought my parents in one at a time for their own quarter hour. I was surprised when he asked to speak to me in private again. He leaned back in his chair as I sat on the other side of his desk. He had one ankle up on his knee and was forming a rectangle with his hands and a pencil. He looked straight at me over the rim of his glasses and said, "Well, your parents are really fucked up."

The words of Chris's letter came back to me: . . . *it is useless to try to explain them to anybody, because they will never believe you. . . . They [will] think that you simply couldn't handle the normal conflicts which all teenagers and their parents go through.* I'd always figured that was the case, too. But now here was Dr. Ray, believing me.

He invited my parents in to sit on either side of me, and he explained the same sentiment to them, but in a more medical manner that would not preclude his being paid. He then suggested that they each come in once a week for counseling.

As I watched the strangers in the cars beside us on the highway ride home and listened to my parents carry on, I could not contain my laughter as they degraded the prestigious doctor to a worthless quack.

Meanwhile, his last private words of advice echoed in my head again and again: "Get out of there as soon as you can."

That was already my plan.

CHAPTER 5

THE SUMMER BREEZE OFF Chesapeake Bay was comforting as I carried my bags down the tall town house staircase and loaded them into my boyfriend Patrick's car. It was midnight, July 19, 1989. My eighteenth birthday. Liberation had finally arrived. My parents could no longer force me to remain locked up in their expensive cage, and I could taste freedom in the salty air.

Patrick squeezed my knee reassuringly as I sat down in the passenger seat. I'd met John Patrick Jaimeson when I worked as a receptionist at a local Honda dealership. He was a car salesman, a college student, and a budding racecar driver from Ireland. His sharp clothes and accent caught my attention. He was small in stature with pale skin and a smattering of freckles you could only see close up. His dark eyes and dark curly hair made his appearance markedly different from the other boys I had been attracted to. But they had been boys, and Patrick was a man. Four years older than me, he commanded my attention in a way I found intoxicating.

When he first started talking to me at the dealership, he was shy but not hesitant. I noticed the other salesmen liked and trusted him and would toss him leads if they were busy with a customer when another potential buyer came in. Patrick was endearingly goofy. He'd start singing the Fine Young Cannibals song "She Drives Me

Crazy" while he danced in this utterly silly way and pointed to me, as I sat laughing behind the reception desk. He didn't have a cocky air about him, no hint of *I'm this sexy European and you're going to fall for me.* Instead, he was self-deprecating, more apt to say, *You like me? Really?*

When Patrick started taking me out, he was kind and attentive, especially when I told him what was going on at home. "That's unforgivable," he said. "I wish your dad would try something in front of me. I'd kick his ass." Within months we'd fallen in love. I felt safe with him.

Patrick's student visa would be expiring soon. He didn't want to leave the country yet, and I couldn't imagine being without him. I was slightly apprehensive when my new love suggested marriage over a casual dinner. We could really help each other, he argued. He needed me; I needed him. I would have no one without him, and without me he'd have to go back to Ireland. When I agreed to the logic of the concept, he removed the green cocktail straw from his rum and Coke and tied it around my finger—a gesture I found romantic, if unconventional. He was kind; he was cute; he was worldly. He handled all the details, making the appointments for us to get a marriage license and be wed.

But first I had to retrieve my birth certificate. It didn't occur to me that I could just order a copy, so I called home for the first time since leaving and told my mother I'd be coming by the Annandale house for the original.

"Carine?" Mom called from the basement office when I arrived. "Is that you? I'm down here."

I walked down the steps, and she looked up from her desk. I assumed she would reach into one of the file cabinets for the paperwork.

"Your birth certificate is in my purse," she said. "But you can't have it."

"I'm eighteen," I replied. "It's mine to have."

"I don't care how old you are," she retorted. "I'm not giving it to you."

I had no interest in arguing with her. I'd seen her purse on the chair next to the front door, and I knew she was baiting me, so I retraced my steps to go get it myself. I heard her a few steps behind me, so I started to run. I grabbed her purse and ran out the door, figuring I could extract the birth certificate before making it to the car, but I couldn't find it at such a fast pace.

Patrick had been waiting in the summer heat with the engine off and the windows down. I yelled frantically, "Start the car! Start the car!"

As I jumped into the passenger seat and started rifling through Mom's purse, she stuck her arm through the open window.

Some neighbors had seen the commotion, and Mom shouted, "My purse! They're stealing my purse!"

"I don't want your purse!" I shouted back. "I just want my birth certificate!"

To my surprise, Patrick put the car into drive with my mom's arm still through the window, her hand now tightly wound around the purse strap. As he slowly drove forward, he yanked on the purse and the top of her head hit the upper window frame.

"Stop the car!" I yelled.

But Patrick just kept driving slowly with this determined glare, his fiery eyes vacant to what was happening. He yanked repeatedly on the purse and my mom's head kept hitting the car.

"Stop! You're hurting her!" I screamed at Patrick. "Stop!"

Finally he stopped the car just long enough to let my mom retrieve her purse and her arm back through the window.

We drove home in silence. I felt terrible about what had happened, and it seemed more like a bad dream than reality. A few days later, I got a call from my mom when I was at work—the only number she had for me. "Come get your birth certificate," she said bitterly. "I don't care what you do anymore."

———————

A MONTH AFTER MY BIRTHDAY ESCAPE, I married my Irishman in the living room of a Fairfax County, Virginia, justice of
the peace. The nuptials were nondescript—certainly not what I had
imagined as a little girl. My long white cotton dress had a wide lace-
trimmed ruffle that fell softly from my bare shoulders. My Aunt Jan,
one of my mom's younger sisters, had sent the dress to me just before
graduation. She didn't intend for the gift to be a wedding dress, but it
was beautiful, and after examining my meager choices, I had decided
it was my best option.

As the marriage vows soaked in through my ears and fell out of
my mouth, I wondered what my brother would say when he found
out I'd gotten married. Everything felt too new to be so definite. I
wished that it were Jimmy standing beside me. I thought about the
very real possibility that I might never see my parents again. I longed
for a way to rewind my life, edit the characters, and push play again.
Some scenes needed less revision than others.

In that outdated living room full of fake flowers, and in the heat of
a D.C. August, the scene that kept replaying was Christmas—one of
them, all of them. Although Dad cancelled Christmas several times
every December, the holy day always managed to prevail. A mass
of presents would spread under the tree like a multicolored quilt of
paper, foil, and ribbon, inviting Chris and me into its folds to inspect
the tags and guess what was under cover. Aunt Jan would always try
to lighten the mood in our house with fun crafts and other creative
endeavors. She was an excellent baker, and Chris and I had special
boxes—his a snowman, mine a Santa face—that she would stuff to
the brim each year with an incredible assortment of delicious cookies, brownies, and fudge. Her little gingerbread boys and girls were
decorated to meticulous perfection.

On Christmas Eve, we would sit with our parents and the rest of
the congregation at Saint Matthew's and read the prayers. Everyone

in attendance would receive a candle. We would sing "Silent Night" as we passed the flame to one another, and each person's voice would get just a little louder the moment their candle was lit. I would feel this incredible crescendo of love and goodwill wrapping its arms around my family. "We're fixing you," it seemed to say. "You're fixed now." *Everything's going to be better from here on,* I thought when I looked at my parents and Chris in the soft candlelight. *Here we are in church; this is so holy; we have our arms around each other; we're passing light to each other; God is going to make everything better now.* I knew we'd go home to our beautiful warm house, our beautiful tree all lit up, and I'd continue to feel safe and warm.

One year when we returned from church, Aunt Jan and her husband, Uncle Marc, had contrived an elaborate production aimed at confirming that Santa was real. Dad threw metal trash can lids up on the roof, making Chris and me believe we were hearing the sleigh and reindeer land. We were both sleeping in Chris's room, and Mom and Jan retrieved us to quietly sneak downstairs. We watched in awe as Santa himself added to the gifts under the tree, played with our train set, meandering through the packages, and then, with a touch of his nose, he seemed to disappear right before our eyes. It was magic. How they managed to make thin Uncle Marc look so much like an authentic fat Santa and vanish like that, I still don't know.

No candles lit my wedding ceremony, no congregation looked on supportively. Reverend Smith was nowhere near, though the justice of the peace seemed like a nice enough guy and wore a suit for the occasion. The aroma of his lunch wafted in from the adjacent kitchen.

What would God think about me now? I wondered.

"I now pronounce you man and wife." The officiant's words cemented me at the point of no return. I was full of smiles as we signed our marriage certificate and prepared to leave and begin our new life together. Another couple walked through the door to get married just as we were walking out. Patrick's father, J.P. (John Patrick Senior), cheered and threw rice at us. He'd flown in from Ireland to be our witness. He wore a fine dark suit that unintentionally trumped his son's, complete with a rosebud in his lapel. His thick silver hair matched his weathered and deep jovial voice. He was a charismatic man, pleasantly thrilled by our union. My parents were not invited or even informed I was getting married.

Our honeymoon was a trip to Ireland, the airline tickets a wedding gift from my new father-in-law. Patrick's parents had divorced long ago, with no love lost between them. J.P. had a beautiful home out in the lush countryside, with gray stone walls and patios that sparkled when the sun's rays hit the rocks during high tea. He also had a very young wife named Wendy. "Winnie," as J.P. called her, had a melodic alto voice and waist-length strawberry-blond hair, and she was simply beautiful without a stitch of makeup. Together they had three very sweet, young, and fun daughters—nicknamed Lulu, Matti, and Izzie—who adored their father. "Daddy!" they cried when we arrived at the house, and they jumped into his arms. He tossed them up in the air and gave them hugs and kisses. When the girls weren't climbing all over their daddy, they stayed at my heels and loved to listen to my accent.

As the evening progressed, I noticed Patrick's father drinking heavily. Wendy grew increasingly apprehensive, and I saw something familiar in the faces of the little girls. By nightfall, J.P. was raging and violent. He pushed Wendy around the house while he screamed at her and the girls. He threw things and crashed into furniture in an unpredictable stupor. I was shocked and looked directly at Patrick, waiting for him to intervene. Not only did he do nothing to stop his father, he didn't seem the least bit surprised at his behavior. He had never mentioned to me that his father was violent.

"Wendy," I said and pulled her aside. I picked up the video camera that we'd used to tape the kids playing earlier in the day. "We're going to record this." She looked at me like I was crazy. "You can't just document the good stuff," I explained. "He needs to see what he's doing." My voice was calm, even strong. "Let me help you." I wanted to do something proactive to stop the violence. Wendy nodded at me, and I started filming.

J.P. sneered when he saw the camera pointed at him, but he was too far gone to tell me to turn it off, and I wouldn't have anyway. I recorded his despicable actions, his violent outbursts, and his nonsensical ranting. I captured the fear and despair in his daughters' eyes as they ran toward the camera to hide behind me. I kept the camera rolling until he had passed out.

In the morning, everyone was up before J.P. When he came downstairs from his room, he didn't look as though he'd been three sheets to the wind the night before. He wore a nice pair of slacks, a shirt with cuffs, and a sweater. As he fixed his tea and we ate breakfast, the table was silent. I spoke up. "Do you remember what happened last night?"

He was jovial and tried to laugh it off. "Oh," he said, "I'm assuming I had one too many."

"I want you to see what you did," I said, looking at him intently. "I want you to understand what it's doing to your family." I brought everyone into the living room, including J.P., who followed without argument. He looked like he had no idea what he was going to see. He sat in a chair while the girls and Wendy sat on the couch, and Patrick stood in a corner, still saying nothing. We watched the disturbing footage of what he'd done the night before in the same room we now occupied.

"Is this the husband you want to be?" I asked. "Is this the father you want your girls to grow up with? Is this what you want for them when they choose a husband?"

"You're right," he said, bowing his head. "That's terrible to see. I'm sorry I put everyone through that. I'll do better. I promise."

I'd helped make a breakthrough; I was sure of it. People *could* change. Breakthroughs *could* happen.

It would be much longer before I knew just how rarely they do.

I HAD NEVER GRASPED THAT PATRICK had a violent side, but it was as if the perfect storm had developed over the Atlantic, and by the time our plane touched down in Virginia, the seawall had crumbled and a deluge swept in. After returning to the apartment that first night home, I made a simple dinner and he became enraged. He accused me of posturing in front of his father.

"You've never cooked for me as well as you cooked for him when he was here!" he shouted. "Eh? Whadya have to say to that, ya tart? That's bollocks, that is!"

"What?" I started to back away. "Pat, what are you talking about?"

"Don't wrinkle that pretty little forehead at me like you don't know what I mean!" he persisted. "My father mentioned he may help us to buy a house and you were walking around here, cleaning and primping the place in front of him, cheffing it up in the kitchen like the perfect little homemaker. You're just after the money!"

He grabbed me by the shoulders and shoved me down onto the couch. When I stood back up, he grabbed my wrists and swung me around like a pendulum. When he released me, I crashed into a small portable oak dining stand I had placed against the wall to hold a jade plant.

His roommate, Glenn, came into the living room at the sound of the commotion. "Whoa! Patrick, what the hell are you doing?" he yelled, seeing me, fragments of the plant and its dirt spread about the beige carpeting.

Patrick snapped to attention. His face fell back into one I recognized. "Oh, Carine. I'm sorry." He apologized as he helped me up.

I didn't say anything. *Holy shit*, I tried to say to Glenn with my eyes. A panic grew in my belly. What the fuck had just happened?

NOW THAT PATRICK AND I WERE MARRIED, Glenn moved into his girlfriend's place, and all buffers were removed. As the next few weeks passed, my husband grew intensely and unpredictably violent. He threw me across rooms, choked me, forced me to have sex. He had fits of extreme jealousy if I even looked in the direction of another man. One day while I was driving down the highway, glancing peripherally at the other cars, he screamed from the passenger seat, "What are you looking at? Do you want to fuck that guy or something?" as he yanked up the emergency brake of the Chevy Z24 and grabbed at the wheel, attempting to put the car into a spin.

In a fog of disbelief and fear, I started my freshman year at Ithaca College with plans to study for degrees in music theory and performance. Mr. Casagrande's letter had helped me gain acceptance into the prestigious school in upstate New York. My tuition was provided by a college fund I had inherited from our family friend Ewie. She was one of the few people our mom had confided in about Dad's true behavior. Perhaps sensing we'd need the help, Ewie had left me and Chris money in stocks that had been put into our names.

"That money was supposed to be mine!" Mom had chided when I cashed in my shares. "Ewie only put it into your names to protect it from your father! That was my escape money!"

"Ewie was smarter than that" was my level reply.

It was a wonderful gift. Chris had managed his college fund astutely. Heading into his senior year at Emory, between the money he had earned from his jobs during high school and his wise investing of these funds from Ewie, he had doubled the size of his account and had plenty to last through graduation. He lived as inexpensively as possible, stayed focused on school whenever classes were in session, and enjoyed his adventures on the cheap during semester breaks.

I would not be as shrewd.

I didn't make it through my first semester at Ithaca. Orientation week was riddled with constant interruptions from Patrick. The blaring ring of the community phone ceaselessly echoed through the dorm hall. I cringed each time a fellow freshman leaned through my open door:

"Ummm . . . Carine, you have a phone call . . . again," then an uncomfortable pause. "From your . . . *husband*?"

I took the embarrassing walk down the hall to pick up the dangling receiver, Patrick's voice still barking through it, yelling at no one.

"You've got to stop calling like this," I pleaded. "I can't even think straight and—"

"Who's that guy who answered the phone?" Patrick interrogated. "Why is he in your dorm? Where have you been this morning? What did you do last night? Who were you with?"

"What do you mean where was I?" I answered. "I was here. Answering this phone every fifteen minutes!"

I had never known what it felt like to be in a drug-induced haze, but I imagined this was close to it. I missed classes. I didn't make any friends. I rarely left my room or got more than fifty feet away from Patrick's only means of checking up on me. He sent threatening letters and showed up unannounced. During one such surprise visit, he insisted I pull my funds out of Ithaca College and transfer to local George Mason University back in Fairfax, Virginia. He made me miserable at Ithaca, and since I certainly couldn't earn an education from my dorm, I didn't think I had a choice. I did think about how disappointed Mr. C. would be. But the person I was most concerned about disappointing was Chris.

Patrick and I went to the administration office together, and the woman who handed me my penalized refund check looked concerned. She eyeballed the stern Irishman hovering over me.

"You understand the choice you're making?" she asked firmly. "And this is *your* choice?"

"Yes, of course!" I said as I signaled for Patrick to stop glaring at the woman.

I returned to Virginia with optimism, convinced that being together again would allow a less stressed Patrick to reincarnate into the gentleman I'd fallen for. I stayed in school at Mason, but I didn't make it a priority, and I returned to my job as a receptionist at the Honda dealership. The violence and threatening behavior continued, and I fell into a deep depression. And like the good student I had always been, I excelled at the cover-up. I decorated our apartment; Patrick decorated me with some new jewelry. I replaced the perfectly good used Z24 with a brand-new speedy Honda Civic Si, white with gray interior, fully loaded. I went to music rehearsals with a smile on my face, usually accompanied by my devoted husband.

One night I answered the phone at work to hear a voice that both elated and devastated me. It was Chris. But he spoke to me in a way he never had before. He was drunk. He was extremely angry. He was not the only person on the line—Jimmy was, too—and they were at the Windward Key house. I could hear Sam, who had recently moved to Virginia to further his education, in the background, trying to calm the situation. My parents had summoned them together during Thanksgiving break for an intervention of sorts, with the uninvited key subject not in attendance.

"Carine!" Chris screamed out in a voice I barely recognized. "What are you doing? Why did you marry that guy?" I was stunned, but still my mind raced. How did he already know I was married? How did my parents know?

"Chris!" I replied with desperate excitement. "I'm so happy to hear from you!"

A continuous wail then roared through the receiver, so loud that I had to remove it from my ear. Chris sounded like an ensnared tiger. Then his words came again. "Why didn't you just marry Jimmy to get out of here? Who the hell is this guy?"

I heard "Oh, please don't ask her that." The familiarity and comfort of Jimmy's sweet voice made me wish I was there with him. There spending Thanksgiving with my fucked-up family but safely in his arms.

"But, Chris, I'm not in love with Jimmy anymore." The words were hard to choke out. I hated to lie like that. I hated for Jimmy to hear it. But I had to stand faithful to my decision to marry Patrick. I heard Jimmy groan and hang up.

"Mom and Dad found out what you've been doing! Why'd you leave Ithaca? You're destroying your life!" Chris accused.

"But, Chris! No—please! You don't understand!" I stood up and pleaded into the phone, tears streaming down my face, customers and salespeople staring at the pathetic exhibition.

Then there was just silence. He was gone again. I stared at the phone, ignoring everything and everyone else around me, including Patrick, who had been retrieved by coworkers. I couldn't understand what had just happened. Why did Chris go to see *them*? If he knew where I was, then why didn't he come to see *me*? Why didn't he trust me? Did he not love me anymore? I felt the weight of the earth compressing me further into my shitty reality.

I sat back down at my desk, transferred all calls to the back operator, took a pad of paper from the drawer, and started to write. I wrote down everything that I wanted to say to Chris. I explained all that had happened, why I had to leave, how wonderful Patrick was, and what a great life I was going to have. I was on the right track; he would see. I mailed the letter the next morning to the last address I had for him at Emory.

Watching the apartment mailbox day after day was agonizing. I knew Chris always took road trips during school breaks, but I couldn't understand why he hadn't visited me and I worried I would never hear from him again—that somehow our seemingly unbreakable connection had been severed. I was thrilled when I finally received his response. I had just returned from a class; Patrick was still at work. I tore the envelope open and started to read his reply in the elevator. His letter began:

Oh my God! I was so happy to get your letter, Carine! I was afraid you would never want to see me or speak to me again!

How he could think that I was even *capable* of not speaking to him was beyond me. Eyes glued to the page, I made my way down the hall.

I am so sorry that I spoke to you the way that I did. I should have known better than to believe anything that Mom and Dad said. I can't believe I was stupid enough to get so drunk and let them manipulate me like that! I'm so sorry for everything you have had to go through alone. Of course I understand why you left and married Patrick. I am glad he is so good to you.

I fell to my knees and began to sob. I wanted to be able to tell Chris the truth. But I told myself everything would be okay. I would be okay. Pat wasn't so bad. Things were going to get better. Why worry Chris over something I could easily handle myself?

My next letter to Chris was one in a duplicate set also prepared for my aunts and uncles—all except Travis. It included pictures from my wedding day, my honeymoon in Ireland, sitting in an Indy car on the track where Patrick had been given a test run, my new Honda Si, and our cushy apartment. All evidence of how wonderful my new life was and how successful I had been since leaving home.

The first letter I received back was from Chris, who politely remarked how nice the pictures made my life look. The careful wording gave me a sense that he was keenly aware that there was a hollowness behind the travel and material possessions. His closing sentence advised me to "Do good in school." I was not yet prepared to disappoint my brother, or myself. I was determined to straighten out my relationship with Patrick before any permanent or noticeable damage was done.

Patrick had changed quickly once before; surely he could just change back.

CHAPTER 6

I LAY NAKED IN THE BED, in silence, focused on how the warmth of my tears turned cold once they soaked into the pillow. Patrick looked back in from the doorway again. He always apologized. I had given up looking for sincerity in his words.

A warm shower helped to wash it all away. My eyes were red, my face flushed. There were no bruises to be dealt with. But I did see something new in the mirror that day. It doesn't take long for a victim to become an enabler, and I was right on course.

"How did you get here?" I seethed at my reflection. "And why the hell are you still here? *Billie!*"

It had only been a matter of months. But that was long enough.

My inheritance from Ewie alleviated the burden of yet another escape. I scoured the yellow pages for local divorce attorneys, female only. I was taken aback by the sheer mass of professionals who could make a living from rectifying poor marital decisions. My finger stopped at a name that sounded tough and gave an impression of someone full of moxie: Jody Badger.

When I first met Jody, I understood why the word "firecracker" was sometimes used as an adjective. A new Miata buzzed into the parking space next to mine as I arrived at Jody's office for my appointment. A stout woman in a snug business skirt and blazer popped out of the convertible and looked me over.

"Are you Mrs. Jaimeson?" she asked. The label felt cumbersome.

"Yes," I admitted.

"Okay, then, let's get to work," she said, and without any welcoming gesture, she walked toward the building's entrance, her thick heels rapid against the asphalt. As I followed behind her, she reminded me of Miss Piggy with shorter hair.

Jody was the sole employee at the Badger Law Office, a professionally appointed yet no-nonsense space. The empathy I had expected to see as I sat and explained my predicament never surfaced on Jody's face. Instead, she sat behind her desk with the same matter-of-fact expression I had observed less than a year prior on Dr. Ray.

She handed me some papers. "First thing you need to do is to take this down to the magistrate's office to file a complaint and request a restraining order against your husband. Once it's granted, if he comes within fifty yards of you, you call the cops," she instructed.

"Um, okay," I stammered and took a deep breath. It felt like she was speaking to someone else . . . or to this hard shell that looked like me while the part of me that could show dread cowered inside. But I wasn't looking for a therapist, I reminded myself; I was looking for an advocate. And there was no doubt in my mind that Jody would help me. I *needed* someone like her to be my bulldog.

"I'll need a check today for a retainer, and we can get started on your divorce."

Divorce.

As I sat in Jody's office writing out my check, I realized that I was the one who held the live bomb now, but this time I could control the end result: sovereignty from Patrick.

I didn't tell Jody anything about my childhood, but she seemed to have a keen awareness of how I ended up in her office that day.

"You've taken your first opportunity at independence and made a complete mess of it," she told me, "and it's going to get even messier before you're through. Pay attention and learn from the cleanup." I didn't say anything aloud, but I vowed I would.

SEEING JODY BADGER was my first act of resolve. Telling Chris the truth about Patrick was the second.

Our letter writing had continued fast and furious. In fact, we had some of our hardest, most intense conversations in letters over the next several months. Chris didn't have a phone, after all—and even if he had, he wasn't the type to talk on the phone for hours on end. And we lived too far apart for a casual visit. "I was wrong about Patrick," I wrote one day, my hand trembling but my words resolute, "and I've filed for divorce." I told him about everything that had happened and how foolish I felt. How I'd tried to make it work, warning Patrick I would leave him, but my husband had only scoffed at the threat. I wrote about how I'd gotten a restraining order against Patrick, and that since he'd been served papers I hadn't heard from him. Our lease had been up at the apartment, anyway, and I'd left it for another, smaller apartment in the same complex. It was a dumb move. It was a luxury apartment I should have realized I couldn't afford, but it was familiar and easy. I needed easy. And I didn't know where else to go.

As I enlightened Chris about the facts of my failed marriage, his understanding words brought comfort. He was proud of my strength to leave an abusive man. "Mistakes are okay as long as we learn from them," he wrote back, without directly pointing out the financial ones that I was now making. He understood I had to come to this realization on my own.

Chris had his own truths to reveal in our letters. He told me that the summer before he'd left for Emory, when he'd walked through the Mojave delivering food, he had also traveled to our old neighborhood in California and visited with former neighbors. He had asked what the neighbors knew about our family, comparing what Walt and Billie had told *them* with what our parents had told *us*. For the first time, Chris had learned the extent of our parents' deception

and the truth behind the photograph on our mother's dresser. Marcia
and Walt had not divorced amicably, as we'd been told. Walt had
still been married to Marcia when Chris and I were born. We were
illegitimate.

My first thought on reading his letter was *clarity*. It was like all
these scattered images from my life—of Quinn, of Shannon, of my
parents' contradictory stories—came together to complete a full picture. Chris had again been senior detective, and he'd given me the
final clue that made everything else make sense. I was livid, but I
wasn't talking to my parents anyway. I wasn't about to pick up the
phone and call them on their bullshit. I knew that would be a waste
of time and just invite more lies. I was leading my own life now,
rocky though it was.

A few days later, though, I began to feel something else: gratitude.
I'd known that something was wrong with Chris when he returned
from that California trip. I could see something weighing on him,
and now it made sense. He'd been furious with our parents and unable to act on what he'd learned. He couldn't confront them and stir
up toxicity that he would then be leaving me alone with. He couldn't
tell me and burden me with the same anger he carried, because I had
no choice but to live with them for the next three years. If he'd been
an only child, I'm sure he would have vented his outrage the moment
he'd returned home from California. But because of me, he'd kept
it all in.

Now I had left, too. I was no longer living under Walt and Billie's
roof, and Chris could tell me the truth. It was a truth that plainly still
haunted him, though he'd had three years to work through it. But as
mad as he was, entirely forsaking our parents was never as easy as we
thought it would be. I'd seen all the rest of our siblings do the back-
and-forth dance of "I'm done with them" and "Well, maybe I'll try
again." It was never simple.

Our mom was many people rolled into one. She was the soccer
mom who brought oranges to all of Chris's games and the epitome

of organization who headed up his Indian Guide and my Girl Scout meetings. She made us elaborate and beautiful Halloween costumes and helped us put the finishing touches on every school project with her artistic talents. We learned how to drive a stick shift under the safety and guidance of her even teaching temperament. And she had a sense of humor, dressing Chris, Shannon, and Quinn up like chauffeurs whenever we went to pick my dad up from the airport after a business trip . . . in the Cadillac, of course.

And our dad wasn't *just* volatile. He also took us to Europe and delighted in watching us experience different cultures and strange gourmet foods, sometimes ordering for us in the local language so we wouldn't be dissuaded from trying something we would normally think was gross. Sometimes when Chris and I built forts in the family room, Dad played guitar and sang his silly songs in front of the fireplace and pretended we were camping. He gave me a children's book about a dollhouse when I had the chicken pox, inscribed with love to his "Woo Bear." He could speak for hours about the wonders of space exploration and had fascinating accompanying visuals, blueprints of his designs, and three-dimensional models of his image-capturing radar systems that now floated about the atmosphere we were orbiting amongst. When I was little, with every trip he returned from, he brought me treats from the plane. I loved the shiny foils and different languages on the packaging, and I loved the taste of the honey-roasted peanuts. Dad could never walk by a snack without eating it, so the fact that he had saved them for me meant the world. I don't remember exactly when he stopped bringing me the peanuts. What I remember most is how I started hiding when he returned home, instead of running for him.

Our parents hurt us constantly, but they were our parents. We wanted to believe the warm moments showed who they genuinely were, not just another part of the show they put on.

But something had changed for Chris, and it wasn't just time. He was finally finished. In one of his letters, he wrote why:

They are just totally beyond hope and there is no way to ever bring
them back into reality. Over twenty years of lies and meaningless
games has reduced them into a permanent state of psychotic insanity.
That's why I don't stay in contact with them and why I don't like
to talk to them . . . [I]t's like a disease which can be caught, if one
is exposed to it too long then one will begin to feel its detrimental ef-
fects upon one's own soul. I don't know how to explain it really, but
what I do know is that ever since I got away from them my life has
been so much more happier and joyful. . . . They always say . . .
"Just wait until you have kids" as if to imply that our family rela-
tionship was a "normal" one, and that we are just immature, un-
learned little brats who don't understand that this is the "normal"
way family relationships progress . . . And I guess they think that
as we "mature" we are going to become more like them, and that
when we have our own families we are suddenly going to "see the
light," and that we will admit that they were "excellent" parents
and that all of our earlier complaints were just the unfounded imma-
ture whinings of little spoiled brats . . . . I bet this is just how they
think. This must be the way they self-rationalize the entire situation
to themselves . . . So I'm finished with them for good.

He'd written them a long letter, he said, that detailed all the emotional trauma and abuse we had suffered as kids. How their actions
had caused him to lose all respect for both of them. He said he'd really laid it all out and explained how damaging it had been to grow
up within a household filled with such painful behavior, so many
lies, such hatred and contempt. He went on:

This was just about four weeks ago. I felt for sure that that let-
ter would finally shake them into some kind of reality . . . . And
then, just a few days ago I get this stupid postcard from Colorado

*where they are skiing, and all it says in reference to my letter is
this: "Thanks for your letter—saving them for your children to
read one day!" Can you believe that? There they go again with
that contemptuous-pompous stance. They just completely ignored
everything I said in the letter! . . . Since they won't ever take me
seriously I'm just going to play along with their little acting game.
For a few months after graduation, I'm going to let them think
they are right, I'm going to let them think that I'm "coming around
to see their side of things" and that our relationship is stabilizing.
And then, once the time is right, with one abrupt, swift action I'm
going to completely knock them out of my life. I'm going to divorce
them as my parents . . . I'll be through with them once and for all
forever.*

Chris had a knack for expressing himself in dramatic letters, and
he always filled both sides of the paper with small print. He'd given
them their last chance in a desperate attempt to be heard, I realized.
His long letter, their quippy response, and his upcoming graduation
made for a perfect break.

I never told my parents of the plans Chris had shared with me to
eliminate them from his life, but I had no doubt that he meant it and
would follow through with the same vigor he did every decision he
made. He wrote to me about hitting the road after graduation. He
said he had not yet decided exactly where to go first. His only plan
was west. He assured me that he would come to visit me before he
headed off on this journey of undetermined length or distance. He
asked if he could stay with me and hoped that I could make arrangements to have Buck during that time. I was ecstatic at his request
and wrote back immediately that my door would be forever open
for him.

Meanwhile, my interaction with my parents was virtually non-
existent. We talked as little as possible. But in May of 1990, in a rare

reunion, I traveled with them to Atlanta to see Chris graduate from Emory. I was vague about Patrick's whereabouts, not wanting them to know I'd filed for divorce. Our interaction was forced but cordial.

I remember being surprised at how tan, fit, and muscular Chris was when he met us at the airport. He was always in great shape—he had a runner's build—but this was different. As he carried Mom's bags, his biceps stretched the limits of his short-sleeve seams. Chris wasn't trying to show off his bulk; he just didn't care to purchase new clothes. I recognized the effort that it took for someone of his relatively small stature to develop such size and strength. He had been building his endurance. He was training for something. I made a mental note to buy him some new clothes when I got back to Virginia.

As I watched Chris cross the stage, diploma in hand, I was so proud and excited for him. After the commencement, the two of us took a sentimental drive in the reliable old yellow Datsun back to his place. It was a shock to walk into my big brother's apartment, so stark and bleak, and different from mine. It was a complete contrast to his childhood room, which Mom had painted blue and decorated with the model planes he used to put together with Dad. In his college room, there was just one picture on the wall, a poster of Clint Eastwood from his favorite film, *The Good, the Bad, and the Ugly.* Even that seemed more symbolic than decorative. His unadorned mattress, absent of the typical comforter with matching pillows, was supported by concrete blocks and two-by-fours. His desk had been created from similar materials, but it did its job—upon it sat his beloved books. The dwelling suited Chris, who was all about substance without ornamentation. It certainly did not look like he planned to stay for very long. As we turned the corner into his tiny kitchen, he was excited to show me how one simple cup of rice could make a huge meal and require such little expense or effort. Later I wouldn't be able to get this detail out of my mind.

I sat on his bed and we talked about all that we had shared through our letters, all that we had shared through our childhood. Although we both were on the brink of a freedom we desperately needed, he had the confidence and solid plan that I still lacked. He had been careful and protective of himself and his goals, while I had made careless choices that had taken me off my own course through an attachment to another. He didn't need anyone else's strength but his own, and I was still finding mine. Still, while so much had changed in both of us because of our distance from our parents, and we knew we would soon be physically heading in different directions, we revisited the past that would keep us eternally and emotionally parallel. We talked more about Chris's trip to our old neighborhood in California. It was the first time we'd seen each other since he'd written to me about all he'd learned.

"Mom told me again yesterday that she wants a divorce," I divulged with a roll of my eyes.

"What? Geez! Why does she always do that? Their lives are just one big falsity, an outrageous, perennial lie," he said, and I noted how like his letters he sounded—slightly formal, intense, assured. "Their whole life is just one big game. They're on this constant cycle of vacillation, switching back and forth between a state of total misery and a state of false happiness. Like one day they will have a huge fight of insane proportions, the kind of fight that would immediately end any normal marriage, and then the next they're pretending that their marriage and family is the very symbol of American prestige and success." He shook his head and let out a lengthy sigh. "I guess that's why I have always thought of them as the most fake people I have ever known. They brainwash themselves into this false sense of security and satisfaction by falling back on their *treasured money* and worthless luxury expenditures to shield themselves from reality. And the worst part of it is they expect you to take them seriously."

"Sometimes I honestly wonder if they just can't help themselves," I speculated. "Like you said—it's like a disease. They invent an alternate reality and dedicate themselves to it completely . . . and blindly . . . like they really don't realize what they're doing. But I can't help but think they'll wake up one day. I mean . . . how can they possibly continue like this forever?"

"I know," Chris replied as his eyes traveled to a distant place. "I used to get very sympathetic thoughts for them, especially for Mom—they used to come to me all the time. I'd be studying and then a sort of vision would pop into my head of Mom as an old lady, deserted by both of her children. I'd picture her all alone in a dark house . . . a dark, deserted, silent house. She's old and crippled, her skin is wrinkled and her hair is white, and she's sitting in this old dusty chair. She's gazing down at her hands, where she's holding a picture of you and me together when we were just little kids, and tears are streaming down her face. I used to get visions like that all the time, and then I would almost cry myself, and I'd feel sorry about all the problems we had, and I'd feel that surely things could be changed for the better and we'd come to have a good relationship."

Chris was still staring off into nothingness. He looked compassionate. Then he tightened up and the look left him as he turned back to me and sighed. "But then," he continued, his voice flat, "I'd remember a time when they acted so irrationally and treated us so terribly, and that sympathetic vision would be blown clear out of my mind." He shrugged. "I no longer get any of those sympathetic visions. They're gone forever. I'd just be fooling myself if I still had them. They aren't ever going to change because they'll never be able to admit that they're the problem."

I was quiet for a minute, taking it all in. "Did I ever tell you about them taking me to see a psychiatrist?" I finally asked. We laughed as I told him about the visit to Dr. Ray. Then we talked about the night I left home, and my wedding. I told him how embarrassed I was about the entire situation with Patrick. How blind I'd been. How I really didn't know what was going to happen next. Chris looked at me intently, taking in everything but saying nothing, while his eyes revealed just how quickly he was thinking and processing. It was harder for me to tell him in person than it had been in letters, especially because I wasn't out of the woods yet. I wasn't focused on school. My job situation was a mess. And I was losing faith in men. In just the few months since I'd left Patrick, I'd been propositioned by my boss *and* by the director of a modeling agency that I sometimes worked for. I was seeing too many Walt McCandlesses in the world and not enough Chrises.

Chris put his hand on mine. "Listen to me, Carine. You can recover from anything. Just believe in yourself and keep your head on straight. You're a pretty girl and men are going to try to take advantage of you. But you're very smart, and you need to focus on that and not so much on the outer stuff. If they don't see what you're worth, then to hell with them. Move on. And I don't mean that just in work. When you know it's time to move on from a bad situation, just do it. Keep moving forward and be true to yourself. You are the only one who can ensure your own happiness."

"I know," I said. "I'm not going to be a victim. That's why I want to have my own business one day instead of just being a stepping stone for someone else's dream."

Chris laughed and said, "Fair enough, but don't let your drive drown you."

WE MET OUR PARENTS out for dinner later that evening. Chris played his part well, and the discussion was meaningless. He was careful to not speak specifically about his future. He was not a hypocrite and hated liars. But out of necessity he'd become skilled at avoidance, and he used his skills to navigate the night's agenda. Just as he'd said he would in his letters, he told our parents what they wanted to hear. When Dad asked about future plans, Chris mentioned law school as one of his many options. He gave Mom a sentimental Mother's Day card, some candy, and flowers.

I supported his performance, but I wasn't fooled by it. I knew that once Chris made a decision, that was it—his discipline and determination ensured that there would be no deviance from the plan. I also wasn't concerned with what he had planned for himself. I already knew that he had not yet determined exactly where he was going or what he was doing after graduation. The freedom of no plan was part of the plan. He just had to keep moving, and I understood that completely. I knew it would be hard to keep in touch, but that didn't concern me, either. I never worried that he would come across anything he couldn't handle. He was remarkably intelligent and always succeeded at anything he put his mind to. As I sat at this dinner theater, I had no idea that this would be the last time I would ever see Chris as the master of strategy, so in control of his own destiny. This was the last time I would see him alive.

———————

UPON MY RETURN TO VIRGINIA, I met with a U.S. Immigration officer who had left me several messages. Apparently Patrick had been evading the divorce papers, seemingly in an effort to delay the process long enough to qualify for American citizenship. Immigration theorized that this had been his intent from the beginning—that his real reason for proposing had little to do with love and everything to do with control, and, embarrassed, I saw their logic.

I was also constantly watching my back, my senses on high alert. While Patrick had kept a low profile right after I'd filed, now he sent threatening letters and left menacing phone calls. He began stalking me, staying just outside the fifty-yard requirement as he followed me from my apartment to work or social functions. If I had anyone over, he'd call up from the lobby phone and yell vile things at me. Jody had been right when she'd said things would get messier before they got better.

I also had more to learn. I was still only eighteen, and I could see freedom within reach once again. Over the past months, I'd surrounded myself with feigned emblems of success. I filled my new luxury apartment with contemporary furnishings and dressed myself in the latest fashions. I learned a hard lesson about easy come, easy go with the lack of discipline I applied to my spending. I jumped headfirst toward independence without any consideration given to building a secure foundation.

One morning I walked to the parking lot and tried to recall where I had parked my little white sporty Honda. It had vanished overnight. I suspected Patrick had stolen the car, and I called the police. Self-reflection hit me hard when they called back to inform me that the car had not been stolen; it had been repossessed. I was two months behind on my car payment.

I had quit my job when the boss's advances became too much to brush off, and I was trying to start my own business selling home-care products. The inventory was sitting all around me, but without a car, I had no way to deliver it to customers. I was struggling to come up with next month's rent. I had no job, no car, and soon no apartment.

I sat on the floor of my fancy apartment, in my designer clothes, amongst my posh furnishings. I was a pathetic and hollow display of vanity and foolishness. I thought hard about Chris's advice to keep my head on straight and to be honest with myself. I needed help fast. I started to sob. I stared at the phone. I wished I could call Chris and ask him what to do. But he had no phone. And soon I wouldn't have an address for him to send a reply to. Besides that, I didn't even know for sure if he was still in Atlanta.

I picked up the phone and dialed the only other phone number I had ever identified with home. I called my parents. Exposing my reality to them was a tough admittance. I was surprised by how calmly they listened as I told them I had left Patrick, and why, and what had happened with school and with work. I was relieved when I didn't hear the words "We told you so," because I did not want to get into the discussion of why I had left them. Maybe they'd learned from the distance I'd kept. Perhaps they had been forced into their own self-reflection and had seen the error in their ways. Perhaps my desperation would provide an opportunity for our reconciliation.

I felt comforted when they quickly came up with a plan to help me resolve my mistakes. I was stunned at their last words to me before we hung up: "It's all going to be all right, Carine. We love you."

I sat and stared at the phone once again, but this time with hope in my heart. In nearly nineteen years I had never heard my parents utter those words. Not to each other, not to Chris, not to me. It was surreal. I wanted to tell Chris what had just happened, the incredible breakthrough that had just occurred.

———————

I MOVED MYSELF and my costly belongings back into the Annandale house, and with my move, Patrick's stalking stopped. Mom and Dad were mostly living at Windward Key and did not spend much time on Willet Drive in those days, other than to work in the basement office. They rented it to me for what they had determined was fair market value. They bailed out my Honda and I was able to sell it quickly to pay them back and pay my rent. I sold my inventory back to the marketing company. I was financially back on track, and I felt like things with my parents were moving in a positive direction.

Chris had recently mailed his final grade report for Mom and Dad to Annandale. He'd gotten an A in Apartheid and South African Society and History of Anthropological Thought, and an A minus in Contemporary African Politics and the Food Crisis in Africa. He included a letter that was polite and civil, thanking them for sending him photos from graduation and other gifts. It was nearing my

birthday, and Chris had also sent a separate box to me filled with
gifts and a birthday card with one final message. He'd addressed the
card "To: The Miss Duchess of York—Carine Zsa Zsa Gabor Ivana
Marie Trump McCandless." Within, he wrote, "Happy Birthday to
my Sister! Rising Successor to Leona Helmsley!" His message wasn't
subtle, really. He knew I was driven and wanted to be an entrepreneur. He had heard me talk about my nice apartment and new car.
He had seen the way I was dressed in Atlanta. He must have gotten
word from my parents that I was moving back home. As usual, Chris
and I did not need words to be able to understand each other. The
early birthday gifts meant he would not be visiting me before his
travels now, and I understood why he wouldn't risk returning. He
was telling me that he was heading out. He was telling me to be careful. He was warning me not to be materialistic like them.

The box held his prized brown leather jacket, which he had worn
throughout every fall and winter in high school and college; a sunlamp; a large assortment of new women's clothing from Britches
Great Outdoors; and a bottle of sparkling apple cider. He was careful
in his note not to say anything that would alarm our nosy parents,
but the contents said a lot to me. The jacket would feel like a warm
hug from him every time I put it on. The sunlamp wasn't practical
for a life on the road. The clothing from Britches made me smile. I
had followed through on my thought during his graduation and had
mailed him a bunch of new clothes from Britches. But he had very
clearly returned every single item, exchanging them for clothes for
me. I could see him walking into the store, tags still on the men's
clothes, and asking a female employee to help him pick out some
things for his sister. Judging by the selections, she clearly did not
understand my style any better than he did. Still, point taken. Chris
was effectively saying *Nice try, sis, but no thanks*. He didn't need fash-
ionable new clothes wherever he was going.

The meaning of the bottle of cider was just as easy to discern: it
was to toast to adventure and new beginnings.

Not long after, a new package arrived, this one for my parents. It was a small stack of letters, stamped RETURN TO SENDER by the post office. My mom and dad soon realized that Chris had left Atlanta, giving them no good-bye or forwarding address. I watched to see worry on their hearts, but instead I only witnessed their resentment and discomfort at the loss of control over their son.

"Did you know about this?" they asked me.

"No, not at all," I said.

I also watched them for signs of self-doubt but saw none. They never asked me if maybe they'd done something to push him away. As far as I knew, they never asked one another this question. Chris left, they maintained, because Chris was Chris. Chris was intense. Chris was selfish.

It was clear the new beginning I had hoped to discover with them was simply a glimmer of fool's gold. If they understood Chris so little, even in the face of such a dramatic gesture, how would they ever understand me? I'd just done what all my siblings had done before me, and I coiled back before it was time to leap again. Soon I was offered a job in Virginia Beach, and I decided to leave Annandale for good.

I knew that while I headed south, Chris was heading west. Although we had no way to keep in touch, we remained connected as we always had. Neither one of us knew exactly where we were going or what would unfold before us. But we were both absolutely certain of what we must leave behind.

PART TWO

STRENGTH

Perhaps strength doesn't reside in having never been broken, but in the courage required to grow strong in the broken places.

—Kristen Jongen, *Growing Wings*

CHAPTER 7

$\mathscr{L}$

$\mathbf{A}$MIDST THE CONCRETE AND STEEL of Manhattan lies the famous woodland of Central Park. The green space, lakes, and playgrounds have long provided New Yorkers an escape from the chaos and noise of city life. The day before I turned twenty-one, I stood in a gazebo near the Oak Bridge inside Central Park's maze of trails known as the Ramble. The trip to Manhattan wasn't to celebrate my milestone birthday. It was for my sister Shelly's wedding.

I had only met her fiancé a few times, but I could tell he was a kind, even-tempered soul—a good balance for Shelly's fiery side. Both were intense, but whereas Shelly was apt to throw a bottle of salad dressing during an argument over dinner, Augustine was more likely to respond with calm, thorough discussion as he finished his meal, staying focused on dessert.

Over the years, Shelly and I hadn't been in close touch. She was busy making her life while I was busy making a mess of, and then cleaning up, mine. But when we did talk, it was different than before. I was no longer the "kid" she delighted in teasing. When we were younger, she loved asking questions of me in front of my siblings. "Carine, do you know what sex is? C'mon, tell us!" And would squeal with glee at my awkward definitions. Now our conversations were much more frank, and she talked to me as a sister, not a *little* sister. I had left home; I was an adult. She talked candidly about things like how her biological clock was thumping—pounding her foot on the floor in emphasis—but how she and Auggie weren't sure they were ready to have children together. I admitted that I was nervous about having kids myself, afraid that I might not be a good parent. It was an equalizing moment, one that cemented Shelly as a friend and ally.

The previous two years had been full of changes for me. I had made the transition to living and working in Virginia Beach, and it was undeniably my home. Three hours south of the Washington, D.C., suburb I was raised in, it had a slower pace and a vibe that felt more real. People couldn't care less what car you drove or what clothes you wore. And it was beautiful. I could step outside my door and see the bay, drive to the ocean in ten minutes and the country-side in twenty. It was still Virginia, so not so far removed that it didn't feel familiar to me, yet it didn't hold the negative energy that I associated with Annandale.

I enrolled in business management and accounting classes at Old Dominion University. It felt good to focus on just myself for a while. Between my studies and a full-time position as a secretary at a busy CPA firm, there was little time for anything or anyone else.

Yet I made the trip to New York to share the joy of Shelly's nuptials with *my* new fiancé, a kind soul who had made me believe in love and trust again. Chris Fish was lead technician at one of the CPA firm's "petroleum accounts"—a gas station with several service bays. We met under the hood of an old 1981 Volkswagen Rabbit, the affordable cash-purchase replacement for my shiny new Honda. I had driven the VW to Chris's workplace to deliver some papers for my boss, but its high-mileage diesel engine decided I would spend a little more time there than I'd intended.

As I lifted the hood and peered into the engine compartment, a deep voice floated into my space. "What's going on with this little gem?"

"I'm not sure yet," I answered, my head and hands still focused on auto parts. "I think it's either the battery or alternator. Not sure if it's charging. The belt isn't in the best shape, but it's still tight."

I looked up to see an incredibly good-looking man standing beside me in a Shell uniform. Tanned and muscular, he had brown eyes and nearly black hair and stood roughly six feet tall. His perfect smile shone brightly under his dark mustache. I felt an instant connection with him. "Oh, I'm sorry . . . Were you asking about me or my car?" I smiled back, then looked down, embarrassed by my flirtatiousness. *Geez, did I really just say that?*

"Well," he laughed. "Perhaps both! You know about cars?"

"Enough to get by"—I looked back to the engine—"but not enough to know what I need to spend my money on. The battery terminals are tight; the cells are full of water. I don't have anything to test the charging system with."

"No worries. You broke down in the right place. I'm Chris."

"Good name," I said as I shook his hand, and he led me into the building. "That's my brother's name. I'm Carine."

"Carine? That's very pretty. Yeah, my first name is far from unique. Everyone calls me by my last name, Fish." He handed me a work order to fill out.

"Well, that's definitely different. Okay, Chris Fish, how long will this take?" I was already worried about the extended duration of this errand.

"We're pretty slammed today, but I can get you in early this afternoon. You work for Thompson, right?"

"I do," I confirmed.

"Okay, how about I drive you back to the office and I'll call you when I know more about why your little white rabbit doesn't want to run for you?" he gallantly offered.

Traffic delayed the short ride back to the office just enough to establish that our interest in each other went beyond the needs of my car. By the time I had paid for my repairs that evening, we had a date for dinner that weekend.

He picked me up on a Saturday night in a freshly detailed Toyota Corolla, apologizing that the Jeep he would have preferred to take me out in was currently in mid renovation. I told him about the classic Corvette still parked at my parents' place. We went to a restaurant called The Hot Tuna, which was known for its great seafood. Since I wasn't old enough to drink yet, he ordered a soda for himself as well. The more we talked, the more I shared with him. He was easy to talk to, a good listener, and not shy about opening up about his life, too.

I could tell Fish was more than just handsome. He was smart and hardworking. He wanted to start his own auto repair shop one day. He was six years older than me, and despite being ages that others would describe as young, we both felt driven beyond our years. We wanted the same thing: a future of our own making, one marked by self-reliance. Fish mentioned he lived alone but had chosen a home one street away from his mother, because he remained very close with her and his sister. His father had been violent, too, and we talked openly about what it was like to grow up strong in the midst of a hurricane. We talked about the hard stuff early, but I preferred it that way. I even told him about Patrick. I felt it was best to be totally transparent. We walked on the beach after dinner, and I knew I wanted to see him again. As I found myself already beginning to imagine what the future might bring with Fish, I thought about Chris's warnings: . . . *men are going to try to take advantage of you.* . . . *You are the only one who can ensure your own happiness.*

The Monday after our first date a dozen roses arrived at the office for me with a card: *Thank you for a wonderful evening and terrific conversation. I look forward to seeing you again.*

Within weeks, we were a couple. We spent almost all our free time together during the week; we went to car shows and the beach together on Saturdays, and to church and dinner at his mother's house on Sundays. I felt safe with Fish and knew he was someone I could be happy with. He was the antithesis of the kind of man my brother had warned me about. He was gentle to the core.

Within months, we moved in together. I was elated, although not surprised, when he proposed. The engagement fell perfectly in line with our parallel paths, and we were stronger when we walked together.

I was excited about my wedding, although no specific plans were in the works. When Fish proposed, I had insisted we not set a date until my brother had returned, because I wanted him to walk me down the aisle.

———————

IT WASN'T LOST ON ME that Shelly, too, had chosen against the tradition of being escorted by our father to her groom.

Her wedding ceremony took place on a beautiful day in the city, with feathery clouds holding perfectly in place to shield the summer sun. Sam stood in the pergola with us, along with his wife and son, our father, my mother, Auggie's mom and sister, and a couple of close friends.

Shelly looked so beautiful and so content. She and Auggie had chosen to have an intimate gathering in this natural setting, a place they had come to often during their courtship. Neither was concerned with formalities or tradition, and since they were paying for the wedding themselves, the reasons to keep things simple were practical as well as philosophical. They'd chosen a female officiant who was not of a strict religious code, and they exchanged vows that focused on being human and sharing love. Both wore black and white, and Shelly held a small bouquet of fragrant white gardenias. The colorless palate was a symbol of their belief about keeping things uncomplicated.

After the ceremony, Billie muttered comments about these contrasting color choices. Augustine was Caribbean and had a mulatto complexion, and she said things like "His coloring is very interesting, isn't it?" I ignored her questions, and I noticed Shelly did, too—or tried to.

Dinner was at Tavern on the Green. Both the bride and groom were well-respected servers at the upscale restaurant, and the many coworkers present helped keep the conversation busy, allowing for safe pockets of side discussion and plenty of opportunities for evasion. The main celebration was to be a garden reception the following week in Denver with Marcia and our other siblings, a gathering of seventy-five or so people, to which Walt and Billie were not invited.

Shelly had confided to me that she'd felt conflicted about inviting Walt and Billie even to the ceremony. But at twenty-seven, she was in a good place. She was attempting to reconcile with her dad and stepmom to whatever extent possible and also felt inviting them would be easier than dealing with the drama if she didn't.

Sam, always the one to analyze and bring order to things, began to sum up Walt and Billie in two words: The Show. Humor had long been a tool Chris and I used to cope with our parents' antics, something we'd learned from our older siblings. What had started as a defense mechanism grew along with the outrageousness of Walt and Billie's behavior to a point where we found ourselves regularly busting out in laughter over the absurdity of their latest actions. For Shelly's wedding, The Show stood unified amongst all that was unsaid.

Chris was noticeably absent from the day's event and from our lives. I wondered, as I often did, where he might be. Our parents had hired a private detective to try to find him, and when he came up empty handed for substantive leads to Chris's whereabouts, I was pleased for my brother. When the detective discovered that Chris had donated the remainder of his college fund to the famine-relief charity Oxfam America, Mom and Dad understood the seriousness of his departure. They finally realized he was *trying* not to be found.

I hadn't heard from him or seen him in over two years. But unlike the rest of those circling around our family during this period, I didn't wonder why he hadn't called. I knew. He'd divorced our parents. And as for me, he knew I'd understand why he wasn't in touch. I had no doubt that once he'd taken the time and space he needed, he'd show up on my doorstep. Even in his absence I felt like he was beside me, and as I walked around the patio after dinner, I made mental notes of what to tell him about this day in the park: How the buildings and towers rose synthetically above the landscape. How our parents seemed just as artificial. How Shelly tried to let my mother's little comments roll right off her back. He'd relish Mom's obvious discomfort with the lack of formality surrounding the ceremony, and when she made the comments about the groom's dark complexion, I swear I could see Chris's customary smirk and eye roll.

If Fish got tired of hearing about Chris, a guy he'd never met but who loomed larger than life in our relationship—who in fact was the reason we hadn't set a wedding date—he never showed it. He seemed to grasp how close we were, and because I talked about Chris so frequently, Fish began to feel like he knew him. Maybe that's why he never pressured me to get married before Chris returned.

FISH AND I WENT HOME to Virginia Beach and got back to work. Fish had been dealing with a lingering dull ache that had been repeatedly diagnosed as an inner ear infection. We knew something more serious was happening when the pain became unbearable and he suddenly felt disoriented. We were faced with the shocking discovery that Fish had a brain tumor. The doctors acted quickly, and it was an incredible relief to learn that the benign growth was noncancerous and located in an area that allowed for its safe surgical removal. Fish was strong and healthy and recovered quickly. It was a blessing and a wake-up call, and it had motivated us both.

Throughout the previous year, I'd encouraged him to follow through on his aspirations to be a shop owner. I was absolutely certain that his expertise, backed by my organization skills, would ensure our success as shop owners. With little more than five hundred dollars cash, Fish's well-equipped toolboxes (which resembled multiple-compartment refrigerators), and some flyers I'd whipped up on the computer at work, we prepared for our grand opening.

We rented a small space with two service bays and a back office. Fish recruited some friends to help him construct built-in workbenches and storage shelves for the garage space. His mom painted the large sign that would hang above the overhead doors. I cleaned and prepared the office to double as a workspace for me and a waiting room for customers. The landlord was pleased by how we'd quickly transformed the dingy space with ingenuity, elbow grease, and new paint.

From the beginning, we aimed to do things differently. Instead of the typical posters of half-naked women lying across or straddling various means of transportation, we gathered industrial posters and metal signs of all colors from the tool manufacturers and parts suppliers to decorate the shop. The paint color scheme was red, black, gray, and white. The office was decorated in softer shades and looked more like a room transplanted from the house Fish and I rented together. I'd used the same wall and trim paint, snagged a portion of the sectional couch from our living room—complete with throw pillows and a blanket—and repurposed our IKEA dining room table as my desk. My mom and dad were proud of these signs of entrepreneurism and passed along some good business advice and a refurbished filing cabinet. Dad recommended I read *The Wealthy Barber* and learn about investing and saving intelligently; despite the luxuries they enjoyed, my parents always saved more than they spent. Mom's filing system and customer-relations skills were ones I aimed to emulate. The shop was tiny, but the environment was exciting. It was a new beginning.

Fish left for work early each morning and stayed late every night. Since the shop was only a few minutes from the CPA firm, I could help out with estimates and phone calls to customers during my lunch hour, then return after hours to do the bookkeeping and prepare invoices. I scheduled most of my college classes at night and on the weekends. During breaks, I helped out even more at the shop. I handled the receivables and payables, recruited new clients, and paid close attention to everything Fish taught me in the shop. We developed a strong following of both male and female clientele, the latter feeling secure and comfortable with my presence. Fish was a brilliant mechanic, while my automotive knowledge was steadily increasing. We did thorough and honest work, referrals spread fast, and the business grew quickly. Soon I was able to quit the CPA firm and work at the shop full-time. I was done working for others, for good. It felt satisfying, empowering to be in control. I didn't even care that I was breaking a rule I'd set for myself, never to go into business with my spouse. I'd seen too much of how dysfunctional that dynamic could be. But Fish was so different from Dad—so complimentary about my contributions and easy to work with.

My parents came down to visit from time to time, usually stopping by as they navigated their sailboat down the Intracoastal Waterway. They would stay with us for short periods, sometimes dropping off Buck for extended visits. They were more or less retired and traveled constantly.

"Have you heard anything from your brother?" they always asked.

"No, nothing," I would answer truthfully as they skeptically examined my expression.

We'd rebuilt a semblance of a good relationship. My time with them was on my own terms and most often in my own territory. And while I felt comfortable with Chris's absence, now I could see how much it wounded our parents. Mom spoke of leaving a note on the door whenever they left town in case he returned, and I saw how she looked twice at any young man walking along the street with a pack on his back. Dad mused over how unbelievable it was, given his powerful government connections, that he still hadn't been able to track down his son. Regardless of what was driving their feelings—whether genuine concern for Chris, discomfort about their lack of command in his new life, or just anger at being left—I felt empathy for them, and I thought if they could feel pain, surely they must feel remorse, too. I hoped that the injury his leaving had caused might force some healing. Chris had hoped for that as well. In his last letter to me he had written, "Maybe it will be different for you, Carine. Maybe once I'm gone they will learn to treat you with some respect."

I wondered if that could happen. And if so, maybe someday, when Chris was back, he'd be open to talking to them again. Surely they'd see each other at my wedding. Even after everything my parents had done, I still longed to have a traditional family life. I was guilty of the same fault as my parents: I wanted us to be who we were not.

CHAPTER 8

In THE EARLY EVENING of September 17, 1992, approximately seven weeks after Shelly's wedding, I took my Rottweiler, Max, for a long run along the sandy edge of Chesapeake Bay, where it opens wide to the expanse of the Atlantic. Fish and I were living in a duplex rental on the beach while we built a new home.

Max loved the water as if he were a Labrador. Whenever I stopped to take a break, I would free him from his leash to race into the waves after the day's toy of choice. He kept up this obsession until he would spot a man, any man, walking toward us. Unwilling to bet that the individual was simply taking his own relaxing stroll, Max would launch himself back onto shore and stand at attention between the trespasser and me. He didn't growl or bark or even flinch. His large frame and the stigma of his breed was enough for the passerby to receive the message. As soon as the distance between the three of us was decidedly safe again, Max's demeanor would return to that of playful puppy. His concentration shifted from the toy in my hand to the water, his legs amped and ready for takeoff, waiting for me to throw it again.

After returning to the house, as was the routine, I began to give Max a bath outside. The grit from the shoreline ran out of his thick black coat, through our toes, and across our concrete pathway to reunite with the sandy soil of our grassless yard. As I worked the shampoo into his fur, I was surprised to see Fish's brown Toyota pull into the driveway.

"Hey! Daddy's home early, boy!" I said to Max as I slapped him on the side a few times and then wrapped my arm around his neck to keep him under the hose. Fish sat in the car a long time after turning the engine off, staring straight ahead. When he finally got out, he walked into the house without so much as a glance in our direction.

"What the hell is he doing?" I asked the dog, who was looking up at me with the same question, as if we could really explain it to each other.

Soon Fish came back out the front door and walked toward us.

"I thought you were working late?" I asked.

He bent down and began to fling the lather off Max. "I need to talk to you," he said, his hands moving vigorously across Max's back and down his sides.

"Whoa, you're washing the dog. That's new," I teased. "What's up?"

"Just come inside," he said and led Max into the house.

I stood there, water still rushing through the hose in my hand, and watched as he walked away. "Um . . . Well, okay, then," I murmured as I turned off the spigot and followed behind.

By the time I came through the front door, Fish had taken Max upstairs and was sitting on the couch in the living room, in silence, his head in his hands, eyes staring blankly at the beige carpeting. I had a guess as to what might be wrong. We had recently hired a couple more technicians to keep up with our demanding workload at the shop. Men enclosed in tight quarters are known to play jokes on one another, some more insensitive than others. I assumed from the injured confusion on Fish's face that there had been some laughable claim that one of the guys had seen me around town with someone else. Fish was far from jealous, and I was far from unfaithful, so I had little interest in entertaining the discussion.

I walked into the kitchen and rinsed Max's collars in the sink. When I walked around the corner, Fish hadn't budged. I came around the couch to sit beside him and put my hand on his knee. "What's *wrong* with you?" I asked with a laugh. "Have the guys been giving you a hard time?"

Fish looked up at me, his eyes red and desperate.

And then my world fell apart.

"It's your brother," he said slowly. "They found him. He's dead."

At that moment I became keenly aware of time and space and my place within all of it. And it was excruciating. My hand left Fish's knee. My eyes blurred as the room collapsed into darkness, and a black vortex started spinning all around me—a sinister mass that somehow slammed me into myself until I became dizzy.

"No," I corrected him, "Chris is not dead."

Then I closed my eyes tightly, threw my hands to my sides, dug my fingers into the couch and began to scream uncontrollably. I could hear Max whimpering and scratching at the bedroom door. I could feel Fish trying to contain me within his strong, calm, kind arms as he searched for the right words to comfort me.

"No! Get away from me! Chris is not dead! He's not dead!" I insisted and pushed him away. I wanted everything to stop. I wanted Fish to stop speaking, the earth to stop turning, my heart to stop beating—anything that forced me further into a life without Chris.

I crawled to one end of the couch and curled up in a fetal position. I shrieked at Fish to leave me alone as he tried to cry with me. He paced around the house for the next few hours as day passed into night and I continued in my hysterical state. Exhausted, I finally collapsed into his embrace, which I needed so badly.

I don't know when I first learned more details—that Chris's body had been found in the middle of the Alaskan wilderness. Fish may have told me then, but the chasm between what I heard and what I comprehended was wide and bottomless.

In a comatose state, I dragged myself up the staircase and took a warm shower. The simple tasks of cleaning myself up and packing a bag so Fish could drive me to be with my parents were agonizing.

I was operating within a murky haze that dragged every action along in painful slow motion. I did not want to go anywhere or see anyone, but I felt a responsibility to be with my parents.

On our way out of town, I asked Fish to stop at our church. It was late but the main door was still open, and as I walked in alone, tears still streaming down my face, I came across the choir director locking up for the night.

"My dear, what is the matter?" he asked softly and put his hand on my shoulder.

"My brother died," I said numbly, hearing my words and finding them absurd. "He was hiking in Alaska and they found him dead."

"Oh dear God. I just read about that poor young man in the paper. That was *your* brother?" He looked at me with wonder. Later I learned that the *New York Times* had published a story, "Dying in the Wild, a Hiker Recorded the Terror," a few days before. The paper hadn't disclosed Chris's identity because until earlier that day, when Sam was shown a photograph, the authorities had not confirmed who he was. On the choir director's face, empathy that had once been theoretical became real and acute as he looked a suffering family member in the eye. It was a look I would see over and over again, for the rest of my life.

"Can I please just sit in the sanctuary for a little while?" I asked, looking down at the keys in his hand.

"Oh, of course, of course," he obliged. "You take as much time as you need."

I walked across the burgundy runner between the church pews, down the aisle that I had envisioned Chris walking me down on my wedding day, and fell to my knees in front of the altar. I thought about us as kids in the pews of Saint Matthew's, trusting in a God that would protect us from harm.

"Why?" I cried out into the echo of the empty, cavernous room. "Why did you let him die?" I placed my head onto the steps below the cross and felt my tears soak into the floor beneath me. "Why?" I railed at my Father. "What am I supposed to do now? How do I do this? Why did you have to take him away from me?"

I didn't know what I was looking for or what I hoped would happen. I thought about the glow that I used to swear I could see around Reverend Smith when I was little. I wanted to feel that around me. It was as if I was expecting the ceiling to open and that light to shine down and heal me, to explain everything, to give me understanding and acceptance. And peace.

I didn't get any of that. I walked out of the church in as much pain and confusion as I had walked in.

I sobbed the entire four-hour drive to Windward Key. I did not want to return there. I did not want to see Walt and Billie.

We arrived in the early hours of a cool fall morning. The walk up the tall town house staircase was laborious as my feet became heavier with each step. But arriving in the middle of the night brought with it the welcome avoidance of an embrace with my parents. I battled with a cruel mix of emotions that teetered between sorrow and exasperating anger.

The next morning, I sat numbly on the couch as Sam explained things to Fish. Chris had covered his identity well, and it had taken the Alaska State Troopers nearly two weeks to find us.

The trail grew warm when an Alaskan named Jim Gallien saw an article in the *Anchorage Daily News* about a young hiker whose body had been found, and he recognized from the details and location that it must have been the same young man he'd given a ride to the previous spring. The Alaska troopers had developed a roll of film they'd found with the hiker, and Gallien had confirmed the young man in the self-portraits was one and the same. Chris had told Gallien he was from South Dakota, so the investigators had searched for his family there.

A South Dakota wheat farmer named Wayne Westerberg, who had been Chris's good friend and employer, heard a radio report about the recovered hiker and feared it was Chris—or rather, Alex, as he had known him. He called the authorities and gave them the social security number Chris had written on a W-4 tax form. Through that social security number, the police learned Chris was from Virginia, and since Walt and Billie weren't living in Annandale anymore, the McCandless number that came up in their directory was Sam's. The authorities faxed Sam Chris's self-portrait, and he recognized his brother immediately, though the young man in the picture looked different from the Chris he had last seen at Windward Key.

So, late in the afternoon of September 17, Sam had been faced with the terrible task of informing Walt and Billie that their son was dead. He had also called our shop, later admitting to relief that I hadn't answered and regret that he had to pass on the awful assignment to Fish.

———————

FISH HAD TO RETURN SOUTH to the long list of cars awaiting his attention at the shop. I stayed in a stupor in the living room of the town house most of the day as events took place around me. Sam and his wife, Michele, took over with strength and grace. They put aside any differences they had ever encountered with Walt and Billie and did what needed to be done. Sam took calls from the police in Fairfax, Virginia, and the coroner's office in Fairbanks, Alaska. Chris's dental records were required to make a conclusive identification, and Sam saw to those arrangements as well. My mom had refused to look at the picture until the dental records confirmed beyond a doubt that it was her son.

She sat in the kitchen when the time came for Sam to bring the picture over to her. He laid it on the table. I watched her entire body tremble as she looked up to see if she recognized the image. Tears dripped from her nose and chin as she tried to fight the release, then an ungodly wail left her body. Sam put his arms around her and she crumpled from the chair onto his shoulder. My father stood by in his own unfamiliar element, trying to figure out how to control the uncontrollable, unsure of how to handle his own pain, much less hers. Their reliable standby of denial was not an option this time. I ran over to my mom and embraced her, finally taking in the common loss.

The phone rang constantly, and Michele drafted a family statement for the press. *Why in the world are people so interested in his story?* I wondered, and I wished there was no story to issue a statement about. Mom and Dad requested I get onto a plane with Sam the following day. We were to go to Alaska and retrieve Chris—his remains, his belongings, anything at all he'd left behind. I was surprised my parents were not going themselves, but I didn't question the plan. I wanted to go. I wanted to fly across the country to discover that it was all a colossal mistake—or perhaps that Chris had succeeded in pulling off a brilliant scheme to finally separate himself once and for all from the oppression of our parents, just as he'd said he would. There would be a note for me explaining his ingenious plan and how to get in touch with him.

I DON'T REMEMBER MUCH about the flight out of Washington, D.C., or the connecting flights that finally landed us in Alaska. I do remember thinking how enormous and distant a single state must be in order to justify having an entire airline named after it. Our first stop in Fairbanks was the coroner's office. I had never dealt with the formalities of death before, and the experience at the bureau was less ceremonial than I had anticipated. As I sat across the desk from the coroner, I found her casual outdoor attire and the rustic environment of her workspace comforting.

She gave us the possessions that were recovered with Chris's body, among them a .22 rifle, a pair of binoculars, a fishing rod, a Swiss Army knife, a book of plant lore in which Chris had recorded a terse journal, his Minolta camera, the pictures the state troopers had developed in order to help identify the body, five rolls of undeveloped film, and several well-read and tattered paperback books. There was no note waiting for me.

I was taken aback by the gun. I had never been that close to one before, and I didn't realize that Chris had owned one. But the books and journal were so representative of the brother I loved, I felt the return of the smile that had been absent from my face for the past three days. Henry David Thoreau's *Walden* and Boris Pasternak's *Doctor Zhivago* were included alongside lighter reads like Michael Crichton's *The Terminal Man* and even some Louis L'Amour.

Chris loved to read and could delve into highbrow philosophy or quick-read westerns with equal zeal. As a kid, he'd had a blue bookcase filled with his perfectly organized Hardy Boys mysteries, and he also loved to read Ray Bradbury. As I sat reading *Little House on the Prairie* or *Black Beauty,* he looked up from "A Sound of Thunder" to tell me about how the simple act of stepping on a butterfly could substantially alter the future of humanity. "Everything we do affects everything," he explained seriously. Then he turned to reading something lighter, like *Old Yeller,* and tossed it to me to read when he was finished.

As the coroner explained things to us, I kept my head up and watched her lips move. Her sentences held little meaning, but certain words sliced through the air like a scalpel: "Starvation." "Sixty-seven pounds." "Decay." "Autopsy." "Cremation." Her description of something called the Stampede Trail and an abandoned bus filled me with confusion. The coroner was polite and sensitive, yet this was clearly routine for her. My rattled mind wandered. I could not imagine having her job, but I supposed she took a certain satisfaction in helping families resolve things and take one more step toward closure. As the process continued, I focused on the nameplate on her desk: FREJA LOVISWEAN. I wondered how far someone with that name had traveled to wind up in the Alaska interior, and why. Sam was on point to verify statistics and sign the necessary papers to take custody of Chris's things. I was responsible for collecting Chris's ashes in Anchorage the next day.

Sam and I went to a hotel somewhere, went to dinner somewhere, talked about the plan for the next day. The restaurant was nice but not overly so. We sat at a table the shape of a half-moon, part of a series along the edge of the large dining room. The concave leather booth had a high back and welcomed me into a feeling of insignificance . . . I could just stay there and hide. I realized this trip was the first time I had ever been alone with Sam, who was twelve years older than me. He was kind and attentive. We didn't talk about what Chris had done or why. We didn't compare notes on our childhoods. We didn't speculate about what had driven Chris to such extremes, nor did we theorize about any of his decisions. It was just time to eat, so we ate.

I had a very difficult time sleeping alone in my hotel room that night. I saw Chris's ghost around every corner, behind every door. But these visions were not warm and peaceful. My traumatized brain invented images of Chris in a zombie-like state, decomposing, his guts exposed through his clothing, his flesh falling from his bones as he walked toward me, his outstretched arms reaching for me. I imagined his suffering. I felt terrible for the pain that he must have gone through, on so many levels. He loved life more than anyone I had ever known, and now his was over. The coroner had said it was likely he had died slowly. That meant he'd been aware of his impending death, and it was more than I could bear. Although there had been no note left for me, Chris had posted one at his camp, explaining that he was too weak to hike out, begging any hikers that might pass by to remain to save him when he returned from his search for food nearby. When the coroner had shown us the desperate message, I immediately thought of that day on the beach when we were kids, watching him shivering in the cold, being helpless to comfort him. I cried myself into a restless sleep.

The next morning Sam and I flew on to the largest city in the largest state, to carry out the largest task of my life. Aside from constantly reminding myself of the need to stay strong and keep it together, I had given up trying to prepare for what would surely be the most devastating and difficult occurrence of my existence. But when the envoy from the mortuary delivered Chris's remains, it was strangely consoling. An absolute relief came over me. *Oh. This is it? This isn't him. This isn't all that he was.* The container was not ornate as I had expected. His ashes weren't even in an urn. They were in a dull dark brown box made of plastic. The container was much bigger than I had anticipated, yet it wasn't daunting. As I held what they claimed was all that remained of my brother, I noticed the plain white label on one side. In neatly typed block letters was the name: CHRISTOPHER R. MCCANDLESS. Chris's middle initial was *J*—Johnson, for our mother's maiden name—and it pissed me off that they had carelessly made such a mistake. But my annoyance was short-lived. Nothing about this package identified who he was to me, and besides, Chris would have laughed at the typo.

Alone for a moment, I took a pen from my purse and respectfully reshaped the *R* into a *J*.

Then I removed from my suitcase a small backpack that I had taken along many trails and had brought to Alaska for one specific purpose. I turned the box from the mortuary on its side and began to gently place it into my pack. Not having realized exactly how the container was constructed, I panicked when the side with the identification label shifted slightly out of its housing, alarmed that my brother's remains might spill out onto the floor, or float into the air, as ash will do. But the vestiges of my closest sibling were contained within a clear plastic bag, complete with a red twist tie that looked like it had just been pulled off a loaf of bread. The ashes were not of a powdery nature at all. They were more like gravel. A final sense of knowing that I was not holding all that was left of Chris ran through me.

Still, I held the backpack close through the entire trip back to Virginia.

CHAPTER 9

S AM AND I RETURNED from Alaska accompanied by the mystery that was attached to Chris's belongings. No one was sure what to make of the items. Dad put every article, from the rifle to the journal, through a thorough inspection. His eyes focused with a detached concentration, dissecting the reasons why Chris would have possessed each one. Once his examination was complete and the display methodically organized, Mom walked around the table touching each item gently. She brought them to her face, one by one, eager to attain some sensory connection to her son. Each family member who arrived at Windward Key approached the anthology delicately and took the time they needed.

We hoped we would have more answers than questions after we developed the rest of his film. He'd been missing from our lives for more than two years, and the snapshots—photographs Chris had never seen—would tell us more about what he'd been doing.

I held that first envelope of photos from the drugstore for a long time before opening it. As much as I wanted to see Chris in them, every image would remind me that I would never see him again, and my mind refused to comprehend it. I didn't want to—couldn't—fathom that I'd never see him in the flesh or feel his protective hugs.

But just as his ashes were an unexpected comfort, as I sifted through the images, they too brought a smile that contradicted my tears. The first thing that struck me was how happy Chris looked. The contemplative, often angry face from our childhood photos was gone. He looked free, completely at ease. No one was forcing him to pose in front of the camera, to wear a suit or a smile. But he did smile. In fact, he beamed. I remembered that look, from a time when we went to Colorado as kids and hiked at Longs Peak with our parents, Shannon, and Quinn. Shawna had come along for the ride into the mountains but opted to stay in the Suburban, perfectly happy to prop her feet up and relax while reading fashion magazines. It had been an idyllic summer day in the Rockies. We stopped for lunch at the beginning of the Boulder Field, a long and wide stretch of stone deposits left behind by the destructive path of ancient glacial flows. My brothers and I scrambled over hunks of sedimentary deposits of earth in every size, testing the stability before putting all our weight onto one, then moving on to the next. It was like an exhilarating puzzle. Chris and Quinn were determined to make it all the way to the keyhole before descending. Dad allowed it but was adamant that they go no farther. The rest of us watched as the two brothers made their way up to the keyhole entrance and raised their arms triumphantly. They gazed through to the abyss for a short time before they scrambled back down to where the rest of us were enjoying the hard sun. The smiles on Chris's and Quinn's faces burned just as brightly.

Now here was that smile again. In one photo that appeared to be taken not long after Chris had left Atlanta, he stood thigh-deep in rich blue lake waters. In another, he wore a straw hat, sturdy hiking boots, and a grin as the Sierra Nevada spread out behind him. A humorous shot showed him holding up a drink as he sat in a beach chair at the side of a road, looking to hitch a ride, and another was of some beautiful wild horses. But the picture that affected me most of all was one in which he stood on an open road with no cars, people, or buildings in sight. The exhilaration in his eyes and the gorgeous snow-covered mountain range that rose behind him left no doubt as to where he had been heading. Despite the images from the last roll becoming more difficult to look at as I neared his final shot, those pictures told me what I'd known the whole time: Chris had left to find peace and happiness. He'd left a good-bye note among his possessions, thanking the Lord and saying he'd had a happy life. I didn't know everywhere he'd been, but despite the dissonance of emotions banging through me, I was glad he'd found what he was looking for.

Otherwise, I was still in shock, wearing a false half smile and trying to keep it together for my parents' sake. Compliant Carine emerged full force, and it felt easier to just go through the motions. My mother gave me and my siblings the task of summarizing our brother's existence onto four poster boards for Chris's wake, to be held the next day.

Mom handed me a large storage box of old photographs without having had the strength to look through it herself first. Shelly, Shawna, Sam, and I dug through the memories, organizing photos by date, and thus began the exhumation of our childhood together.

Board one was dedicated to Chris as a baby. "Well, here's the beginning." Shelly sighed and handed me a small picture of my mother, dated in April 1968. Mom stood proudly in a bathing suit, holding Chris—a tiny, underweight seven-week-old—up for the camera. Shelly's lips tightened, and I knew why the photo upset her. While Mom was showing off her postpartum figure, Marcia had also just given birth—to Shannon. An image of Marcia at this time—exhausted after her fifth delivery and under command of our dad—would tell a very different story from the one Billie was aiming for.

"Oh my gosh, look at this one," Shawna quickly intervened with a giggle. "I forgot just how cute he was as a baby!" She held up an eight-by-ten sepia-toned image of Chris, caught in what would prove to be a rare formal pose for the camera. He rested tummy-down, and the onesie he wore melded so perfectly with the white puffy blanket that he appeared to have been inserted directly into a marshmallow. Chris had propped himself up on one arm to have a look around, his hand in a gentle fist just in front of his ear. His huge brown eyes smiled cleverly at the camera while his lips appeared ready to say something well beyond his years.

Board two was for early childhood and grade school. I picked one of Chris with me in front of a spindly Christmas tree. We were dressed for church, our arms wrapped around each other, our grins wide as we stood among the gifts Santa had left behind. I found another seasonal picture of us, this one with our parents, taken when I was just one and Chris was four. On the back, in my mother's handwriting, was "Us at beach Christmas Day 1972—waiting for turkey to finish baking at home." I thought about how all our siblings must have felt that day, at home with Marcia, wondering where their dad was. I buried it deep into the not-for-wake pile.

The next up for assessment was another picture taken at a beach. This was years later with several of our siblings at a waterfront house on the West Coast that Dad had rented for a family vacation. After the photo was taken, we'd all been locked out of the house. Mom and Dad were fighting inside, and an audience was not wanted that day, so we were forced to stay out on the sand. All Marcia's kids, who had inherited her fair complexion, burned terribly in the sun and spent the rest of the vacation nursing huge blisters on their backs and shoulders.

I found another picture of Chris and me—we were buried in a colorful shed of autumn foliage, Chris's hands entangled in Buck's fur. "We used to make gigantic piles of leaves in the backyard at the Annandale house," I said, "and run into them again and again." My siblings smiled and passed it around so everyone could see.

Board three was for high school and college. Sam found a photo of Chris standing on the high school track with Andy. It was picture day at Woodson and the yearbook club photographers were out in droves. Chris was barefoot, running shoes slung over his shoulder. Both boys were posed for the opportunity, yet Andy's wide smile contrasts with Chris's pursed lips and squint toward the camera lens, as if the request to pause had interrupted something more important.

"Do you remember how he would wear that *exact* same shirt and shorts to running practice *every single day*?" I asked Shelly.

"Hell yes!" She laughed and wiped her eyes. "I think that outfit could have run around the track on its own."

Shawna pulled out a photo from Chris's high school graduation party at the Annandale house. "God, I remember that night," I said. Chris was dressed like a young Tony Bennett and stood next to the piano where Dad sat. The party had been held under a big blue, white, and yellow tent on the back deck, and you could see blue and white balloons—our school colors—in the background.

I remembered how Chris had sung "Tender Is the Night" while Dad played the piano. Chris had an amazing voice, but when he sang, he always turned away just slightly . . . almost shyly. But he wasn't ever nervous—he usually turned away so he wouldn't start laughing. He had an embarrassed grin he'd get whenever he noticed someone looking at him, and he wasn't always successful at hiding it.

Number four was the board dedicated to the man we did not get to share experiences with, who'd separated himself from our painful past. This was the man who smiled on that open road, doing exactly what he wanted to do. What he needed to do. I wished I knew more about what he'd done and whom he'd met. But in the absence of that information, we did the best we could to put the fourth board together. Though Shelly was still in denial, she also recognized something in those last photos of Chris. She'd heard mutterings of how foolish he was to go off the way he did, with such limited resources, to "find himself," but she understood that she'd done the very same thing. She would never have dreamed of getting lost in Alaska but had loved getting lost in New York, where she'd moved alone and with very little money. They had both been on a journey, and the thought made her feel closer to him.

As we looked at the photographs, we didn't need to speak to know we all felt the same way. We mourned the loss of this strong, dynamic human being. And we also knew why he'd felt he had to leave so decisively.

I believed that there was a part in all of us that wanted to march down the stairs and blame Walt and Billie for what they had done, for driving Chris to leave. But we couldn't talk about it. Not there. Not then.

Throughout the rest of the afternoon Mom alternated between being catatonic and manic. At one moment I would see her sitting in a chair, alone, staring off into the distance, loneliness filling her face. Then something would snap and she would move about the house like a Tasmanian devil cartoon character, a swirl of nervous energy with vacuum and dust rags in hand, stressing over cleaning the town house meticulously before the guests arrived. Dad rearranged furniture. Then, after Mom stopped her spin just long enough for them to swap spats about placement, he rearranged it again. The stage was set for another show, one that none of us wanted to be in. Still, I was determined to say my lines and smile on cue.

Although I could see the intense pain on my parents' faces, I could not bring myself to take them into my arms. To mourn and cry with them should have been the natural thing to do, but even the thought of it felt illusory. Those emotions only felt honest and cleansing when shared with my siblings, with Fish, or in quiet solitude. I was awaiting a sure reaction from my parents, expecting a breakdown and an apology at any moment. A request for forgiveness. I was certain the loss of their son would bring about this long-awaited change. I was grasping for anything positive in this devastating situation. *They'll see now,* I thought. *They'll change. They had to lose a son to make this happen, but it will happen, and I can help make it easier for them.*

The wake played out as programmed. Friends and neighbors filed into my parents' home to make the rounds and give their condolences. They ate fine finger foods and lingered on the decks overlooking

Chesapeake Bay. Unasked questions floated in with the breeze off the water and circulated amongst careful discussion.

I was up in the loft at one point during the gathering and heard my mother's voice rise with a lift I had not heard in days. She wanted me to come down to see Chris's friend Brian Paskowitz. Brian had been a neighbor on Willet Drive, a kindhearted but tough kid with a bulky football player's build, noticeable especially next to Chris's slim runner's physique. While I was still in grade school, Chris and Brian went to Frost junior high together. On every fair-weather day, after the bus dropped them off at the corner of Braeburn and Willet, right in front of Brian's house, the boys would sit in his front yard and practice their French horns, waiting for me to come walking home from Canterbury Woods Elementary. I would sit and listen for a while, and when it was time to go home, Chris would carry anything heavy I was lugging along with his horn.

Though my memories of Brian were vivid, I hadn't seen him in several years. I ran down the stairs, eager to greet him. When I walked into the kitchen, he was on his knees, weeping hysterically. I tried to calm him with rehearsed words of reassurance that felt hollow on my breath, but his keening was inexorable. At that moment, seeing his raw emotion break out in the midst of my family's performance, I was forced to acknowledge that my brother really was dead. He was dead and never coming back.

Not long after, several of Chris's college friends arrived, including a couple of guys I remembered hearing him mention: Josh Marshall and Lloyd McBean. Lloyd had been Chris's roommate and closest friend during his sophomore and junior years at Emory. Having them there was a welcome diversion. I brought them to the dining room to view the photographic display of Chris's life. I smiled and pointed to different pictures and shared anecdotes, giving a varnished account of their friend's life before they knew him. Lloyd followed directly beside me with an air of circumspection, listening to everything I had to say. He studied the photographs carefully. Then he raised his eyes, looked directly into mine, and with an expression that appeared to be wrestling sadness and anger, said to me slowly, "Chris would hate this."

Compliant Carine crumbled. Of course Lloyd was right. Chris wouldn't have wanted to be memorialized this way, or perhaps at all. If he had, it likely would have looked much different.

But, for the day, I was an automaton, submitting Chris's very private persona for examination by many who had never even met him, on assignment from those who didn't even understand him. I noticed how many of my parents' neighbors and friends were there compared to people who really knew and loved Chris. I understood exactly what Lloyd was saying to me, and I envied his freedom to express it.

———————

THE NEXT MORNING the poster boards were replaced with fine china and fresh linens. My siblings and their spouses remained at the town house with Fish and me. We passed the scrambled eggs, toast, and bacon in silence. Fresh fruit and pastries were piled up on silver trays. It felt wrong to have this abundance of food traveling across the same surface that twelve hours earlier had displayed images of my brother slowly starving to death.

Mom didn't eat much. She stared at the plate in front of her and scattered the food around the edges.

"I think the reception went very well," she said softly.

"Absolutely, Billie," Dad concurred.

"Everyone was so kind and forgiving of Chris for what he's done to this family," she continued.

"Excuse me?" I about choked on my eggs. "What did you just say?"

My mother's eyes, wide and hurt, met mine. She was expecting pity. The compassion I felt the day before evaporated.

I looked straight back at her and sternly asked, "Do you want to talk about why he left?" Then I turned to my dad. "Do you?"

I knew my siblings were willing to have the conversation. That didn't mean we *wanted* to. We felt weakened, exhausted—sad for Billie and Walt, and for ourselves—but we all sat up to attention, ready to defend our fallen comrade if necessary.

Mom didn't say anything. She just looked down and continued moving her food around on the plate. Dad acted as if he hadn't heard. There would be no battle today. The table fell silent again.

I RETURNED TO VIRGINIA BEACH with Chris's paperback books and a few other items that Mom and Dad had decided Chris would want me to have. Although I did not feel the need to have his things with me to feel close to him, they were precious cargo. I would look through his books from time to time, paying close attention to the passages that he had underlined and his notes in the margins. In the back of *Tanaina Plantlore*, a field guide to edible plants, he kept a brief, abridged journal of his days. *He was planning to stay a long time,* I thought, noting how carefully he'd conserved space; typically, there was nothing brief about Chris's writing once he got going. He spoke about wanting to write a book someday, and so documenting important specifics from his experiences made complete sense.

On Day 43, his entry read: "MOOSE!" He'd successfully taken one down, and with only a .22, but over the following days, he recorded his difficulty preserving the meat. On Day 48, he wrote, "Maggots already! Smoking appears ineffective. Don't know, looks like disaster. I now wish I had never shot the moose. One of the greatest tragedies of my life." The following day he was clearly still chastising himself, because he wrote, "Must revamp my soul and regain deliberate consciousness. Trying to salvage what can of moose, but henceforth will learn to accept my errors, however great they be." I thought about Mom telling us how Grandpa Loren, an experienced hunter, had cried every time he had to shoot a deer to feed his family. I wondered if Chris had thought about this, too, as he agonized over the disrespect of killing the animal without purpose.

One of the entries that affected me the most was on Day 69: "Rained in. River looks impossible. Lonely, scared." He had tried to leave. On Day 67, he recorded that he'd departed the bus. He'd planned to return the same way he'd come. But after a two-day trek back to the Teklanika River, he found that the waters he had simply waded through ten weeks prior were now wide and raging with the snowmelt brought by summer. It haunted me. He had tried to come back. It would have happened around the beginning of July, as I was anticipating my trip to New York for Shelly's wedding.

I also noticed how celebratory his entry was when he reached a particular milestone. "Day 100! Made it!" he wrote. That had been a goal, clearly. But it was accompanied by several entries about how weakened he was. Those were the hardest for me to look at.

In his tattered copy of Boris Pasternak's *Doctor Zhivago*, Chris had highlighted a paragraph that read, in part:

> *And so it turned out that only a life similar to the life of those around us, merging with it without a ripple, is genuine life, and that an unshared happiness is not happiness. . . . And this was most vexing of all.*

Chris had written, in the same block-letter format he always used when he felt something was of principal importance:

HAPPINESS ONLY REAL WHEN SHARED

Given my awareness and understanding of Chris's deep beliefs in self-reliance, his warning that I was the only one who could make myself truly happy, and the great comfort I knew he took in the purity of nature rather than from human relationships, these words from him surprised me. Was he actually missing the communal feel of the society he had shrugged aside for its conformity? Had he felt regret for leaving home the way he did? Could he possibly have been thinking about our parents and trying again to find some resolution with them? My reflections were in total discord with the finality of the statements Chris had proclaimed in his last letters to me. Up to this point it had never occurred to me that he felt regret over anything he'd done.

Then, as I turned the page, I saw there was more, and any discrepancies between Chris's jotting about shared happiness and his final letters to me fell away. He'd written, also in block letters:

<u>RELATIONSHIPS</u>: THOSE <u>REAL</u> / THOSE FALSE

No one but Chris could know why he wrote these specific things. But I saw these powerful notes, when put together, as both hopeful and cautionary.

———————

DURING THE FIRST FEW MONTHS after Chris's death, I witnessed some changes within my parents that I was confident were reconnecting us in a positive way. Though I had questioned their motivations in looking for Chris when he'd disappeared, their grief now was unmistakably real. My mother was losing weight while my father gained. Their eyes were gaunt and tired. Whether or not they actually took responsibility for the loss of Chris, they were suffering. I was suffering, too, so I felt closer to them than ever before.

At home one day I received a call from a writer who identified himself as Jon Krakauer. He was working on an article about Chris for *Outside* magazine, and wanted to know if I would talk to him. I was conflicted about the idea.

I wanted to know what Chris's life was like after he left Emory, where he had been, what all he had done, and here was a journalist willing to find some answers. But Chris had had a very private nature, and I feared him being exploited, which I was quick to inform Jon during our short interview. The cause of my trepidation, however, I did not explain to him on the phone that day.

The article Jon wrote for *Outside* received an extraordinary amount of attention and generated more mail to their offices than any other article in the magazine's history. This was as much a surprise to Jon as it was to my family, which increased his already strong desire to explore Chris's story further. The next time I heard from Jon was in May of 1993. He had just made a formal agreement with my parents to expand his efforts into a book, and asked if he could come to Virginia Beach to interview me at greater length. I was cautious.

Since it was my parents who had granted him permission to tell Chris's story, I doubted that much of the truth would be told. I was also unsure how much *should* be shared. I still held out hope that my parents would see the error of their ways and regret the course of events that had led to a story at all. In the end, I agreed to at least meet with Jon in person. He was not very well known, and I didn't understand why he felt that there would be enough public interest in Chris's life and death to write an entire book about it, much less sell many of them. I doubted that anyone beyond our own family or the occasional reader of *Outside* would even pick it up.

Jon Krakauer flew to Virginia to interview me at the new house Fish and I had recently finished building. Upon meeting him, I was struck with an unexpected sense of trust of the kind that only comes from having years of history with someone. He seemed much like I would have expected Chris to be in his late thirties. He wasn't particularly tall, and he had a wiry yet quite muscular build that he did not make any effort, visual or otherwise, to boast about. His hair was dark, like Chris's, though his eyes were lighter. Overall, though, his similarities to Chris were more internal. He had an inquisitive nature that seemed to be in constant conflict with skepticism.

There was not much public information on Jon to be found. I had learned only that he was a literary, journalistic-style writer and an active outdoorsman, highly respected within the obscure world of first-rate climbers.

Although Jon had a reserved demeanor, I could almost see the current of fervent energy flowing behind his eyes. The mystery surrounding my brother's story was one that seemed to intrigue him to a point of obsession, but in a very private way.

He never asked me directly, but I could discern from Jon's questions that he believed there was much more to Chris's story than he had previously been told. He wanted to know about our family dynamics from my perspective. I recognized his intense quest for truth. At first, I spoke vaguely around the issues he was attempting to dissect, but this strategy did not last long. Not because I was unable to speak in soft circles around the specifics of our childhood—I had been doing that for years—but because, for the first time, I felt obligated to tell the truth. I had kept so much private, and even the notion of coming clean about our family history offered me a sense of relief.

I trusted that Jon wanted honest answers for the right reasons. I told him about Walt's coinciding "marriages." I told him about the awful fights, the manipulations, the violence. As I treaded into the unexplored territory of exposing the reality of our past, I became more and more comfortable with Jon. Resolute, I explained that truth was of paramount importance to Chris—and why that was. In Chris's own words, there was "nothing more crucial to a pure and happy existence." I wanted to honor and do justice to Chris, and I felt I could only do that by describing everything in the most finite detail, telling Jon the whole story so he could represent Chris fully, even if not explicitly.

Jon was grateful to my parents for allowing him to delve into the mystery of Chris's journey, and he was also sensitive to their pain. But I perceived an even stronger obligation within him to understand Chris and be fair to him. He was clearly not party to what I feared might be my parents' agenda.

While I told him almost everything, I asked that he keep much of it private. I still wanted to protect my parents from full exposure in case they could change for the better. I wanted to spare my siblings from having to deal with the painful mess of our family history in a public way. We spoke about the delicate line we would need to define and walk together. He would quote me describing my relationship with my parents as "extremely good," and at the time, I hadn't stopped believing that it could be.

Just as Jon was preparing to head back to the airport, I felt an overwhelming reassurance come over me. I decided to let him read Chris's letters, which I had never shared with anyone else—not my parents, not Fish, not my closest friend, not even my siblings. I would not let Jon make copies or take any photographs of the letters. He was restricted to handwritten notes only.

Shortly after reading the first letter, the others spread out on the table awaiting their turn to speak for Chris, Jon's mood became anxious. His eyes darted across Chris's impassioned handwriting, then back to his notepad. I knew he would need time to digest what he was reading and that there would be hours of discussion ahead. I invited him to have dinner with Fish and me and stay in the guest room for the night. His acceptance was understood as he quickly rescheduled his flight and informed his wife, Linda, of the change in plans.

Before handing over the letters, I made Jon promise that he could not include anything from them in his book without my approval, and even as I said the words, I felt that they had been unnecessary. I sensed a deep respect from him and that he was very aware that having my trust was his key to truly understanding what had made Chris tick. I had given the author of the story Chris did not live to tell the enormous responsibility of knowing the truth yet not writing it.

CHAPTER 10

OVER THE NEXT YEAR, Jon began his journey on Chris's trail from Atlanta to Alaska, and he sent me updates from the road. One letter included some snapshots of Chris's Datsun. I wondered what had happened to that car. Chris had loved it so much that he'd referred to it as a traveling companion he would never part with. Jon had tracked it down in a National Park Service maintenance yard in Lake Mead National Recreation Area, where he found it parked next to an ambulance. The Datsun had 133,788.9 miles on the odometer. Chris had abandoned the car within weeks of leaving Emory, after it had broken down in the Detrital Wash of the Mojave Desert. A note left on it reportedly said,

THIS PIECE OF SHIT HAS BEEN ABANDONED. WHOEVER
CAN GET IT OUT OF HERE CAN HAVE IT.

It reminded me of Chris's brash reactions at the bowling alley, in the racquetball court, or on the golf course. He could get very mad at things. Even the Datsun.

Jon wrote:

Here are some photos from my last trip to the desert.

It's probably a little strange for you to see Chris's car like this—washed, parked nonchalantly, looking like it must have looked when Chris was still driving it.

It certainly felt strange to me when I sat in it. I could almost feel Chris's presence.

Jon said the Datsun's engine had fired right up when it had been discovered. I studied the photos he'd sent, seeing the appeal Chris had found in the tranquil desert landscape. Imagining Chris there, giving up on his car so easily, I was slightly amused—I knew he had probably just flooded the carburetor in his frustration. And Jon was right—it was strange to see the Datsun again, and without its companion.

While Jon was busy researching Chris's travels, my family welcomed the distraction of planning my wedding. Discussing the plans at all seemed wrong, and my emotions were in constant flux. Did I deserve to enjoy this happiness in the midst of so much sadness? Was it justifiable to be planning a party so soon after Chris's death? And how could I possibly get married to a guy he'd never met? I'd envisioned getting Chris's nod of approval after he'd spent some time with Fish. But I knew Chris would have liked him and surely would have been happy for us.

Mom and Dad wanted us to have the wedding amongst the rolling hills and waterfront communities that bordered Windward Key. They were footing the bill for the wedding and wanted their business associates and friends to be able to easily attend. But since they weren't members of a nearby congregation, we couldn't use a local church. I was relieved, because Fish and I hoped to have our wedding in Virginia Beach, where his family and our friends were. So, I pointed out how hard we were working to build our own business and that a nearby venue would allow our employees and many of our best customers to attend. My parents commended my ingenuity and agreed.

Jon Krakauer called me often from the road as he discovered new information that led to new questions, all while Mom and I shopped for my dress and chose flowers, cake, and caterer. I wrestled with my loyalties: my mom and dad were providing me with a beautiful wedding while I was telling Jon what terrible parents they were.

On the surface, the possibility of reconciliation with my parents seemed promising. Mom and I laughed together for the first time in years when I tried on dresses that were ridiculously poofy. When I went with my parents to check out possible reception sites, Dad pulled me onto the dance floor and started practicing our father-daughter dance. He already knew what song he should choose, and he began to belt out "Unforgettable" in his strong baritone voice as he twirled me around the empty room.

At the same time, the relationships had an expansive hollowness—like a balloon on the brink of exceeding its limits—yet I couldn't help but blow in a few last breaths. Once again I felt that I was their last chance to maintain some semblance of a family, and I was not prepared to have them lose another child.

I HAD TROUBLE SLEEPING THE NIGHT before my wedding. My excitement to marry Fish was distanced by the immeasurable chasm that accompanied Chris's absence at such an important occasion. Still stirring in the early morning hours, I climbed out of bed and knelt to pray. I asked for peace, guidance, and strength, and for the presence of my brother.

On July 3, 1993, with nothing left to wait for, I prepared to be escorted down the aisle by my dad. My long gown of raw silk had a ruched bodice and covered buttons down the back. Wisps of soft rosettes wrapped closely around my shoulders, and behind one I tucked a silver locket, a gift from my mom. Engraved on the front was a *C* encircled by forget-me-nots—Alaska's state flower. Inside the locket I'd placed a lock of Chris's hair that we'd found inside a storage box of old photos. The envelope holding it had read "Bucko's first haircut"—a nickname my parents had used when he was a baby and his vivacity had reminded them of a bucking bronco.

When the music began, I walked to the main entrance of the church to meet Dad. He smiled and offered me his arm. Before the doors opened, he turned to me and asked, "Are you sure you want to go through with this, Woo Bear? Because if not, we can just walk right out of here. Right now."

I waited for his deep laugh and for him to add, "But you'll owe me fifteen grand!"—but he didn't. He just looked at me solidly, until I realized he was serious. I was touched, and also confused. Up to that point he had voiced no concern over whether I was ready for this moment. I felt the nerves that had collected in my shoulders and neck release as I tilted my head and smiled at his selfless offer. "Thanks, Dad, but I really do love him, very much."

Although I would have preferred to walk alone, my parents expected my father to have the honor. How would they explain any other choice to their guests? It really wasn't optional. As the doors opened wide, the crowd of smiling faces rose. When we began our pace with Mendelssohn's "Wedding March," I was glad I hadn't gone solo. I wasn't sure I would have made it down the aisle without someone to walk beside me in Chris's place.

I tried to focus solely on Fish. He looked incredibly handsome, standing at the altar flanked by the groomsmen and bridesmaids. Ten months earlier I had knelt there, crying in anguish over the loss of my brother. I knew this association was not lost on my soon-to-be husband. As I walked up the steps and his eyes met mine, he flashed that great smile that always made me feel amazing, and I was lost in the happiness of the day and how lucky I was to be marrying the man of my dreams. Reverend Keever walked us through the nuptials, and we declared our vows. With that, there was officially a new man in my life, who had promised to love and protect me forever.

Most of my siblings attended, and it gave me great comfort to see my sisters in the pews, though I felt a little uncomfortable about the grandeur of my wedding as compared with theirs. But if they felt anything other than pure happiness for me, I didn't see it on their faces that day.

The reception was gorgeous—perfect in almost every way. I was disappointed, though, that the roses on the cake were pink—not peach, as I'd requested. Almost as soon as I had the thought, I laughed. That was just the sort of thing Chris would have teased me about, and he'd have been right to. What did it matter? The cake was still beautiful, it would still taste great, and the wrong flowers wouldn't change the meaning of the day. Though my mom had tried to represent Chris with the locket, and my dad had too by using the "Woo Bear" nickname for me, it was the moment of prioritizing substance over ornamentation that reminded me of him the most.

When the party was over, Fish and I made for the mountains. Fish had suggested we avoid expensive airlines and opt for a road-trip honeymoon westward through the Appalachians. It was far from the romantic tropical retreat we had originally discussed, but I was delighted to hike on some of the same trails I'd walked on with my brother, and it seemed to be an incredibly sweet gesture on Fish's part. We took in beautiful summer views of the Shenandoah National Park and the Blue Ridge Mountains. We continued on into Kentucky and stayed a couple of days with his maternal grandparents in Louisville. We toured Churchill Downs, where Sea Hero had recently pulled off his valiant win of the Kentucky Derby. Our final destination was the massive Opryland Hotel in Tennessee, where we enjoyed relaxing spas, acres of meticulously manicured golf courses, fabulous dining, and nonstop country music shows. The hotel boasted a vast assortment of gardens and atriums, and Fish regularly departed our hotel room for long walks. I thought it was strange but also quite considerate of him to give me space as I primped for our next outing—he knew it irritated me to be hovered over while getting ready.

When we returned from our honeymoon, we quickly adapted to a comforting routine of working hard and enjoying our time together—a lifestyle we maintained over the next three years. At play, we were adventurous and took every opportunity to get outdoors. At work, we were earning an excellent reputation within the industry and we continued to expand the business. I had significantly boosted my business management and accounting knowledge at Old Dominion University, but I'd left the program when I was still two years shy of earning a degree. I worried I'd made a mistake by leaving school. I found myself still wondering if Chris would be proud of me. But I wanted to concentrate on the business opportunities at hand, so I focused on my big brother's advice to stay true to myself.

JON HAD DECIDED ON A BOOK TITLE for Chris's story. It would be called *Into the Wild*. Once the research was completed and he began the writing phase of the book's development, he sent me chapter drafts and excerpts to check for accuracy and content where the family was concerned, and to ensure that he was remaining within the boundaries I'd requested.

Through Jon, I constantly learned new information about Chris's experiences, where he'd been, and the people he'd met. During his two-year trek, he'd traveled across the United States and as far south as Mexico before heading toward the destination he'd idealized since his first read of Jack London's *Call of the Wild* in grade school: Alaska. He had visited the Land of the Midnight Sun once before, during a semester break from college, and was hooked. On his second venture, after a long journey through the Yukon Territory, he arrived in

Alaska and made it to Fairbanks, then hitched a ride toward Denali. He hiked into the wilderness through tough spring terrain on the Stampede Trail. On the fourth day of hiking, he was amazed to find a deserted bus, oddly parked amongst overgrown dormant buckbrush some twenty-five miles from the nearest highway—"Magic Bus Day," he'd written in his journal.

In the summer of 1961, the bus had been part of a camp of gutted vehicles towed out into the wilderness to support workers who were building a road intended to ease access to proposed mining efforts in the area. But conditions proved too unstable to support the project and it was abandoned within a few months. The crew broke camp and left as they had come, but Fairbanks City Transit bus 142 remained behind with a broken axle to be used as a shelter for local trekkers and moose hunters, and to be stumbled upon more than thirty years later by my brother.

From Jon, I learned that the strong magnetism Chris had had in high school and college had endured during his travels. He'd always been good-looking and charming without an ounce of egotism. His self-confidence was apparent. He spoke out against human rights atrocities and global political injustices, and shared strong opinions about social imbalances he witnessed—whether within our local government or at our high school. He did it all without sounding self-righteous. He had conservative values and was cofounder of a young Republicans club in college, but not being one to adhere to labels or blind allegiance, he fervently authored derisive articles about both sides of the political aisle as an assistant editor of the school paper.

Individuals who had picked Chris up while he was hitchhiking had been profoundly moved by their conversations. Regardless of whether their time with Chris lasted only a few hours or developed into brief relationships between fellow vagabonds, wanderers, employers, or friends, they all reported feeling an unexpected connection to this young man, who had struck them as intelligent, polite, and hardworking—even while he had often remained evasive and mysterious.

One individual he seemed to have made an enduring impression on was an elderly man named Ron Franz, who Chris spent time with over a two-month period in the winter before he left for Alaska. Ron was a former military man who told Chris he had lost his wife and only son in a car accident over thirty years prior. He lived alone and didn't have many friends when he offered Chris a ride to a desert campsite in Anza-Borrego. Afterward, he couldn't get Chris out of his mind. He thought he was a smart kid and later went back to find him and talk him into a better direction for his future. Unsurprisingly, my brother rebuffed the offer, but the two became good friends. Chris—whom Ron knew as Alex—frequently went to Ron's house for meals, to do laundry, and to learn from Ron the art of leatherworking. As they grew closer, Ron put together the small pieces of information that Chris let slip in conversation and came to understand that Chris no longer had a family. They weren't deceased, Ron realized, but Chris had actually *chosen* to denounce his parents and leave his family behind. Given the respect Ron had gained for the boy, he accepted it must be for good reason. Ron offered to adopt my brother, suggesting he fill a grandfatherly role in Chris's life. Chris declined the offer; keeping people at arm's length was a necessity for him to continue his solitary journey to Alaska.

Chris had a tendency to lecture Ron about the importance of getting out and experiencing the world instead of treading a predictable path from church to grocery store to home. Ron listened. After Chris left his life, Ron moved out of his apartment and began living as a "rubber tramp" out of the back of a GMC van he'd outfitted with a bunk, a kitchenette, camping gear, and a portable toilet.

One day when he was driving back to his campsite from gathering supplies, he picked up two hitchhikers and started talking to them about his friend Alex. One asked if the friend's name was Alex

McCandless, and when Ron said yes, he told Ron that his friend had died. The hitchhiker had just read Jon's article in *Outside*.

Ron was devastated. He immediately wrote to the magazine, asking for a copy and explaining that he knew "Alex" and wanted to talk to the article's author. Jon was soon in touch with him.

Through Jon, my parents contacted Ron, and he sent the family a letter in return, describing his time with Chris and the impact Chris had had on his life. I could sense Ron's strong disappointment in Chris, his words deliberate despite the shaky handwriting, as he asserted that he had had no idea that Chris had come from such an admirable family with such loving, Christian parents. He seemed to be apologizing for Chris. I saw the satisfaction my parents gained from reading the letter and showing it to others, and it offended me.

I immediately drafted my own letter to Mr. Franz.

> Please keep this letter just between us, but I feel it is important
> to correct any inaccurate impression you might have of the family
> life Chris left behind. Our childhood was violent—physically and
> emotionally—and very difficult.

I offered just a few more vague sentences but succeeded in getting the message across. He replied:

> Dear Carine,
>   I can sense the honesty and sincerity in your words, and find
> you sound a lot like your brother. So much of what you wrote
> makes the bits and pieces of what Chris claimed to be so angry
> about ring true.

He complimented my brother on the fine young man Ron believed he was, thanked me for helping him to understand Chris better, and promised to safeguard anything that I shared with him.

When Mom and I traveled together to California to visit with Ron in the Anza-Borrego Desert, my pen pal and I communicated many knowing glances during our group discussions about the friend, brother, and son we remembered. Ron was still grieving deeply over the loss of his companion. Several times he stopped in mid sentence, tears welling in his eyes, and stared out across the desert.

Ron brought us to the landlocked Salton Sea and other areas that he and Chris had explored together around the outskirts of Borrego Springs. The desolation seemed endless. We passed a small group of fellow migrants, but other than that, we saw only the crimson blooms on the cholla and ocotillo cacti and some passing tumbleweeds. It was difficult for me to grasp what had attracted Chris to the place.

It wasn't until darkness fell that I understood. Around our diminutive campfire, the desert flats were perfectly level as far as the eye could see. As the sun vanished beneath the horizon, the blackness exceeded the parallel of the parched sands and seemed to completely wrap around me. The night sky offered the most breathtaking view I had ever witnessed. It was as if I had been raised up to touch the ceiling of a planetarium, and the display of stars swallowed me up. I sat alone on the surface of the earth in a cheap lawn chair, like just another infinitesimal speck of sand.

COMPARABLE TO THE VASTNESS of the starry sky of Anza-Borrego are the seemingly endless northern plains of South Dakota. Fish and I traveled to the Badlands state to visit another individual who'd become a close friend of Chris's during his travels, Wayne Westerberg, in Carthage. It was clear to me why Chris had felt comfortable with the measured pace and blue-collar virtues of the small farming community, which covered an area of only one and a half square miles. It boasted one grocery store, one bank, and a solitary gas station. The closest international airport was almost two hundred miles away.

From the letters that Chris had written to Wayne, it was obvious that he had forged a strong bond with him, as if Wayne had been somewhat of a young father figure. In one letter, Chris encouraged Wayne to read *War and Peace.*

> *I meant it when I said you had one of the highest characters of any man I'd met. That is a very powerful and highly symbolic book. It has things in it that I think you will understand. Things that escape most people.*

In his last postcard to Wayne, he wrote:

> *If this adventure proves fatal and you don't ever hear from me again I want you to know you're a great man.*

Clearly my brother was drawn to Wayne, much like others had reportedly been drawn to my brother. I was eager to meet him and understand the man's appeal for myself.

As Fish and I drove our rental car along barren highways through continuous crops of corn, wheat, hay, and sunflowers, the drive reminded me of the cross-country trips my parents took us on, Airstream trailer in tow. Once when we were driving through the Midwest, we watched anxiously as an ominous dark cloud made its way across the plains. As it approached, we realized it was not the storm we had expected to drive through. Instead of heavy raindrops, the windshield wipers sloshed around a paste of yellow-green mush. Even with the wipers going at top speed, it was nearly impossible to see through the glass. I marveled at the ghastly display as the swarm of insects perished explosively, smacking against the surface with a *thunk* like hailstones. Dad said they were locusts, just like the eighth plague of Egypt.

Fish and I arrived in Carthage in the afternoon and met up with Wayne, who took us to see the grain elevator and other places where Chris had spent time. Wayne drove fast—with one beer in his lap and one in the console. I looked over at Fish, but he seemed unconcerned, so I double-checked my seat belt and tried not to appear terrified. Later we all met up with Wayne's girlfriend, Gail, and a group of Chris's friends and went to the places Chris had liked to hang out after work—the Cabaret bar, the bowling alley. I shared childhood stories about Chris's intense bowling antics, and his friends all laughed knowingly, remembering the friend they had known. The group was kind and welcoming to me and Fish, and I found them to be incredibly genuine.

Wayne drank heavily all night, and at some point switched from beer to whiskey, so Fish took the wheel when it was time to head back to town. We'd been invited to spend the night at Gail's house, and she led me and Fish upstairs to our room. As she opened the door, we saw that her teenage son was already fast asleep in the bed.

"Oh no. I feel terrible taking his bed from him," I said.

"No, it's fine," Gail said as she roused him. "Hey, get up! We've got guests sleeping in here tonight."

Her son awoke surprised and a bit annoyed, but he muttered a kind "Hello" as he stumbled out of the room, half-conscious and half-naked, to find an available couch space downstairs.

"Okay, see you guys in the morning," Gail said melodically as she closed the door.

I stood there looking at the door. "Do you think she's bringing in new sheets?" I asked Fish.

"What? Of course not." He laughed as he put his bag down and rearranged the pillows.

"But don't you think that's kind of gross? I mean, geez. He was in his underwear! And we don't know what's happened in that bed!"

"You know what, Carine? Sometimes you're just like your mother—everything has to be so prim and proper," Fish snapped. "Why can't you just be grateful to the kid for giving up his bed for you?"

I was taken aback by Fish's abrasive response. It pissed me off when anyone drew similarities between my mother and me beyond our big brown eyes, and he knew it. But before I could object, we heard a full-blown fight outside the room. I heard Gail hurrying down the hall and screaming. Fish looked away from me, his glare turning to concern and alarm. He rushed over to open the door, and I saw Wayne attacking Gail, battering her as he pinned her up against the wall. In a flash, Fish was out the door and, without the slightest hesitation, had pulled Wayne off her. He picked Wayne up by one shoulder and his belt, carried him down the flight of stairs, and literally through Gail's storm door. I stood at the top of the staircase, frozen. I could see Fish had pinned Wayne down on top of a patch of grass and was yelling in his face "You do not hit a woman!" over and over again.

I was horrified, and devastated by the thought of Chris escaping our home only to see this. I began to cry hysterically.

Fish released Wayne and stood over him for a moment. Wayne made no attempt to get up. Fish turned quickly, walked back through the doorway, took a stash of cash from his wallet, and handed it to Gail. Gail stood with her eyes wide and her hands clasped at her chest.

"I'm sorry about your door," Fish said sternly. "I'm taking Carine out of here." He continued back up the stairs without pause.

Fish shot me a look that said, *Everything will be okay. You can stop crying,* and I did. We both had too much baggage tied up in what we'd just seen, and it was time to go.

I hadn't even processed everything before Fish was in and out of the bedroom with our bags. I numbly followed him to the car, not saying a thing to Gail or her son. Although Fish had not struck him, Wayne appeared lifeless as he lay drunk in the front yard.

I had no idea where we would go. Fish's only concern was to go *away.*

Rural South Dakota is pitch-black at night if there are no lights from the cosmos to help guide you. We drove around aimlessly, as if the car and roadways were tightly wrapped inside a swath of thick black velvet. With no hotels nearby and nowhere to stay, we pulled over to the edge of a cornfield to sleep in the car until the sun came up and we could find our way back to the airport and to Virginia.

We didn't talk about the scene we'd just left. Tears streamed slowly down my face and I remained silent. As I laid my head on Fish's shoulder, I attempted a fitful sleep. I couldn't believe what had just happened. I'd hoped to come to Carthage to feel closer to Chris, to spend time with those he'd grown close to in the years we were apart. Instead, I only felt confused.

All I could think was *Did Chris ever see Wayne do that? And if so, why in the world did my brother stay in Carthage?* No one who'd witnessed Wayne's drinking throughout the evening had seemed concerned. It seemed to be his typical behavior. Did those drunken nights always end in violence?

Had Chris ever had to pull Wayne off Gail as Fish did? Would he have done what I had tried to do with Patrick's father—to make him see his errors and repent? Had he ever encouraged Gail to leave? Chris had been on a pursuit of lightness and peace. I couldn't understand why he would have felt so connected to Wayne.

Perhaps, I thought as I finally drifted off, it was the same thing that kept me connected to my parents.

CHAPTER 11

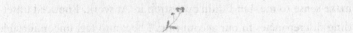

A FTER OUR RETURN from South Dakota, I relied on Fish more than I liked to admit. Despite the emotional roller coaster I was on, I managed to remain comparatively grounded, and I owed much of that to his love and support. Even when we argued, he was even tempered and gentle hearted. We had a successful business and a beautiful new house; we'd acquired a girlfriend for Max—another Rottweiler named Shelby—and with that, we'd established our little family at home to add to the family we'd created at work. We spent time with our employees socially, and many of our customers were also our friends. We traveled to visit with my siblings, and when we saw my parents, Fish was a welcome buffer, always keeping the mood light.

While I still struggled to imagine a world without Chris, I wanted for nothing. I saw my entire future before me, and it involved a long and happy life with Fish. Our days were routine at times, and I would recall my brother's cautionary advice that if you plan everything out completely from beginning to end, you destroy your chance for adventure. But Chris and I were as different as we were similar, and the fluency of the monotony felt comfortable to me.

Sometimes, though, even if you don't seek change, it finds you.

Throughout the next several years, I started to notice changes in Fish. He became arrogant in ways he'd never been before, and I knew something wasn't right. We had built up our business with a solid staff, and as we continued to grow and expand, I felt strain from the employees. I heard sideways comments that I should be around more.

I frequently found small pieces of foil in Fish's pockets when I did his laundry. When I asked him why, he said he'd been "experimenting with a new way to test electrical connections." His answer didn't make sense to me, but I didn't question it. At work, I noticed unsettling discrepancies in our accounting. I began to feel uncomfortable with some of his new friends, the ones who hung around the shop at night. I dealt with dissatisfied customers for the first time.

Whenever I questioned Fish about these things, he had a reasonable explanation for himself or an accusation toward one of the employees. One employee in particular—Lee—was a problem, according to Fish. When it came time to fire Lee, Fish left all the talking to me, though all three of us sat down together. Lee gave me a piercing look—not an angry one, but one that seemed to say, *You've got it all wrong, honey.* It was unsettling. After Lee walked out, I turned to Fish.

"You were so adamant about firing him," I said. "Why did you just sit there? You didn't say anything. You didn't even look up."

Fish shrugged. "It was just hard to look at him after what he did," he said, and I chose to believe him.

Even once Lee was gone, the imbalance in the books continued, so I questioned our receptionist, Cindy. Cindy had worked for us for two years. She was hardworking, pretty and sweet, thorough and trustworthy. I put her on task to ensure that every part that was delivered was matched up to a customer invoice.

Then receipts started to disappear.

One day while hovering over Cindy's desk, I tracked her organization to see if I could solve the puzzle.

"Somehow we're losing receipts between your files and mine," I said. "Show me how you track what still needs to be billed out."

"After every part comes in, I assign it to that customer's invoice, just like you instructed me to," she replied, "and then I label it accordingly and put it in the relevant folders on your desk, exactly like you asked me to."

"Well, how in the world do I keep getting bills from our suppliers for parts we've never charged out?" I interrogated. "Here are the carbon copies of what the suppliers sent me, and your signature is on them as the person who received the parts. I just don't understand how these are falling between the cracks, and it's costing us a fortune!"

Cindy was noticeably flustered as she looked up at me with red eyes. She was a wonderful employee, and I wasn't trying to accuse her, so I softened my tone. "I know it gets busy up here sometimes, so just please try to keep better tabs on the receipts."

"Are you going to start spending more time up here during the day?" she asked.

"Well, I was going to," I answered, "but Fish prefers that I join him at night. I like having the quiet in the office while he works back in the shop. It's more productive that way. He assured me he's not overloading you up here."

Cindy rolled her eyes in a rare display of dissent.

"What is it?" I asked.

"Nothing. Just . . . never mind."

"No, tell me."

She was hesitant but continued. "Fish takes those parts from my desk, and the receipts, before I can enter them into the computer," she said softly.

"But don't you ask him which customer they're for?" I inquired. "I showed him what's been missing each month, and he said he doesn't understand how they aren't getting billed out."

Cindy stood up and looked at me for a few more seconds. Then she sighed and walked out to the shop. I hoped she wasn't quitting.

I felt extremely uneasy, like something awful was about to happen. My instincts were validated when she walked back in a few minutes later, following our lead technician, Greg, who was also Cindy's husband.

Greg was an excellent technician. He wore long black braids, was a rider of Harley Davidsons, and hosted an elaborate annual Halloween party laden with terrifying, fantastic theatrical props. He was small in stature but big in heart, well-read, and enjoyed listening to an eclectic mix of disturbing rock and classical music while he diagnosed automotive ailments. He'd worked for us for several years, and I had grown to respect and trust him.

"Listen, we need to talk," he said. "I hate to be the one to tell you this, but you're being really naïve. Your husband has a real problem. He's been using crystal meth up here at the shop."

The words coming out of Greg's mouth rattled around in my head, my brain void of comprehension. "What?" was the only response I could muster.

Greg explained that he'd witnessed the drug use on several occasions and had confronted Fish about it but to no avail. Cindy tearfully explained how she often had to talk to him about customers' cars through the bathroom door. They explained how inventory was being sold for cash or traded for drugs, as was most of the after-hours work. Fish's mood swings were making all the employees nervous, as were his implications that they would all lose their jobs if I became aware of the situation.

I stood there, taking it all in. Greg was right; I had been incredibly naïve. I had never used any drugs, never smoked a cigarette, never even had a cup of coffee. I was completely ignorant about the signs of addiction all around me—but I shouldn't have been. The pieces of the puzzle all slid into place. It all made perfect sense in its absurdity. The only thing that made no sense was how Fish could take such a perfect life, such an amazing opportunity, and risk it like this.

I waited until Greg, Cindy, and the rest of the staff had left for the day before confronting Fish. Although Fish had claimed that Lee's job performance was the reason for his firing, I was now worried that he had been a victim of Fish's deceptions, and I did not want that to happen again. I walked into the shop where Fish was working, or where I'd *thought* he was working; he was slumped over, apparently sleeping, in a red barber's chair in front of the intricate parts of a Ford AOD transmission sprawled across a workbench. A day earlier I would have marveled at how he could sleep in such an uncomfortable position, with his large, muscled body all slumped over itself. *He must be so tired from working so hard,* I would have thought.

"Fish!" I said loudly and shook him.

He rubbed his eyes. "Hey, hon," he said, smiling warmly.

"Hey, we really need to talk. I want you to tell me what's been happening with these receipts. I want you to tell me why we're not getting paid for these parts. We're not getting paid in the books for these after-hours jobs either, so what are they being paid for with?"

"What's going on, Carine?" he asked, confused and still waking up. "We've talked about this—I don't know what the problem is with the receipts."

"Listen to me, Fish. I know you are lying. Please give me the respect I deserve and tell me the truth."

"What exactly are you accusing me of?" He was wide awake now. "Did someone say something to you?"

"It doesn't matter how I know. I just know. You're using drugs. You need help."

Fish was caught, and he knew it—there was no sense trying to deny it. What he did deny was that it was a problem. He was only doing a small amount, only occasionally, he explained. "Carine, come on, hon, it's me. I'm fine. Look at me." And he did look fine—muscular, tanned, healthy. Not what a meth head was supposed to look like. "Look, we work so hard, and I need a little pick-me-up to get through sometimes. But it's not a problem—I can stop anytime I want."

"Great," I said. "Then stop." I couldn't enable him to ruin himself completely, destroying all of us in the process. I had a responsibility to our customers and staff, and to all that Fish and I had worked so hard for.

I had faith that Fish would stop using, but I wasn't going to depend on seeing change in someone—I had learned that lesson already. There was no time to feel ashamed or sorry for myself. At the shop, I went into survival mode. I became very methodical while making a point to stay completely fair. I changed the computer passwords on the accounting and check-writing programs at the shop to protect the company. I went to the bank and entered instructions that neither Fish nor I could withdraw any cash from the business or personal accounts without both of our signatures. I kept the books and financial reports completely transparent.

I became heavily involved with the operations of the shop during regular business hours, working alongside the staff, watching Fish closely—who still assured us he could stop cold turkey, no problem, even though we were all "clearly overreacting."

Fish now served in a diagnosis and service management role only. He seemed normal and was still functional in the shop, but we could not have a drug abuser repairing brakes or installing wheels. I monitored when Fish was there and who was with him. If he worked late, so did I. I banned certain persons from the property.

At home, I moved into one of the guest rooms. Fish agreed to counseling and we began to see Reverend Keever once a week, the same man who'd guided us in exchanging wedding vows on that hopeful summer day. After months of listening to Fish lie and deny throughout our sessions, I worried that he had no intention of quitting his drug abuse. Though he claimed he already had, the signs were still there. The employees confirmed my fears, since they had become watchdogs themselves.

I finally told my parents and his what had happened. I felt that exposing Fish fully would take away his hiding place, and once forced to see himself—to really analyze what he was risking—he'd make the positive change that only he could make. I organized an intervention at our home with his entire family. I knew how much they all meant to him, and I had no doubt that together we could get Fish clean. At the intervention, Fish said that was what he wanted, too, while still insisting that his habit was under control. His sister tearfully pleaded with me to not leave her brother. I looked back at her, stalwart, knowing that I was preparing myself to do exactly that.

"Please," she begged. "He loves you so much."

But I didn't believe that anymore. How does someone love you and lie to you? How do they choose drugs over you? How could that lead to an outcome where I wasn't left feeling like the fool who should have been smart enough to leave? I was determined to remain honest with myself about what I really wanted out of life. A comfortable lifestyle and financial success were not enough. I wanted a partner in love I could always trust.

Not long after the intervention, Fish's father, a retired marine colonel, came to stay with us for a weekend. On the second night of Colonel Fish's stay, I sat with him on the front porch while he smoked a cigarette. After chatting, I walked inside the house to look for Fish. I headed upstairs to our bedroom. As I rounded the corner into our large walk-in closet, I saw him hurriedly putting something away inside a shoe.

"What is that? What are you hiding?" I accused.

"Nothing!" he spewed, his voice laden with guilt.

I ran in as he picked up the shoe again. I wrestled it out of his hands and found a plastic bag of white powder stuffed inside.

I shrieked at him, "I knew you were lying! Why are you doing this to yourself—to *us*? How dare you bring this into our home!"

I sprinted to show it to the colonel. He inspected the contents, and when his eyes returned to mine, they were heavy with disappointment. "This is cocaine," he said.

It was the first time I had seen Fish's drug use firsthand. With irrefutable evidence that he was still lying to me, something in me changed. I felt exceptionally disrespected. Honesty was not too much to ask for. I went back inside to find Fish sitting on the couch. His father followed me, waiting for my reaction. I walked slowly over to Fish and laid down an ultimatum.

"That's it," I said sternly. "This is your absolute last chance. It's the drugs or me. No compromises."

After that night, Fish started to spend less time at the house.

I HADN'T SLEPT WELL since my brother's death. If I didn't go out with friends to pass the time, I would come home late from work, feed the dogs, and just sit in front of the television for hours. Lying on the couch with remote in hand, I would run through the broad range of cable channels from bottom to top and back again, watching nothing, until it was time to go back to work. On the nights I made it up to bed—still in the guest room—I would read through one of Chris's books until my eyes gave in to my exhaustion and I could no longer focus. One night as I read from Leo Tolstoy's *Family Happiness,* I came across a section where Chris had placed an asterisk in the margin and brackets around the following excerpt:

> *"It is a bad thing," he said, "not to be able to stand solitude."*

Farther down the page it continued:

> *"Well, I can't praise a young lady who is alive only when people are admiring her, but as soon as she is left alone, collapses and finds nothing to her taste—one who is all for show and has no resources in herself."*

My tired brain tossed these phrases back and forth, from left side to right. When I lost Chris, I'd had Fish to help me pick up the pieces.

Who would I have when I lost Fish? For so long I'd been afraid, I realized, of being alone.

I'd also been afraid of not having money. I looked around the large guest room and thought about its place in my four-bedroom house. I examined the decorative items on the walls and shelves and couldn't remember where half of them had come from, or why I had felt compelled to purchase them.

I thought about the past six years of my life and their place within all twenty-five. I wanted to learn something valuable from this experience. I wanted it to be worth it. I wanted to remember it all and understand why it was happening to me—again.

I did not feel close enough to my parents to share my feelings with them. I was embarrassed that the money they had invested in our wedding was all for nothing. I was so young and I already had two failed marriages, but I couldn't let the fear of that failure make me stay. My mother had stayed. Once again, I determined I would not.

The supportive phone calls from Fish's family had stopped. I had no family locally. My siblings all lived halfway across the country. I was very alone—but I felt more empowered than lonely—and I gained a further understanding of what Chris had experienced out in the wilderness. *It is a bad thing not to be able to stand solitude.* It is a wonderful thing to embrace it, and I was ready.

––––––––––

FISH'S BEHAVIOR AT THE SHOP became erratic. One day he came flying through the waiting room on Rollerblades, maneuvering quickly from one side of the shop to the other, then back out to the parking lot. A clownish smile filled his face. "Hello!" he said in a bizarre tone as he entered the room. "Good-bye!" he said as he exited, in the same strange tenor. The customers sitting nearby got a chuckle out of the oddity. Cindy and I looked at each other, dumbfounded.

What the hell is he doing?

I walked outside to find him working inside a white Chevy G20 that neither Cindy nor I had on the schedule that day. As I opened the passenger side door, I saw him hunched over in the driver's seat, his skates repeatedly sliding upward with a screech as he pushed against the floorboards, trying to pull the steering column from the dash.

"What the hell do you think you're doing?" I asked.

"What does it look like I'm doing, Carine?" he retorted. "I'm fixing the ignition on this van!"

"Like hell you are! Get out of it. Now!" I demanded. "You're high!"

"You're mean," he complained as he came out of the van. Then he promptly declared a slogan from a bumper sticker he'd recently installed on his Jeep: *"Mean people suck!"*

"Are you serious?" I scoffed back at him. "You can't come to work acting like this! I don't even want you around here anymore!"

"Fine!" he said, then stuck his tongue out. "That will just give me more time to spend with my new girlfriend," he continued. "She hates you!"

"Oh, please," I laughed. "You really think I care? She's never even met me! And I doubt you've been honest with her about why we split."

"She's much cooler than you!" he shot back. "She'll party with me!"

"Lovely," I said as I walked back toward the shop. "Now get the hell out of here."

"You're just a hard-ass—Little Miss Can't-Be-Wrong!" was his last jab as he got into his Jeep and took off.

I'd already known Fish had a girlfriend, and it didn't bother me. I was still in love with him, but I had also moved on with someone else, possibly before he'd even met her. Although we were still married and sometimes still under the same roof, we had been living separately for a long time, and the distance between us was too destructive. I did what I'd done with Jimmy but this time with stronger ammunition to justify my disreputable decision. I moved forward because I knew it would keep me from stepping back. Intimacy with another had put me safely past the point of no return.

Fish was so far gone. One night, months before it had come to this, we'd had a heart-to-heart about whether there was any chance we could stay together. At one point Fish pointed out our extreme differences on the matter at hand. I was against any drug use, even the occasional pot smoking. He said that my standards were tough to live up to.

"But I don't understand," I said. "I haven't changed. You've known I was that way since the day we met. *Why in the world* did you ask me to marry you?"

"I guess," Fish said with a smile and a shrug, "I thought you would fix me."

His words made me feel like I'd been cheated. I didn't enter into our marriage with the intention of changing him and I hadn't known he needed to be fixed. Besides, I already knew that change doesn't come to someone who doesn't really want it.

————————

AS THE ZEN SAYING GOES, "After enlightenment, the laundry." And Fish and I had a lot of the latter. We had incorporated our business as C.A.R. Services before we were married, and since we had started the company as a joint effort, we'd split the corporate shares down the middle. I had to figure out how to keep him away from the shop even though he had just as much legal right to be there as I did. Since I controlled the finances, I struck a deal with him that he would continue to receive his full salary and any profit sharing *only* on the condition that he did not show up for work.

I hired an attorney to begin divorce proceedings. Fish finished moving out of our house completely. He stayed away from the shop, and communication between us returned to being nonexplosive. We even consulted an attorney together to decide what to do about the business, which was still small but strong. Given the circumstances, it was impossible for us to manage it jointly. Our attorney advised that either we sell the company or one of us would have to buy out the other. We agreed to meet again the following month. I continued to run the shop, but I began to look for other employment options.

Before our next appointment with the corporate attorney, Fish called a meeting at the shop after hours to speak with me and all our employees collectively. Apprehensive, we all took seats on the couches and chairs in the waiting room. Fish proceeded to explain how he was going to force me out of the company and take over. Apparently he had not paid much attention to what it meant to be incorporated as equal shareholders—he couldn't just force me out.

Everyone, including me, just sat there for a few minutes listening to him. Then Greg stood up, took a measured breath, and said, "I'm not going to stay here and watch you run this place into the ground. I'm following Carine. I'm going wherever she goes. We asked her to make some changes around here and be present, and she did that. She's made it a good shop to work in again. I simply don't trust you anymore. I trust her."

One by one, the employees announced their faith in me and asserted their disappointment in my business partner. Fish sat there listening, flabbergasted. My jaw gaped even more than his.

Finally Fish stood up, called them all fools, and walked out.

The meeting was over.

I muttered out a "Thanks, guys" as the staff dispersed. Still in shock, I went back to my office and collapsed into my chair to collect my thoughts. Maybe I didn't have to leave. Could I actually buy Fish out of the business instead? It hadn't seriously occurred to me to own the shop by myself. I had just been trying to maintain everyone's jobs and keep things operational until the attorney told us what to do next. But as I sat, staring at the idle papers on my desk, which may as well have been blank, it occurred to me that this was my decision to make. I'd already been running the shop on my own, and I'd loved it.

Then Fish walked in—a ghost of the man I'd stood with at the altar, just a shadow of the man who'd stood up for me in South Dakota. He looked at me with utter disdain. "My customers will never stay with you," he said. "This is a man's business. You can never run it by yourself. You're just a *woman*."

I knew my employees could easily fill out a W-4 form at another shop down the road, put on a new uniform, and count on a paycheck—and they knew it, too. And I could easily do the same. But the way Fish said the word "woman" motivated me—I heard echoes of the way my dad had talked to my mom. *Billie, you're nothing without me.*

I wasn't eager to bust my way into a male-dominated industry as a solo female owner. But I wanted to see if I *could* do it. I thought about my big brother and what advice he would have given. The risks were great. But I was prepared and would proceed cautiously. I figured Chris would have said *Easy is boring,* and I went for it.

CHAPTER 12

MONEY WAS NEVER JUST MONEY in my family. Money was power, it was loyalty, it was leverage. It was a truism that Chris understood early. When he was home one summer from college, working at Domino's Pizza—more to stay out of the house than anything else—Shelly came to stay with us for a few days. Despite her tumultuous history with my parents, she had a good reason for the visit: she wanted to go to college, desperately, but couldn't afford it, and our mom and dad had offered to pay.

"Don't take the money," Chris warned her. "There are strings attached—there are always strings attached. If you take the money, you will feel obligated to them for the rest of your life, because they'll *make* you feel obligated to them for the rest of your life. Is that what you want? Go to school, but find another way to do it."

Shelly listened to what Chris had to say—he was so adamant and she couldn't deny his logic. But she didn't have an inheritance from Ewie like we did. She couldn't do it without Mom and Dad's help. So, she accepted the money. In the end, Chris was right. Their demands proved to be too daunting and Shelly didn't finish college.

Still, she accepted a gift of a trip to France years later, as did I, as did Shawna and Stacy. "Please come," Dad had said when he invited me. "You and your sisters. Your mom and I want to treat you to this trip—it will be good for all of us."

My sisters and I discussed it. Was there a catch? Should we go? Was this really a bid for familial connection, for closeness? If so, how could we say no to such a generous offer? Why had I spent so much energy protecting them if not to take any opportunity to preserve and improve our relationship?

In the end, we all accepted the invitation. We had a wonderful time together touring the French Riviera, enjoying cultural delicacies and historical architecture. We lazed in the sun on beaches overlooking the Mediterranean Sea. We strolled through villages and their quaint shops, which offered fine cheeses and beautiful works of art. The conversation remained lighthearted and safe. It was the kind of time spent with Mom and Dad that convinced us that a deep bond still existed that could withstand any solvent.

But soon after we returned stateside, the old dynamics were back in place. Dad called his daughters separately and told us that it was looking like he had no choice but to leave my mom. His reasons alternated from the insensitive to the ridiculous, including his own diagnosis of her state of mind being enough evidence to prove that she was bipolar—and that he couldn't be expected to stay in such a difficult relationship. He reported negative things she was saying about each of us and reminded us of hurtful things she had done in the past. He was trying to pit us against Billie, and while my sisters didn't have a good relationship with my mom, we all thought his treatment of her was unfair. We recognized he was laying the groundwork to discredit her, which probably meant that she was threatening to expose something he'd done. It reminded me of when my parents had said my older siblings were doing drugs: *Don't believe them—they're high and demented.* Any construction of a hopeful future was eroding again.

I knew the dangers of taking my parents at face value as well as Shelly and Chris did, but I still struggled with accepting more than just their financial advice. My parents were proud of my accomplishments, and they constantly boasted about them. Dad wore C.A.R. Services T-shirts around town almost every day. I needed help to buy Fish out of the business, and I had been wary yet still receptive when my mom called one day with a plan. She suggested that she and my dad loan me the money. I could pay them back with profits from the shop, the sale of the house with Fish, and my share of the royalties Jon had agreed to pay our family for the right to publish excerpts from the letters, diaries, and other documents Chris had written during his journeys. I accepted the offer and was able to pay them back quickly.

It wasn't long, however, before the same tragically comedic scene started to unfold at work at least once a week:

"Here they come again!" whoever spotted them first would warn when Walt and Billie's Cadillac sped into our parking lot. Immediately after the car jerked to a stop, both front doors would fly open as my parents tried to beat each other inside. They looked like little kids scrambling to be the first to tattle on the other, and I was the judge.

The opening line was always the same, gender interchangeable depending on who'd won the race to find me first. "Carine! Do you know what your mother/father just did?" . . . and it would go on and on in the same way it had for more than twenty years.

"How many times do I have to repeat myself?" I would scold. "You guys absolutely cannot do this here. This is a place of business—*my* place of business."

"Oh, really? Is that so? You think you got here on your own? After all we've done for you, now you won't help us in return?"

"Keep your voices down," I would say, trying to contain the scene. "You two don't want help. That's why you keep having the same fight over and over again. You actually prefer this misery. I do not. Please leave."

Eventually they would leave, but not until their tantrums had dissipated. I'd then apologize to any staff and customers who'd been in the line of fire. Luckily, Mom and Dad were out of town a lot during this time and would just leave me phone messages. And I, feeling obligated, would always call back.

I was grateful for their generosity and support, but their constant reminder of it was enough to make me regret the favor. I now felt like it had been offered simply to keep me appropriately aligned and permanently obliged to them. I was working hard to make my own money, and I was determined not to drown in the materialism Chris had warned me about.

I thought of how, when Chris and I were adolescents and my parents' business became successful, they had purchased a deluxe Airstream trailer. Our simple camping trips to the Shenandoah were replaced, and we covered more distance by tires on pavement than with boots on dirt. We went to visit extended family instead of wooded trails. We stayed at manicured resort campgrounds in vacation destinations across the country. Chris would grumble that we were missing the best stuff by driving through it rather than walking into it. Once we were set on a long expanse of highway, it allowed ample opportunity for our parents' attention to revisit the issue of debate that had sparked the most recent uproar. When we were finally settled for the night and one of Mom's delicious hot dinners came out of the oven, Chris couldn't help but reminisce about how much better everything tasted when cooked over a campfire, and how the sleeping bag and tent felt so much more rewarding after a long hike than our plush bunks in the back of the Airstream felt after a long drive. My parents considered his comments to be ungrateful and inconsiderate after they had worked so hard to provide us with what they regarded were the nicer things in life.

Before I was mature enough to make the connection, as Chris did—that the more luxury we had, the more fighting there seemed to be—I silently agreed with my parents. I only missed the natural settings of our past adventures when the weather and all other conditions were perfect. I thought Chris was crazy to prefer a tent over a climate-controlled camper, a bedroll over a mattress, a tree over a real, flushable toilet, and half-smushed SPAM-and-cheese sandwiches over Mom's saucy ham casserole served with fresh-baked rolls and warm fudge brownies for dessert. We even had a television to watch and ColecoVision and Atari to play with. But Chris complained that the light from the campground made it difficult to see the stars, that the noise scared away the deer, and when he wasn't trying to top his own record at the controls, that my Pac-Man obsession was disturbing his reading.

Not long after Chris left Atlanta, in what seems to have been a ceremonial offering after he'd abandoned the Datsun, he set fire to his remaining cash—he even documented it in photos and a journal, so important and symbolic was that act to him. Of course he had to earn money again later in order to eat and survive, but his complex relationship with money and possessions was easy for me to understand. Just as Chris had done before me, I resolved to never accept my parents' help again.

———————

ON MY TWENTY-SIXTH BIRTHDAY, my employees gave me a small cake, some balloons, and a card that read:

> *Happy birthday to a great boss—from the rest of us pathetic, aimless souls wandering with you through the valley of the damned . . . but enough about work.*

We'd been through a lot together. The changes in the business, while for the better, were financially stressful on all of us, leading to adjustments in our personal lives as well. When I first bought C.A.R. Services from Fish, I ate mainly bulk foods from grocery warehouses and went without luxuries like cable television, visits to the hair salon, and tickets to the jazz concerts I'd once enjoyed regularly. But there were also plenty of opportunities to relieve the pressure with laughter.

One day a new recruit from a local parts supplier paid a visit to the shop. There was a sliding glass window between Cindy's reception desk and my office, and we both watched as he came through the door buoyantly.

"Hi, there!" he greeted Cindy with a smile.

"Hello," she replied. "Welcome to C.A.R. Services. How may I help you?"

"Well, I'm the new sales rep in town from Primary Products," he continued, resting some suspension parts on the front counter. "We've got a new line of Monroe in stock. Can I speak with the owner for a few minutes?"

Cindy glanced over at me and I nodded my head.

"Sure. No problem." She directed him with a wave of her hand. "First door on your right."

I stood up to greet the man as he came into my large L-shaped office. "Hi, I'm Carine."

"Hey, there!" he answered. "Is the owner around?"

"That's me. What can I do for you?"

He looked around the corner. "Is your husband around?"

"No." I paused and smiled. "I'm not married. Is there something I can help you with?"

"Oh, I see. Okay. Is your father here?"

My extended right hand returned to its partner in a fold as I curled my tongue and pursed my lips. I heard Cindy struggling to not spit out the pasta she had warmed up for lunch, her hand slapping against the counter.

"No," I said sharply. "I am the sole owner. Now, what may I do for you?"

"Oh. I'm sorry." He attempted a recovery. Then he crashed and burned. "I'm here to talk about auto parts. Maybe I should speak to one of the guys in the back."

I looked over at Cindy, who now had both hands tightly clamped over her mouth, her wide, laughing eyes staring back with the same questions I was asking myself. *Is this guy serious? Did he really just say that?*

I looked back toward the poor bastard. "I'm sorry, but you seem confused," I said slowly. "Let me try to explain this again. I am the one who makes the purchasing decisions for the shop. I am the one who pays for the parts that you want to sell to us."

He stared blankly at me for a moment, then fumbled to open one of the boxes in his hands.

"Wow," I stopped him. "Are you really gonna try to sell me shocks and struts right now?"

"Oh . . . Um," he stuttered. "I guess not."

"How about you come back another day?" I suggested. "And when I introduce myself as the owner, you shake my hand, and we can move forward from there."

He left with his head down and his strut between his legs. Cindy and I loved reenacting the story to the technicians for laughs, but it was also revealing, and it was just one of many incidents like it. If I wanted to succeed, it was clear I would have to turn what Fish considered a disadvantage into an edge.

A single female shop owner was unique, and it got people's attention. We just had to earn their business. I would sit at the stoplights on my way to work each morning, watching the variety of cars pass by in every direction: a colorful compilation of metal, fiberglass, and plastic in every form; big and small, new and old; sports cars, sedans, trucks, family vans—obvious job security if you're doing things right.

We were. The schedule was consistently booked solid and all new business came from referrals. I was doing fine without Fish—actually, I was doing better than fine; I was excelling.

I loved my independence. For the first time in my life, I felt completely self-reliant.

HAVING A CUSTOMER BREAK DOWN and cry in the waiting room of C.A.R. Services was not a typical occurrence. But as I sat typing an invoice at the reception desk—wearing a T-shirt with a smiling car dancing above our slogan, WE KEEP YOU AND YOUR CAR HAPPY—I noticed Pam Stoltz starting to crumble. She was waiting for us to complete a state inspection on her Toyota Camry. Pam had been a customer for years and certainly not someone I'd describe as emotional when dealing with automotive maintenance.

"Hey, Pam? They did already tell you that your car passed, didn't they?" I asked from my seat.

"What?" she answered softly. "Oh . . . yes, thank you." Her eyes lingered for a moment on my concerned expression but then returned to her lap and the book she was reading, *The Secret Art of Dr. Seuss*—not exactly a tearjerker.

"I'm sorry to intrude," I continued, "but are you okay? Is everything all right with Mike and the kids?"

She looked back up, her face flushed. "I'm so sorry," she said and removed the book's jacket. "I started reading this a few days ago. I knew I had this appointment with you and I wasn't going to bring it, but I just haven't been able to put it down."

In her hands was a now-naked edition of *Into the Wild*. Her face wore the same expression that I'd first seen on the choir director's face the night I learned of Chris's death.

Into the Wild was flying off store shelves at a pace no one had anticipated. Apart from my long talks with Jon Krakauer, I'd remained mostly silent about the story and my relation to it. It was a surreal experience every time a customer figured out that the protagonist's sister was actually the same Carine they took their car to.

I was puzzled by the amount of attention Chris's story received, and from such a diversity of people. And as interest grew, the number of questions grew exponentially with it. The article that Jon had written about Chris for *Outside*—"Death of an Innocent"—had generated more mail than any other in the magazine's history, and now the book was proving to have the same powerful draw. Many admired Chris for his courage and felt inspired by his transcendent principles, his charitable heart, his willingness to shed material possessions to follow what he believed was the path to a pure existence. Others considered him an idiot and admonished him for what they felt was obtuse, reckless behavior. Some simply believed that he was mentally unstable and had walked into the wilderness with no intention of ever walking back out.

Chris had not concerned himself with the opinions of others, so I told myself the negative judgments shouldn't bother me—and, for the most part, they didn't. But when critics claimed his disappearance was little more than an incredibly selfish act of cruelty toward his parents, I took note. "Why would any son cause his parents and family such permanent and perplexing pain?" wrote one *Outside* reader. Another wrote, " . . . while I feel for his parents, I have no sympathy for him."

My parents drank in the sympathy they received. They attached themselves to those who said things like "My son was selfish, too. How sad that yours didn't live long enough to grow out of that teenage rebellion." They still showed no accountability, no ownership over anything that had happened. When people asked them why Chris had been so angry with them, they just sighed and said, "Well, as Jon wrote, 'Children can be harsh judges when it comes to their parents.'"

I was unsure if I'd been right not to allow Jon to write the whole truth about why Chris had left with such impudence. Then again, I didn't feel that anyone outside the family was owed an explanation—and the family already knew. Plus, I still felt Chris would have wanted my parents to have the opportunity to prove that he didn't

die in vain. But with all the criticism and "Why?" questions circu-
lating around me, it was tough not to shout from the rooftops the
real reasons Chris had left the way he did. I wanted to explain that
going into the wild was far from crazy; it was the sanest thing he
could have done.

Chris had known exactly which emotional demons he needed to
slay. He had observed firsthand how people often placed their own
needs before others', and he wasn't about to do that himself. He loved
people, and he wasn't going to be a hermit for the rest of his life. But
he needed some time and space to heal before he could grow too
close to anyone. I believe that he would have approached his role as
a husband and father with his typical quest for perfection. He was
disciplined and determined enough to do whatever it took to get
to a place where he could be open again. Far too many applied the
cliché that he was *finding himself*—but Chris had known exactly who
he was. I believe he had ultimately wanted to find a place in society
he fit into while remaining true to that knowledge.

As *Into the Wild* remained at the top of numerous bestseller lists,
my parents became more vocal about our family history, but they
always made it sound as though Walt had divorced Marcia before
becoming involved with Billie, eliminating the stem of our family
dysfunction. They repeatedly claimed to have no idea why Chris
had left, or why he had been so angry with them. They portrayed
themselves as martyrs working hard through religious missions and
charitable endeavors to bring honor to their son despite the terrible
pain he had caused them.

I called them out, in private, on every infraction. I told them that
Chris's siblings would not stand quietly in the face of such disrespect.
I warned that if they pushed the family too far, their veil was going
to fall, and the rest of us would fall away with it. Dad would widen
his eyes, then recite Bible verses and the commandment to honor thy
mother and father. Mom would try to equate their position with mine.

"Oh, Carine," she would say. "Isn't it *you* who's inventing things to protect your own image? You know, he left you, too."

But I knew better. Even though Chris's path and my own were so different and often didn't intersect, we had shared an emotional parallel. I understood *why* our childhood had affected him so severely, yet he'd always been so strong in my eyes that I'd never expected it to. Perhaps, for all the abilities in which my brother had surpassed me, one I surpassed him in was resilience.

THE YEARS PASSED WITH ME WORKING constantly at the shop and trying to keep my parents at a safe distance. I also made more of a concerted effort to connect with my brothers and sisters. It had been too easy in the past years to neglect those relationships. Outside of work, these were the people who understood me, the only people who made me feel like a part of something bigger than myself, something that I somehow completed.

One summer day I arrived at Shawna's house in Denver for a visit. Her six-year-old daughter, Hunter, had crafted and strung a colorful banner along the iron rail on the front porch that read, WELCOME, AUNT CARINE! A chorus of chatter was coming from the backyard, and as I approached, I could pick out the various tenors and altos of almost all my siblings and their families. I had not traveled to Colorado for any specific family occasion, and as I rounded the corner to see the most siblings together in one place at one time since Chris's wake, I realized that I was the occasion. I was deeply touched.

Everyone had taken time from their busy lives to gather together for the impromptu reception—the Denver pack didn't need to do things with a lot of notice or formal planning. My sisters in particular were eager to talk about the new man in my life. I'd kept my distance from any serious relationships in the years since my divorce from

Fish, but Shawna and Shelly had deduced from my periodic phone calls that this one was different. And it was.

Robert was not my usual type. Despite his adequate mechanical abilities, as a self-employed masonry contractor he worked nowhere within the automotive industry. And he was my first blond. He also had a romantic sense of humor I found irresistible. Not long after we'd started dating, he sent me his "résumé" to pass along to my father. In addition to citing his weight, height, occupation, education, and references (one of which was his mom), the résumé covered his "Current Intentions" which were "to see Carine McCandless. I have found she is an extraordinary woman who is very independent. I hope she will share her free time with me . . . If anyone cares to discuss this matter with me, I can be contacted at the following numbers."

I was definitely in love but hesitant about thinking too far ahead. I had already told Robert that although I felt comfortable committing to him for the rest of my life, I had no intention of ever getting married again.

As the sun lingered low in the west and Marcia played with the kids, my brothers and sisters and I gathered on the front porch. We lazed in comfy chairs and spoke about work and hobbies and the Broncos versus the Redskins. Chat amongst those who already had children led to inevitable jokes about various embarrassments we had all either caused or earned in our own adolescence. And just as certain, the discussion found its way to The Show, as it always did.

The Show was also in Denver during this visit, staying at the upscale condo they'd bought a few years earlier. My parents knew I was spending the day at Shawna's. They also knew they were not invited. I planned to have dinner and stay the night with them, knowing it would be easier than the repercussions of refusing their invitation.

I began to vent about the things Walt and Billie were doing in Virginia, and we all joked about their various idiosyncrasies. I brought up their obsession with having a sparkling toilet to return to after their travels. Before they got home from a trip, they'd call me and ask me to go over to their house and "swishy" the toilets so that they wouldn't have to see an ugly ring. Shawna cracked up, because she'd been the "swishy" point person in Denver once upon a time. We all agreed the worst thing to do was "poke the bear," which is what we had termed responding to one of our dad's email missives. We tallied who was in the lead for the most times written out of his will. I was pretty sure it was me, but Sam made a compelling argument that he was the front-runner. We also talked seriously about everything that we had yet to discuss together in person, like why Chris had left in the first place and what he had shared with me about the mysteries of our childhood. I spoke about the lies and manipulations, the violence and bullying. I acknowledged my awareness that they had all experienced the same thing growing up. I recognized their mother's willingness to put an end to it as well as the pain that my mother's acceptance had caused for us all. I told them how Chris had tried to salvage a relationship with Mom and Dad with his long emotional letter and their rejection that had caused him to leave in the manner he did. We talked about *Into the Wild*, the success of which they found as surreal as I did. We were all upset that Mom and Dad were giving people the wrong impression about Chris.

Surrounded by the warmth and support of my siblings, I was reluctant to continue on to my parents' place, and I pondered aloud the various excuses I could use to stay at Shawna's instead. *Too tired?* That wouldn't work; their condo was only ten minutes away. *I've had too much to drink to make the drive over?* We decided that there were two major flaws with that one. First, everyone knew I rarely drank, and when I did indulge, it was never in excess. Second, what if they insisted on coming to pick me up? That would be a most unwelcome but very plausible result of my trying to get out of my commitment.

"I'm a little surprised to finally hear you talk like this," Sam said, looking at me thoughtfully. "I honestly was concerned that you might be coming here tonight to be their mouthpiece—to try to convince all of us to give them another chance."

I sighed deeply. "I think I've just grown so weary from trying to promote peace throughout an endless war."

All my siblings had taken this path before me. Some of them had completely cut off my parents, while others had intermittent contact that was strained at best. Shelly, Shawna, and Stacy hadn't seen them much since the trip to France. But they all understood I had to make that decision for myself, on my own terms and at my own pace. While they had always remained open to talk about things I needed to discuss as I cautiously navigated my way through my own minefield of trials and tribulations with my parents, none had ever tried to deter me from maintaining a relationship with them.

I ARRIVED AT MY PARENTS' CONDO to find my dad in a jovial mood. He was standing in the kitchen whipping up a four-course meal, wearing his new chef's coat, his black and gray hair tied back in a short ponytail. Dad and I shared a tongue-in-cheek humor about his culinary ego. He had asked for a real chef's coat for his birthday, complete with an embroidered insignia: GREATEST CHEF IN THE WORLD. I, in turn, had ordered him a casual apron with an iron-on that read: I THINK I'M THE GREATEST CHEF IN THE WORLD! He would wear it in good humor for a fun picture—maybe while barbecuing a chicken—but not for the impressive spread we would share that night. He'd been on one of his health kicks lately—fish this time—and the smell permeated the air.

"Look at what Hunter made for me. Wasn't that so sweet of her?" I said as I walked over and spread the banner across the counter.

"Hey, wow! Those are great!" Dad agreed without looking up from the intense action taking place on the stovetop.

Mom glanced at the banner. She looked away quickly, but her eyes rolled as she turned her face. One look at the empty wine bottles on the table told me what she'd been doing during my reunion with my siblings.

I hadn't even removed my purse from my shoulder before she floated by me with one hand in the air, as if conducting a symphony only she could hear. "Carine, come with me."

She led me into their bedroom and proceeded to show me a beautiful and very large panoramic print of horses in a snow-covered field. "See this, Carine? See this? Your father and I picked this up at a gallery in Utah. It cost eight hundred dollars." Then she pointed out two other pieces of artwork and told me how much each of them had cost. Her alcohol-infused tour took me through every room, up to every item sitting upon a shelf or hanging on a wall, telling me where they had been traveling when they found it and how expensive it had been. I had always admired my mom for her keen bargain shopping—she was never one to shy away from advertising that the great dress she was wearing was a significant find at a consignment shop—but that wasn't the mood of tonight's performance. I recognized the mammoth crystal bowl from the Annandale house—the peace offering Dad had brought home from Germany to squelch the threat of divorce during the infamous Shelly debacle. Mom reminded me, again, of how valuable it was and how I was on track to inherit it one day. She was, I realized, presenting me all that she could offer.

Dad called us to dinner. As we sat passing the sautéed fish, the steamed vegetables and rice, the gourmet greens with Dad's always-delicious homemade dressing, I felt cold. I wanted to be at Shawna's, where the air was warm and the food less discriminating. Dad hinted for compliments about the spices used on the bluefin fillets. Mom excitedly asked how things were going with the shop and with Robert. They didn't ask a single question about my siblings or their grandchildren.

My parents couldn't conceptualize that they were ten minutes away from the richest bounty they could have ever hoped for.

I looked at my mother's tired eyes, the sag of age that was starting to come into her chin. She struggled every day with my father's hot-and-cold temperament and with her own constant, barely concealed bitterness. I wanted to take her by the hand and lead her out of her lavish confines. But I reminded myself, as I had done so many times before, that she chose to stay. Marcia had left. It had taken years, and it had been difficult, but Marcia had left for good, and her kids were better for it. Mom had opted for what she thought was a fair trade, allowing harm to come to children in exchange for a more comfortable life . . . until she herself became an abuser.

My mother was pregnant with Chris and my dad was still married to Marcia when this announcement was published in Mom's hometown newspaper.

WED RECENTLY—Miss Wilhelmina Marie Johnson, former Iron Mountain resident, became the bride of S. Walt McCandless, of Los Angeles, in a recent ceremony performed in Palm Springs, Calif. The bride is the daughter of Mr. and Mrs. Loren A. Johnson, currently of San Diego, Calif. The bridegroom is a UCLA master's graduate in electrical engineering and is employed by Hughes Aircraft Company, space systems division. The paternal grandparents of the bride are Mr. and Mrs. Edward Gunderson and maternal grandparents, Mr. and Mrs. Phillip Sundin, all of Kingsford. Mr. and Mrs. McCandless are residing in El Segundo, Calif.

Chris and me in the front yard on Willet Drive. Aunt Jan snapped this picture as Chris was leaving to go to school.

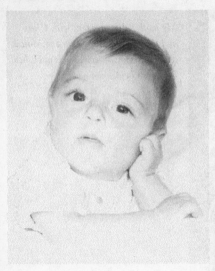

Chris was a cute baby. This was one of the pictures displayed at his wake. Even at such a young age, he looks like he has something important to say.

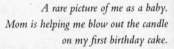

A rare picture of me as a baby. Mom is helping me blow out the candle on my first birthday cake.

I love this picture. Chris was always my protector. Aunt Jan captures a Christmas hug during our early years in Virginia. Every time I look through our childhood photos, I'm struck by how many of them show Chris hugging me

A break in the fighting to take more pictures before church. It was very rare for Mom to show her true emotions in photos.

(left to right) Mom, me, Shelly, Shawna, and Stacy in the notorious green dresses, at a summer party.

Quinn, Chris, Shannon, and me at the beach. Chris and Shannon were both older than Quinn, but Chris was small for his age, so he looks younger.

Chris making a sand mountain on vacation.
Sand castles were much too pedestrian and
formal for his taste.

One of my favorite pictures of Chris,
taken at a time when he began to ask
the hard questions about our family.

Chris and best friend Andy on the track at
Woodson High School. Chris was captain of
the cross country team.

Chris with his girlfriend, Julie, at
prom. Chris adored Julie. He was never
a big spender, but he saved up to treat
her to a gourmet dinner and an
expensive orchid corsage.

Our senior portraits from Woodson High School, circa 1986 and 1989.

...amily portrait taken during Chris's senior ...r of high school. I remember he was not in ...osing mood and wanted to leave.

At dinner following Chris's graduation from Emory College. Although noticeably aggravated, Chris was still playing his part, never indicating to our parents that he was planning to head west and cut off all contact with them. This is a powerful scene in the Into the Wild movie.

Taken during my first visit to Bus 142 in August 2007. It took me fifteen years to gather the emotional strength to make the trip.

Sitting on the bed in Bus 142 where Chris died, Jon writes in the journal I left behind for visitors to the bus to leave their own messages.

A tame early spring view of the Teklanika, the river that stranded Chris in the wilderness. He tried to cross back over in late summer at a time when the raging waters were swollen above both banks.

Chris's backpack was returned to me fifteen years after his death, with his wallet tucked inside. Examining these items gave me peace and insight into what he intended to do after his journey was complete.

Spending time with Chris's beloved books, reading the notes he left in the margins, was a great source of strength for me after his death.

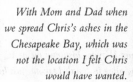

With Mom and Dad when we spread Chris's ashes in the Chesapeake Bay, which was not the location I felt Chris would have wanted.

Jon sent me this photo in January 1993. He was researching Into the Wild *and following Chris's trail out west when he found his beloved Datsun, all cleaned up and recovered from where Chris had abandoned it in the Detrital Wash of the Mojave Desert in Arizona*

Shelly, Chris, and I shared a strong connection. His absence was palpable whenever the two of us were together. Here we are after Shelly's wedding.

Gail and Wayne, Fish and me at a bowling alley in South Dakota, just before the incident at Gail's house.

Mom and me visiting Chris's friend, Ron Franz, in Anza-Borrego California, in 1994.

Me in the shop, showing my admiration to a customer's 4.1L GM V8 engine after it had put in years of hard work and high mileage, with a kiss on the valve cover.

Mom and Dad in front of their first RV after upgrading from the airstream trailer. Dad loved wearing my C.A.R. Services company T-shirts to show his support.

Robert and me at our intimate Kauai wedding, where we committed to being Heather's parents together.

Heather's first Christmas morning with Robert and me. She was an immediate and adorable teacher of lessons about pushing the limits of your comfort zones.

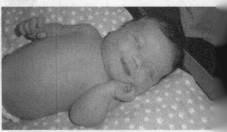

Christiana at two weeks old. She has been smiling since day one.

At my baby shower when I was expecting Christiana. It was taken at a time when I still hoped very much to salvage my relationship with my mom, while sensing it was deteriorating.

Marcia holding Christiana, in a sweater she knitt for her. Despite painful part of Marcia's past th I resulted from, has always been wonderful to me and my kids.

A very pregnant Shelly, Robin Wright, Sean Penn, Shawna, Christiana, me, and Emile Hirsch during the filming of Into the Wild in 2006.

With Jon Krakauer and Sean Penn at the L.A. premier of Into the Wild. The three of us shared a close bond while making the film.

With my siblings at a fund-raising event in Denver. From left:
Quinn, Shelly, Sam, Shawna, Stacy, and me.

With gracious Eddie Vedder and my girls on a tour bus in Baltimore, Maryland.

PART THREE

UNCONDITIONAL LOVE

He was right in saying that the only certain happiness in life is to live for others.

—Leo Tolstoy, *Family Happiness,*
passage highlighted by Chris

Oh, how one wishes sometimes to escape from the meaningless dullness of human eloquence, from all those sublime phrases, to take refuge in nature, apparently so inarticulate, or in the wordlessness of long, grinding labor, of sound sleep, of true music, or of a human understanding rendered speechless by emotion!

—Boris Pasternak, *Doctor Zhivago,*
passage highlighted by Chris

CHAPTER 13

O N ROBERT'S AND MY first Christmas morning together, he had a very large and heavy gift under the tree for me, wrapped in a hodgepodge of inharmonious papers and tape that one might expect from a man who works in construction. It was a new toolbox—just what I needed. As I opened the easy-glide drawers in delight, examining the new home for my various screwdrivers and ratchet sets, a small red velvet box slid out across the smooth, cold metal. I jumped back at the sight of it as my hand released the drawer. I looked at Robert.

"What was that?" he asked, failing to seem surprised.

"I don't know," I replied. "What *was* that?"

"I guess the Craftsman quality inspector must have left it in there," he continued with a smile. "Better check it out and see if it's a problem."

Around our fifth date, Robert and I took a long walk down the beach and I tried to talk him out of seeing me again. As much as I enjoyed being with him, my growing feelings made me nervous. He could already tell I was falling, and he teased me politely as I presented my case against being in love. At twenty-eight, I already had two failed marriages, and I'd made it clear on more than one occasion that two was enough. I was happily independent, was financially self-sufficient, and had a successful business, a new condo, and a couple of canine kids—too much to risk losing within the drama of a serious relationship.

But my argument wasn't convincing enough for him, or for myself. A container plant bursting with fragrant blooms of blue and white hyacinths arrived at my shop the following week. Attached was a card from Robert:

> *Hyacinths symbolize sincerity and constancy of love. I've been*
> *married before, too. From that experience, and from being an*
> *expert in masonry, I know a lot about walls. Those rising high*
> *around your heart were built by amateurs. I intend to take*
> *them down.*

He'd chosen Christmas morning, apparently, to stage a major demolition event. As I slowly opened the tightly hinged lid of the little red box, Robert bent down on one knee. The diamond solitaire sparkled against the satin lining. I knew I would say yes if he ever asked. He wanted the commitment; I did too. He understood my fears, and I understood his. Our relationship was perfect. We made each other blissfully happy, shared incredible passion, respected one another's independence and the constraints that came with self-employment. We had as much fun together stuck indoors on a stormy weekend as we did traveling to every NASCAR race and NFL game we could fit into our schedules.

I accepted the ring under the condition that we never actually get married. He understood my reasoning and didn't care much about formalities. He just wanted to be together, forever, and so did I. I figured, with my luck, we had a better chance of reaching that goal if we just stayed eternally engaged.

OVER THE NEXT TWO YEARS, Robert and I remained inseparable. Though we maintained separate households, we were always together at one home or the other. Both of our businesses were growing, mine to the point that I needed more space again. Robert was the one who first spotted the FOR RENT sign on what would become the newest location for C.A.R. Services. It was twice the size for close to the same price, but it needed a lot of work to bring it up to the standards my customers had come to expect. Robert drew up the architectural design plan, I dug into my savings, and renovations were under way. Once again, it was an inspiring experience to see how my staff came together. We worked hard all day at our current space, then drove to the new location for the second shift, with Robert and many of his employees showing up to help.

Cindy and Greg had both moved on to managerial positions elsewhere. My new lead master technician, Ron, was like a big brother to me, and he disliked every guy I dated—until Robert came along, that is, and the two became fast friends. The guys created lots of noise and dust in the shop as they redesigned the service bays. Our receptionist, Missy, and I, along with her parents and Ron's wife, Susan, installed new flooring, cleaned, and redecorated the front offices and waiting room. Within two weeks everything was completed and covered with a fresh coat of paint, our equipment and tools were all in place, and we were ready to open our new doors. It was a wonderful family-style effort that I was extremely grateful for. The schedule filled up quickly and stayed consistent. Our honesty and first-class customer service earned us nominations for several excellence awards, and I was asked to host an "Ask the Expert" forum for the local newspaper. Life was great.

On a beautiful summer night, I was over at Robert's place making dinner as he headed home from a job site. It was the kind of night that always put me in a great mood. Temperate winds blew in through the large kitchen window and danced with the silky melodies from Ella Fitzgerald floating through the speakers. The vivid sunset offered a full spectrum through every shade of red and purple. Just as I was pulling my self-proclaimed "world's best" homemade chicken potpie out of the oven, Robert came in through the front door.

"Perfect timing!" I called from the kitchen.

"Hardly," he replied quietly and turned off the stereo.

"What was that?"

If Robert and I were apart for more than a few minutes, once we were reunited in the same space, it was all of two seconds before we were in each other's arms again. He had yet to greet me in the kitchen and I knew right away something was wrong. I came around the corner to see him sitting in the living room, clearly distressed. The way he called me over to the couch was strangely reminiscent of when Fish had told me Chris was dead. I could tell something bad was about to happen, and I moved very slowly.

He stared straight at the ground while he uttered words that would, again, alter the course of my life through no instigation of my own: "I just found out that I have a two-year-old daughter."

I paused for a few minutes and stared at him in disbelief. I could have guessed almost anything *but* that. Of all the questions swirling in my mind, there was one I needed the answer to most.

"Just tell me," I struggled to form the words. "Just tell me it's not with Amber."

When Robert looked up with tears in his eyes, I knew the answer.

"No!" I cried out. "Oh my God. No! Anyone but her!"

Aside from being Robert's ex-wife, Amber had been his childhood sweetheart. Like Fish, she had had some serious problems with drugs. In fact, that's how Robert and I had met; a mutual friend who felt we were sure to understand each other's trepidations had brought us together. There was one difference between us, though. Regardless of her problems, Robert had been completely devastated when she'd left him for another man. I knew somewhere deep down, despite the pain, and aside from the true love that he felt for me, a part of him still pined for her.

My mind raced to irrational thoughts. I cried and asked if he was going to leave me, thinking he might try to patch things up with Amber for the little girl to have a family. He cried too, in relief, saying he had been terrified to tell me for fear *I* would leave *him*. We held each other for a long time before calming down and trying to figure out where to go from there.

Robert explained that he had received a call at his office from Amber two weeks prior. He wanted to believe she was lying, so he hadn't told me about it. He had taken a paternity test and had just learned the positive results. He had done the math and figured out that she was pregnant when she left him. I'd heard that Amber had a young daughter, but I'd never seen the child, only Amber herself from time to time when she would show up on Robert's doorstep, preying on old emotions to beg for some cash. To my dismay, he would always give her what she wanted quickly in order to diffuse the awkward situation.

The little girl's situation was dire. Amber's boyfriend—the man she'd left Robert for—had recently caught her cheating. In the breakup, Amber lost her main source of income and had to move back into her childhood home. With her drug problems, a declining interest in employment, and pressure from her parents, she had decided that child support from Robert was her next endeavor.

I immediately felt protective of this little girl, who clearly needed a healthier home life. I had a huge decision to make. Harder yet, I had to make it fast, and not just for myself. I started to examine myself as a potential mother, and I was terrified at the thought. Despite my even temperament and being calm under fire, I feared that violence hid somewhere deep within me. I worried it was part of my DNA, still untapped, waiting for an opportunity to show itself. Robert and I had never intended to have children. He felt that it didn't fit our lifestyle. I figured it didn't coalesce with my decision to never get married again. But most of all, I had decided that the best way to never become an abusive parent was to simply never become a parent.

Part of me wanted to run. I already had everything I needed for a happy life, outside of the one I shared with Robert. I was deeply in love with him, but could that be enough to make it through this? In my romantic experiences, love hadn't exactly prevailed. I didn't need this relationship.

But another, bigger part of me opened up to the possibility that maybe, this time, this relationship needed me.

My new daughter's name was Heather.

Robert wanted to get married, and I knew why that was import-ant now, but I asked him to wait two more years before making it official. I felt that was enough time to determine if I could really be a loving mother. If I proved to have abusive tendencies, I wanted to be able to do the right thing for his daughter and walk away.

I called my sisters for advice. Shelly didn't have any kids yet but was always a source of balance and strength. Stacy, a devoted mother of two, was wonderful about absorbing Heather into the family, al-ways the one to send birthday cards and presents and whip up the McCandless siblings' yearly calendar.

Shawna was more reflective. She told me to be prepared for changes deep within myself. When she became a mother, she said, her per-spective on so many things shifted—particularly when it came to her relationship with Walt and Billie. Shawna had always been the family peacemaker. Petite in stature but large in heart, she was quick to forgive and first to diffuse tense situations. As Shawna's daugh-ter, Hunter, grew up, though, things changed. Once when Shawna, Hunter, and Billie were all in the car together, Hunter threw up. For the remainder of the drive, Shawna was preoccupied with cleaning Hunter up and making sure she was okay, while Billie was preoccu-pied with whether Shawna was going to have the car fully detailed upon arrival. But aside from their predictable insensitivity, Shawna saw pain in Hunter's face when they were around Walt and Billie's erratic behavior. Shawna's well-known tolerance plummeted.

Shawna's words stayed with me as I began my journey into motherhood. And so did Chris's. His faith in truth above all else reminded me of how important it was to be completely honest with Heather, always. I asked Robert and Amber to agree that no matter how bad it made anyone look, we would all be honest with Heather about her past.

———————————

ROBERT AND I BOTH SOLD our places and bought a larger home together, complete with a swing set in the large backyard and a yellow room with a floral wallpaper border that I knew was perfect for Heather the moment I walked into it. Soon she was spending a lot more time with us. I picked her up from day care and took her shopping for new clothes; we decorated her room and made milkshakes of every flavor combination until we figured out her favorite. I also took on the more practical, less amusing stuff: potty training; child proofing every cabinet door, drawer, and electrical outlet in our home; and struggling through multiple bouts of car-seat wrestling until I was finally victorious in strapping the heinous contraption into my truck.

Heather was twenty-eight pounds of blond-haired, brown-eyed toddler cuteness who wanted everything she wore to be pink, as well as jeweled or sparkly in some way—not something my dedication to a life in the auto-repair industry had prepared me for. I marveled at how quickly aspects of my personality changed. Or perhaps they had always been there and I just had yet to discover them.

On the first Christmas Heather spent with me and Robert, I decided it would be a great bonding opportunity to make traditional sugar cookies with her. I resisted my tendency toward perfect detail as I watched her pour half a container of edible Barbie glitter on a single snowman cookie. "Oh, okay," I said, pulling out another snowman, "but we can also do it this way. Look, we can give him a little hat, a little scarf, and three little buttons. That's how you're supposed to do it, see?"

"I think it looks better this way," Heather said confidently. She proceeded to create a dozen more multicolored, lumpy snowmen; several Santas wearing glittery blue coats, purple pants, and pink boots; and a slew of reindeer that were donned with enough red frosting and silver balls to look like they had suffered through a shooting massacre.

"Okay, then," I said, taking the blobs of colored sugar over to the fireplace. "These are so beautiful! I'm sure Santa will love them."

Heather and I hung candy canes on the tree together, because I'd told her that the elves and reindeer needed snacks, too, during the long night of helping Santa deliver presents. When she was asleep, Robert and I put tiny chairs by the tree, to make it seem like the elves had climbed on them in order to retrieve the striped treats. We sprinkled red and green glitter all around, so Heather would see exactly where they had been. The glitter trail extended down the hallway and into Heather's bedroom and even her bathroom. After being conditioned by my mother that a home should always be kept immaculate, I was surprised at how easy—and how fun—it was for me to purposely make tomorrow's vacuuming difficult. I was also well aware that I'd soon need to sleep while it waited there for me on the floor, a sparkly mess that would grind further into the carpet with every morning step. Shawna, I knew, would be impressed.

In Heather's bed, I put an elaborately wrapped gift from Santa—her very own Christmas storybook—nestled just so within her plethora of stuffed animals, so that it would seem like Santa had hidden it there just for her.

When she emerged on Christmas morning, wearing her footie pajamas and a colorful reindeer antler headband we'd found at the mall, she looked as sweet as Cindy Lou Who. She walked slowly into the kitchen, her little fingers pointing down the hallway.

"Merry Christmas, sweetie!" I said, giving her a squeeze. She stared back at me with eyes as wide as saucers. "What, honey? What is it?" I asked.

"Mommy Carine! It was Santa!" she finally blurted out, practically hyperventilating. "Come look! He was really here! He was in my room!" She tracked the glitter trail and followed it into the bathroom. "Daddy! The elves used my potty!"

The ruse had taken some effort and had the exact effect we'd hoped for. Robert smiled at me, and I smiled back. But as the day progressed and Heather carried on to everyone we saw about her special visit from Santa, all I could think was *Oh my gosh, what have I done? I lied to her! I have to tell her the truth right away!*

Thankfully, my rational mommy instincts prevailed. We propped ourselves up in her bed that night, reading the special Christmas gift for her bedtime story. I kept the magic going while explaining to her that one day she would learn how everyone gets the chance to be Santa. She smiled and fell asleep in my arms.

———————

SHAWNA WAS RIGHT—Heather changed me in ways small and large, to the extent that I didn't miss my independence at all. It seemed to have been replaced with a new mission—and a greater purpose. Regardless of the fact that Heather was not related to me by blood, in many ways I felt like my own past had been preparing me to not be just her mother—but also her advocate.

Through child support and custody issues, stressful court filings and uncomfortable testimonies, I had to tackle an entirely new set of issues that I had never expected to deal with in my lifetime. Conflict was never Robert's strong suit, and he was too amenable to Amber's demands and legal proposals, which provided her a steady income without accountability while she retained primary custody of Heather. I was uncomfortable with the future I saw developing. I had my eyes on the door, envisioning my getaway, but something kept me from leaving. It wasn't just about walking away from Robert anymore. I was falling in love with Heather even faster than I had with him.

It was unnerving to witness Robert's avoidance of tough circumstances, but I tried to understand how difficult it was for him to deal directly with Amber after the way she had left him. He had always said that for any relationship to function at one hundred percent, one person had to make up the difference when the other dropped below their fair share. He'd done that for me many times since we had met, and I resolved that it was my turn. Although I had no legal rights as a parent to Heather, I was practiced at dealing with emotional issues under pressure and was happy that I could help Robert and Amber work through it all by keeping us focused on what was best for Heather. It felt good to be needed.

Through the years with my daughter, I kept myself in check by asking *What would my parents have done in this situation?*—and then usually doing the opposite. At first, my fear of failure constantly lingered in our household, though I was the only one aware of its ominous presence. But with my love for Heather, every obstacle became surmountable. And, as I expected it might, as Heather grew up, the task fell upon me to answer her questions about her past. It wasn't always easy, but I cherished the opportunity to develop that bond of mutual trust and respect.

In 2003, true to my self-imposed two-year maternal probationary period, Robert and I flew to Hawaii for an intimate wedding ceremony attended by only the two of us and the officiant. On a secluded cliff bluff nestled on the island of Kauai, overlooking blue crystalline waters, we exchanged vows committing us to coming together as Heather's parents forever. Motherhood was my drug of choice, and I was addicted. I knew then I wanted more of it.

BECOMING A MOM CHANGED ME significantly in another way, as well, outside of my maternal responsibilities. When asked questions about my family history, I began to speak more openly and honestly. I stopped declining invitations to speak at local schools where *Into the Wild* was required reading. When students asked about Chris's childhood—which happened at every visit—I was careful not to condemn my parents, but I spoke the truth. I would remind the audience that my parents were human, and humans make mistakes. I gave examples of the good things they had done along with the bad choices I felt they'd made. The line I was walking felt increasingly narrow and slippery, however, especially as Mom and Dad started doing more of their own outreach, with a very different story about our family and what our childhood had been like.

Mom and Dad spent part of each year living in the same city as me, and it wasn't long before they heard about the discussions I was now having about our home life. They began to say disparaging things about me within the community and their church, and one of their favorites was "Carine's just upset with us because in our wills we're leaving all of our money to charity." We did not attend the same place of worship, but word travels fast between congregations. I found their comments very hurtful but not surprising.

The greatest violation was what I saw as an unforgivable encroachment on Chris's faith. Mom would consistently use Chris's last written words against him. "Carine, I don't know what you're talking about," she would say if I brought up a painful memory from childhood, her melodic tone piercing my gut. "Don't you remember the good-bye note Chris wrote? He admitted to God that his life was happy. He had nothing to complain about." They informed the family that they were born-again Christians and told me the slate had been wiped clean—that there was nothing to discuss. It revolted me to see them use religion as a pardon for their crimes and to know that I had allowed the opportunity for them to use Jon's book as their new Bible; if it wasn't in there, it didn't happen. I was disgusted at the ease with which they exploited Chris's incomplete story in an attempt to rewrite their own.

"You're wrong to use God in this way," I cautioned them. "Chris said in his last letters to me that his life began during college after he left you two behind. *That* is the life he was talking about. You know that's true—he said he told you that himself, and I don't know how you can claim otherwise."

Mom laughed. "God will punish you for not honoring your father and mother, Carine. Don't you remember His commandment? I feel sorry for you because you will not get to join Chris and us in heaven."

And so it went on every occasion I interacted with my parents. As they became more vocal in the limelight, my siblings and I became more exasperated by the mistruths they were spreading. I couldn't protect Mom and Dad anymore, and they needed to stop making it so hard for me to try. Surely it must be possible to come together in some level of compromise in fairness to Chris, and to ourselves. But I needed backup. All my siblings dealt with these feelings in different ways. Some of us were willing to sit down and visit with an anger that the others found easier to move away from. Perhaps those of us who held on still hoped for change, while others were smart enough to stop waiting.

When everyone was in Denver at the same time, I took the opportunity to "pull a Shawna" and bring the two sides together to talk things out. I invited Mom and Dad to join Shelly, Shawna, and me for dinner to discuss these matters, to try to improve our relationships and prevent further abrasions—or at least to slow the bleeding. Although history had taught me we likely wouldn't get through to them, we were still honestly hopeful we could reach an understanding. As my sisters and I headed down the highway toward the restaurant, we devised our strategy. I would do the talking. Shawna would lighten the mood when the tension rose to dangerous levels, which she was well primed to do because she'd had an uncharacteristic cocktail or two before we'd picked her up. And Shelly—she would do her best not to explode.

We arrived first and sat at the table to review our plan again. We predicted how Walt and Billie might act, complete with imitations. We analyzed the menu to see what food would make the least mess if Shelly wound up flipping the table over, and we all had cash in our pockets for a quick exit. The jokes cleared away our discomfort, until a tense fog rolled in with the arrival of The Show.

Dad greeted the table with a jovial "Hello!" as if we had all comfortably broken bread together last week. In reality, Shawna and Shelly had had very little contact with them in recent years, and my last interaction with them had been through the Virginia Beach gossip mill. Billie placed some homemade bread on the table for us, each carefully preserved in plastic wrap and each one decorated with a different colored ribbon. Aside from that, my mom did not acknowledge me.

"Why don't we decide on some appetizers?" I said, hoping to warm up with some meaningless group discussion.

"Oh look, Walter," Mom said. "Shawna's wearing a scarf just like the one Hannah always wears."

"Who's Hannah?" Shelly asked. Mom didn't answer. It wasn't for Shelly's ears anyway; it was for mine. Hannah was a woman a bit younger than me, a devoted fan of *Into the Wild*. She had befriended my parents, and Mom had started taking her to mother-daughter church luncheons. She had recently informed me that Hannah was their new daughter—my replacement. Hannah's friend Allan, also an *Into the Wild* enthusiast, was Chris's replacement.

"Hmmmm. They don't have any vegan options," Dad said.

"You guys are vegan now?" asked Shawna with surprise.

"No. But Hannah is," he answered.

Mom arched her brows and gave me a *So there* look. Shelly and Shawna were perplexed and looked for my reaction, but I didn't give one.

We ordered our nonvegan appetizers, and I began. "So," I said, "there are some specific things we wanted to talk to you about with regards to Chris." I explained what was bothering us—how the misleading information they were giving about our family, and their not acknowledging the true past of Dad's history with Marcia, was resulting in Chris's actions appearing to be those of an immature rebel with no cause to leave the way he had.

"Look," Dad said, trying to take control of the situation. "I didn't agree to come here to talk about any of these things."

"I told you when I invited you that was why," I said, following it up with the obvious, "Why else would we be here?"

I pulled out a list I'd made of times they had publicly misrepresented our family—either in talks they'd given or in text they'd published. "Instead of putting out all this nonsense about what a perfect childhood Chris had," I said, "all we're asking is that you not say anything at all. It's terribly sad that you lost your son. Sympathy for you is fair and automatic. Why can't you two just accept that instead of lying?"

"I don't know what you're talking about," Mom said.

I got up from my seat and sat next to her. I showed her some of the things that had upset the rest of us so much: lists that conveniently misreported our birth order; words that ignored how Walt was impregnating two women at once, not to mention beating them; pictures that showed us as smiling children in one big happy blended family, images frozen in time that told an incomplete story. "You guys are publicly insulting this family," I said, tears forming as my voice wavered. I was so overcome I was practically whimpering, and I felt decidedly pissed off that I was allowing myself to appear weakened. "You're using Chris's story to try to reinvent our history"—I took a steadying breath—"and in doing so you're bullying Chris in his death."

Mom stared at the evidence in my hands and slowly shook her head in denial. "Hmmm, I really don't see a problem," she rebuffed.

I went back to my own seat, frustrated, my face flushed. On cue, Shawna stepped in. "I think what Carine's trying to say is that we'd rather you didn't talk about our childhood at all if you're not going to do it honestly."

"Do you know," Mom said, looking at Shawna and Shelly, "that Carine has made a lot of money from all of this *Into the Wild* stuff?"

"Yes, actually," Shawna said quickly. "She shared some of it with us and told us to consider it a gift from Chris. It paid for my daughter's braces."

One divisive tactic shot down, Mom tried another. "Oh, Carine, isn't it you who's making up false family scenarios just to get attention?" she said. "You're not as smart as you think you are. I don't even understand what wrongdoing you're talking about. Besides, when I met him, your father had his own apartment and lots of girlfriends."

Shelly was sitting on my left and turned to me. The force of her hand on my knee told me her fuse had been lit. Her angry green eyes peered into mine as she said, "I'm not gonna make it, Carine. I'm not gonna make it!" She stood up, went over to my mom, and bent down until their faces were nearly nose to nose. "You started your affair with my dad when my mom was pregnant with me," she said loudly, disregarding the close proximity of neighboring tables. "You have insisted on telling lie upon lie, and at some point it's got to stop!" Dad looked on calmly, as if nothing that was going on had anything to do with him.

Shelly went out to her car. We thought maybe she was just having a cigarette, but when our dinner came—served with a side of uncomfortable silence—Shelly still wasn't back. Shawna had now had one glass of wine too many and was considering one more. She and I looked at one another, wondering, *Should we go, too?* Mom finally got up and walked outside, returning a few minutes later with a seething Shelly.

Dinner resumed, but it was clear our mission had failed. We finished eating as quickly as possible, insisted on paying for our own meals, and got the hell out.

As soon as my sisters and I got into the car, we started talking all at once. "Can you believe she said that?" "Can you believe he did that?" "Unbelievable!" After a moment of dumbfounded silence, we all looked at one another. Then we burst out laughing.

"Who the fuck is Hannah?" Shelly asked.

I started imitating Shelly. *"I'm not gonna make it, Carine. I'm not gonna make it!"*

"Look at me!" Shawna slurred from the backseat, imitating the way Mom had approached the table. "I'm Suzie Homemaker and I made you bread!"

"Shit, the bread!" I cried. I had the loaves of freshly baked bread sitting in my lap. "What the hell are we going to do with all this bread? Why did I even take it off the table?" We certainly didn't want it. We laughed as the car sped away from the restaurant, away from The Show and into a saner world.

CHAPTER 14

I CAN'T REMEMBER the first time Heather called me "Mommy," instead of "Mommy Carine." Not because it wasn't momentous in my mind. It was just something that happened progressively, and naturally.

For a long time, following my mantra of what was best for Heather, I'd tried to include Amber in everything we did with her. So, I invited Amber over for tea and dinners and to work on school projects together, and occasionally she would accept. Together we planned Heather's birthday parties and attended school assemblies and dance recitals. Robert understood that it was important for Heather to feel surrounded by love and support and not dysfunction, but the arrangement made him uncomfortable. As a result, oftentimes it was just Amber and me together with Heather at community events, looking like *we* were a couple, which made me uncomfortable instead.

I worried that Robert and I were allowing Amber's parenting efforts to be sporadic at best. It was almost as if Heather had come with a troubled big sister. I didn't want to enable Amber; I wanted to encourage her to clean herself up and move in a positive direction. I found her job opportunities that she didn't pursue. When she lost her lease, I found her a new place to live. I tried to help her with her budget and with saving for the future. I hoped she would become someone that Heather could look up to, and there were promising moments when I believed she would. But by the time Heather was in elementary school, Amber had taken a bad turn and was spending less and less time with Heather.

Eventually she signed over full custody to Robert and me. We all knew that this was best for Heather, and while a part of me was relieved by her decision, I feared it was a sign that Amber would disappear from Heather's life completely. She promised that she wouldn't, but soon her phone was disconnected and she had moved with no forwarding address.

A few months later, Heather and I were standing in the refrigerated section of the grocery store, discussing what we might want to cook for dinner.

Suddenly she reached one of her hands over to mine. "Mommy," she said, her eyes enlarged to the size of the plates our dinner would soon be on.

"What's wrong, honey?" I asked.

Heather's stance became rigid, and without moving her head, she answered, "I think I see Mommy Amber over there."

I turned my head in the direction of Heather's frozen gaze, and there was Amber, smiling as she strolled through the aisles, her blond hair piled high on her head, tanned, wearing a white tank top under a man's flannel shirt. She looked over to us but then away again and continued pushing her shopping cart at a slow pace.

I gently turned Heather's head to mine. "Sweetie, listen to me. Do you want to go over and talk to her? It's okay if you want to."

"No," she said quietly.

"Are you sure?" I asked again. "Please don't think I'll be upset if you want to talk to her. Trust me. I understand what you're feeling right now."

Heather looked into my eyes and said directly, "I know. I'm sure." But I sensed that she just wanted Amber to be the one to make the first move.

We continued to retrieve all the items on our list. Several times we passed within a few feet of Amber as we traversed the same aisles between brightly colored cans, boxes, and jars. Each time we were within earshot of her, my voice grew louder, begging the opportunity for Amber to reach out to her daughter. "How about any of these soups, Heather?" "What kind of juices do you want for your lunches this week, Heather?" "Do you want me to make some spaghetti tonight, Heather?"

Heather knew what I was doing, and she didn't try to stop me. It was obvious that Amber saw us and heard us. But each time, she simply looked in the other direction and continued passing by as if we were just a couple of strangers who had volume-control issues.

I imagined it was a torturous experience for Heather, but she showed no signs of weakness whatsoever. I was amazed at her strength and resolve at such a young age. Tears came into my own eyes for her, knowing what it's like to grow up so fast, but I quickly wiped them away. Before we left the store, I felt I should offer to bridge the gap one last time.

"Heather?" I asked. "Do you want me to go talk to her?"

"No, thank you," she answered and placed a box of macaroni and cheese into the cart. I struggled with an incredible impulse to walk over to Amber, knock her upside the head, shake her by the shoulders, and ask her what the hell was wrong with her. But I didn't want to violate Heather's faith in me. We finished our shopping and went home.

Birthdays and holidays passed by with no contact from Amber, though our address and phone numbers always remained the same. I marveled at how she could possibly make a conscious choice to eliminate herself from her daughter's life. I remembered hearing Amber tell Heather she loved her every time she dropped her off at our house. How could someone allow a love like that to evaporate?

I hurt for Heather, and then I remembered that distance, in certain circumstances, was sometimes healthier.

I wanted to give Amber the credit for having perhaps realized this. But still, it seemed unfathomable to me that she was able to let go that way. Maybe there were different levels of love, even amongst moms. I told Heather that I loved her every single day, and I worked hard to make sure she never doubted just how much. To ever leave her, I would have had to be dragged away, dead, after having been skinned alive while kicking and screaming to get back to her.

We never saw Amber again.

ROBERT AND I WERE BOTH working hard and running our businesses. He began to return home later and later into the evening. With Amber out of her life, Heather, I felt, needed more attention from me than I could give with the long hours I was putting in at the shop. I wanted to volunteer for all her school events and holiday parties, to be the room parent for her classroom, to chaperone her field trips. I also knew that I could not run my company the way I wanted to and be that involved in Heather's life every day. I had been so driven to succeed in my industry, but now I found myself more interested in tackling the challenges of motherhood with the same determination.

Robert and I spoke about it at length. We agreed it was more important to have extra time together as a family and less important to have the stuff that the long hours at work bought for us. I would do consulting work and had plans for other ventures that would keep my schedule more flexible.

I talked to my employees before making the final decision to sell C.A.R. Services, because I wanted the blessing of those who'd helped me have such an option in the first place. My team was surprised that I could give up all that they'd seen me work so hard for. But they had also seen the changes in me that motherhood had brought, and they knew my priorities were different now. They granted me their understanding and support. Potential buyers lined up quickly, and I was able to structure a deal that protected my staff's salaries and benefits as well as our customers' warranties. I wanted to do right by all of those who had helped the company be so successful over the past twelve years. When the deal went through, I sold the company for ten times what I had bought Fish out for seven years earlier. It felt nothing less than monumental.

But even greater was being able to fully embrace the promise I had made to Heather to be a consistent force in her life. In the past I had dissolved my loyalties to two husbands and a business partner, altered course in my education and career choices, and seen important friendships come and go. But motherhood was an altogether different kind of commitment. A connection that circumstance never severs. A bond not unlike that of siblings.

I thought about Chris and all he had taught me about self-awareness. He'd written in a letter to Ron Franz something I'd heard him say many times:

> So many people live within unhappy circumstances and yet will
> not take the initiative to change their situation because they are
> conditioned to a life of security, conformity, and conservatism, all of
> which may appear to give one peace of mind, but in reality nothing
> is more damaging to the adventurous spirit within a man than a
> secure future.

I thought about the courage it takes to do whatever is necessary to see your true path and follow it, no matter how far outside of your comfort zone it leads. I could see my true path more clearly than any other that had ever been before me.

THE WARMTH OF FRESHLY DUG DIRT always makes me feel centered and connected with a larger world outside my own worries. I
had been in Heather's class that morning and then busy organizing
renovations on two rental properties I had purchased. The work necessary at the rentals had caused me to fall behind on things at my own
home. As the afternoon approached, I was working to beautify my
own acre of the planet before picking Heather back up from school.
Mom had always kept a beautiful yard at the Annandale house, and
even though our relationship was constantly on edge, I accepted her
offer to come over to help me in my garden.

I was at a crossroads with my parents. On the one hand, as Shawna
had foretold, motherhood had made me more protective and even
more guarded around Mom and Dad. On the other hand, now that
I was a mom I *wanted* a mom even more. I knew Billie would never
provide easy or unconditional love, but I wanted to maintain some
connection with her. And there were times when I believed she
wanted that, too. In between the peaks and valleys of our emotionally charged relationship, she would sometimes send me messages
that sounded incredibly heartfelt. In one, she wrote:

> It is my hope that one day you will come to realize that even through
> the difficult times, I loved both you and Chris with all my heart,
> wanting nothing but the best for you, albeit not always making the
> right decisions to achieve that. I can't even promise that I'll never
> disappoint you again, because I'm only human and mere humans are
> known for often leaving even the people they love most hurting and
> wanting. I can promise that I will continue to try to do better.

Although I had heard such sentiments before, I remained hopeful.
I felt that if I was able to manage our interactions on my own terms,

with enough distance from emotional topics, I could protect myself while saving our relationship from complete collapse.

In the garden, I was careful not to lift anything too heavy, and Mom launched a couple of lighthearted slacker comments in my general direction. She did not know I was pregnant. Robert and I had decided to wait a few more weeks before informing the family, because our last pregnancy had ended in a devastating miscarriage. There was enough anxiety in the air without those extra concerns; talks of making a movie out of Jon's book were turning into plans of substance. Jon and actor-filmmaker Sean Penn were due to arrive that weekend to discuss Sean's vision for a film.

We had met Sean once before, ten years prior, and had declined his and everyone else's offer to make a movie about Chris's life. The main reason was that Mom had had a bad dream about the concept coming to fruition. In her dream, Mom explained, she was young and was holding little Chris in her arms while I toddled around them. For some reason Chris was so weak that he couldn't even hold his head up. Mom kept having to put her hand under his chin—she was trying to look into his face and ask if he was okay, but he wouldn't respond, and in her distraction, she'd lost me. She awoke in a panic, with her last memory of the nightmare being that she was desperately looking for me while Chris's energy continued to diminish. She saw the dream as a sign from Chris to her that he did not want a movie made. I interpreted it as more of a warning.

Of the many pursuers over the years, Sean had been the most reverent and the most eager. Though he had respected Mom's reasoning, saying, "Hey, if I didn't believe in dreams, I wouldn't make movies," he also hadn't given up hope completely. I was curious about his plan to convince us this time, and I wondered how much I would be willing to share with him if we decided to move forward with the project.

"Hand me that extra shovel and let's get all these petunias planted, petunia girl," Mom said while pulling on her gloves.

"I know. I bought too many. They were on sale and so pretty I just couldn't help myself," I replied, handing over the tool.

After we dug the holes, we got down on our knees, emptied the pots, and arranged the flowers in their new bed. Mom had recently returned from a trip to Michigan to visit her mother, and she was telling me about it.

Grandma was a bit of hoarder, the exact opposite of how Mom kept her own home. She could not accept that Grandma was perfectly happy living that way. Whenever she visited Grandma, she cleaned the entire house, organized everything, threw out piles of trash, shopped for fresh food, and performed a personal beauty make-over on Grandma. Mom was always disgruntled that Grandma didn't respond with overwhelming gratitude. Although the reason why was clear to me, I kept quiet as she complained. Despite the good intent behind Mom's hard work, I knew she embarrassed Grandma by wearing a mask on her face and rubber gloves up to her shoulders. While Grandma sat in the same room crocheting and watching TV, Mom made constant under-the-breath comments about how "disgusting" everything was. She took before and after pictures, which she'd then share with her friends and the rest of the family.

While Mom had been in Michigan, she'd also seen Uncle Travis, who was still a drunk and living in Grandma's basement.

"You should see how repulsive that basement is," Mom said. "You can't even see the floor; there are piles of beer cans everywhere and ashes all over the place. Travis is going to burn the whole house down the way he passes out while smoking down there. He's always drunk. I don't even think he has a real job."

"Sounds lovely . . . and typical," I chimed in.

"And do you know what he did to me? I was upstairs talking to your grandma, and Travis and I were both sitting on the couch next to her crochet chair. When I got up to squeeze by him, he grabbed my ass! I mean he really held on to it for a couple seconds! Can you believe he would do that to his own sister?"

I looked at her in amazement, but she continued.

"I turned right around and said, 'What the hell do you think you're doing?' and he just mumbled back, 'What? Oh geez, Billie, y'know, c'mon, don't get so bent outta shape.' Can you believe that?"

I was still stunned, but not for the reason she thought. I repeated her words: "Can I believe that."

"Yes?" she stopped primping the petunias. With a look of complete violation, she paused and waited for my sympathies.

She did not get any. I stood up and dropped my gloves to the ground.

"Can I believe that?" I railed back at her. "Can I believe that? After what he did to me, you actually want me to stand here and feel sorry for you because he grabbed your ass? Are you fucking kidding me? I was just a kid—and you and Dad did nothing!"

She tilted her head and thought for a moment, her eyes focusing on nothing as they traveled back in time. "My goodness. I'm sorry. I'd forgotten all about that. But you really are overreacting, Carine. It's not like he raped you or anything."

I touched my hand to my stomach, where my baby was no larger than a blueberry. My attempted reconciliation with my mother through a day of stress relief in the garden was over, and I went inside. Mom left in a huff over how unappreciative I was that she not only had been doing the heavier work but had given up her day to come and help me.

———

I SAW MY PARENTS AGAIN at the meeting with Jon and Sean. I put my emotions aside and stayed focused on the task at hand: deciding if this was the right person to speak for my brother through such a vast medium. I didn't know much about Sean personally, aside from his rumored short temper and his outspoken political views—the latter far from parallel to Chris's. As we spoke, he struck me as very intelligent and with high principles when it came to his work. Chris couldn't have cared less if anyone ever took notice of his accomplishments, reflected on his opinions, or regarded him as brilliant, and although Sean embodied the exact opposite, I could tell that he cared much more about the quality and integrity of the film than about selling tickets to it. He spoke passionately about his vision for the project, the message he wanted it to convey, his admiration of Chris, and his consideration of the family.

Although I was impressed with the previous films Sean had written and directed, I still had a lot of questions about why he felt his past experiences qualified him to bring the story of my brother to the big screen. At one point after complimenting him for being such an incredibly talented actor, I asked him politely, with that in mind, how were we to know that he wasn't simply blowing smoke up our asses and telling us whatever we wanted to hear. My parents looked at me with wide eyes, aghast at my dry and direct approach. Jon smiled at me. Then he turned to Sean, waiting expectantly for his answer. Sean wasn't the least bit offended by the interrogation. He answered all my questions—thoroughly and patiently—and seemed to genuinely appreciate that I didn't treat him like he was above anyone else sitting in my backyard that day. I believe it started our relationship out with clarity.

After much discussion with Jon, we all felt it was time to take the next journey with Sean. While Mom and Dad tried to discourage my involvement with the filmmaking process, Jon was quick to inform Sean that my input would be invaluable, and thus I was contracted as a consultant.

When I sat down with Sean for the first time in private to tell my brother's story, it was a very different experience from when I had sat with Jon so many years before. Maybe it was due to the obvious differences between the two men—compared to each other and to Chris—or the differences between books and movies. Or perhaps it was because I was older, wiser, and wary from the immense success of *Into the Wild*.

I gave Sean the same information I had shared with Jon, but this time I asked that not all of it remain unsaid. I requested fairness for Chris and my siblings. And while I had not seen the changes in my parents' behavior I had hoped for, I still did not intend to vilify them on the silver screen, especially in what was sure to develop into a high-profile project. Sean understood my concerns. He explained it would not be possible to tell the entire story and maintain the beautiful spirit of the film, but he agreed the film should include enough to allow for some understanding that there was more to the story.

I allowed Sean to read Chris's letters. He was deeply moved by their content, and with that came a lot more questions. He asked me to also share them with actor Emile Hirsch, who would play Chris in the movie. Filming was going to be a demanding process for Emile, both mentally and physically, and he was working very hard to prepare for Sean's obsession with having every scene be authentic and precise. The wilderness scenes were, of course, going to be some of the most arduous. I wanted to teach Emile everything I could about Chris's personality so that he could emulate him as faithfully as possible.

One day Emile and I were sitting in my living room, going through Chris's pictures from Alaska. There were several self-portraits Chris had taken of himself with the animals he had killed for food, and it was important to me that Emile did not mistake the barbaric expressions on Chris's face—as he stood over a carcass with his rifle or machete—to be ones of disrespect for the animals. This was especially important to me when it came to the moose that Chris failed to preserve, which I knew would be a pivotal scene in the film. Chris had stated in his journal that taking the life of the animal was one of the greatest tragedies of his life.

Emile then said something that humbled me and made me realize that there was a part of Chris that he understood much better than I did, even though he had never met my brother. This handsome, smart, talented, and ambitious young man—who was about the same age as Chris was when he died—sat on my couch with images of my brother spread out all around him and said, "Don't worry, Carine. I don't get a vicious impression at all from these photographs. Chris didn't have much experience with hunting. It's hard work; it's exhausting—especially when you're all alone and hungry. I get it. This wasn't sport for him; it was survival."

And then Emile slid into character and went to a place in his mind that only a young male can get to.

"Yeah!" he called out boisterously. "Look at me! I'm a fucking hunter!"

The glint of innocence and excitement in his eyes reminded me so much of Chris that it hurt and comforted me at the same time.

———————————

SOON THE FIRST DRAFT of the script arrived at my door. As I opened the package, the first thing that caught my eye was "Carine VO." Sean had sent me his screenplay copies of *Mystic River* and other familiar films so I could learn about scriptwriting and how the content on paper transitioned to the screen. I knew "VO" meant voice-over, and I called him immediately.

"What's this?" I asked. "You didn't tell me that my character was going to narrate the film."

"I know," Sean said. "I didn't want it to influence your initial approach. But it has to be you. Your voice is nuanced throughout Jon's book. You understood Chris more than anyone."

Tears sprung to my eyes. *He gets it,* I thought. I also felt the immense accountability of being placed in a position to help him genuinely portray Chris. It was important enough to me to welcome the weight that it brought.

I collaborated with Sean and renowned poet Sharon Olds to draft the final narrative along with actress Jena Malone, who would portray me in the film. When all was said and done, there was only one segment of the narrative that I did not approve of, because it was something I never would have said.

Sean faced the difficult task of referencing Chris's discovery of our true family history, and in such a way that made clear it had been the catalyst for his distancing himself from our parents. But he also did not want to completely expose them. As a result, there's one section that mistakenly implies that we did not know our brothers and sisters growing up. I discussed this with Sean extensively and even wrote some different lines as well as an entire scene that I felt were plausible options to take the place of the objectionable narrative. Sean decided that to completely flesh out the details of how our two families overlapped within the time constraints of the film would seem to be just an intent on his part to sensationalize the family drama. He felt that it wasn't his place to tell that story. I worried that I had let down Chris, our siblings, and Marcia by protecting my parents in the past, and I did not want to make that same mistake again.

Finally Sean said, "The moment I interrupt the story of Chris and his journey to try to explain all that happened within your two families, the audience will immediately lose focus on Chris, and the movie then becomes about your parents. Yes, the truth is important, but it's so wild on its own that it would take another entire movie to explain, or another book, or both."

I conceded that Sean knew a thing or two more about making movies than I did, and I certainly did not want this stunning visual representation of Chris's life to become all about the painful past he had worked so hard to escape from. Whenever we discussed how to handle these difficult issues, I could tell through Sean's impassioned words that he believed his beautiful movie would spark some healing in my family. But Mom and Dad had not learned anything from

Chris's death, nor had they been appreciative of the restraint in Jon's book, and I was skeptical that this would turn out any differently.

———————

SO MUCH OF THE ATTENTION surrounding *Into the Wild* had been placed on me, and I felt as if my siblings had always been swept under the rug—that their relation to Chris was glossed over and thus viewed as less important. Yet their existence in our lives was essential to understanding why Chris had acted so intensely on the raw emotions that wove throughout his childhood.

During one of my visits to Denver, while the whole family was at Shelly's, I sat at the dining room table across from Stacy. We'd just finished clearing the plates from dinner, and our other siblings were busy in the kitchen or in the yard with the kids.

Marcia sat quietly in her chair in the other room, knitting. As I glanced at her, I remembered a certain sweater I had often swiped from Dad's closet while in high school. Warm, soft, and comforting, it was my favorite, and I wasn't surprised when I learned Marcia had knitted it. Tonight she was making a sweater for whichever grandchild was next in line to receive a new one. I knew Heather and the child I was carrying would be included on that list, too.

Marcia was always quiet and rarely spoke first, but she was quick to join in a card game and laugh along with everyone else. I loved to see her happy. I knew my existence was part of a painful chapter in her life, but she was too kind to ever acknowledge that connection.

So, as I sat with Stacy, guilt was heavily on my mind.

"When Chris and I got older," I confided, "and we came to understand about the affair, about the things that Mom and Dad had done . . . we felt so bad. We'd been completely ignorant as to what we must have symbolized, as your mom babysat Chris or you guys came over to our house. When we were kids, you never looked at us with resentment. And still you guys don't see me as even a step or a half. I'm your *sister* and I feel that. And Heather feels that. You guys never got pissed off or jealous or treated Chris and me poorly. You never took any of that out on us, and it would have been so understandable if you had."

"Don't you get it?" Stacy said sweetly, reaching her hand across to mine. "It's because of who raised us."

Tears streamed down my face as she continued. "Our mom got us away from all of that. It's true that we didn't have much money, and that was tough sometimes." She looked toward the family room, where Marcia sat focused on the rhythm of her yarn and needles, and she lowered her voice. "Maybe our house wasn't always spotlessly clean and Mom sometimes struggled with providing structure. It's hard work to be a single mom and keep up with six kids. But she always provided us with plenty of love, and we learned that was the most valuable thing we could have ever hoped for. You and Chris may have had it better financially, but we got the better deal."

———————————

WHILE THE SCRIPT PROCESS was nearing its end and before filming of *Into the Wild* began, we had occasion to make an entirely different kind of movie. I was one day past my due date when the contractions started. Robert videotaped the cheerfully decorated hospital room and each noisy machine hooked up to me, along with my alternating expressions of excitement and wide-eyed preparation for pain, all while providing his typically humorous commentary.

I had announced my intention to continue my clean streak of a life without drug use during childbirth. That quickly changed to an assertion that I certainly deserved synthetic relief after having held out for so long, now that I was facing the task of pushing something the size of a watermelon through something the size of an apple.

"Can you please go find the anesthesiologist?" I saw my pathetic expression looking back at me through the camera lens.

"Oh, yeah, yeah, sorry," Robert said, putting the camera down. "You're sure about that?"

"Oh God, yes!" I winced and hunched over as much as I could while a foot tried to come through my belly button.

After the epidural fairy came to visit, all was good and peaceful and right in my world again. Robert held my hand and coached my breathing, and it was nice to have that quiet time together. I had denied his mother's request to be in the room for the birth, and I knew she was upset by it. I actually would have had no problem with her presence, but I was very strongly against my own mother being in the room. Robert and I had decided that it would be less stressful to avoid invitations and explanations, and just make the broad statement that we wanted it to be just the two of us.

Our baby girl came out about an hour after the doctor instructed me to start pushing. The nurses put her to my chest almost immediately, as I had requested, and I tried to comfort her while she cried a hearty wail. I put her to my breast to see if she could get some milk, but it was too early. The nurse took her away quicker than I expected. They tagged her arm and carried her out of the room to clean her up and weigh her. My doctor smiled as she continued to work on me. Everything seemed routine.

A few family members and friends started to make their way in. The doctor disappeared for a moment while the nurse finished cleaning me up. Someone walked Heather in, and while I hoped she hadn't seen anything that scarred her for life or made her promise herself to never have kids, I was glad to see her.

Then a nurse walked into the room, one I'd never seen before. She gave me her name—which I did not register—and told me she worked in the neonatal intensive care unit. *That* I got.

"Where's my baby?" I asked.

The nurse looked around the room and asked someone to take Heather out. Heather looked straight over to me.

"No. She can stay. What's wrong?" The words fell out of my mouth in a slow cadence, not really wanting to be answered.

That's when they told us our little girl had Down syndrome. I was in shock. I had been so cautious during my pregnancy—coping well with stress, exercising properly, eating healthily, never drinking any alcohol or even a single soda. There had been no signs of trouble at my doctor visits, and screening tests for common concerns had been negative. I didn't know anything about what caused Down syndrome. The doctor explained that it happens at conception—it was part of her DNA.

I looked around the room to my husband, to my friends, to anyone, for strength. Everyone was staring at each other or straight ahead, not knowing what to say. The nurse proceeded to explain that our baby had been taken to the intensive care unit because she likely had heart defects and gastrointestinal disorders.

"I want to see her right now!" I insisted.

"I'm sorry," said the nurse, "but she has to stay down there, and you can't be allowed to get out of this bed until you can move your legs on your own."

"Damn it! I knew I shouldn't have asked for the epidural!" I said and started to sob.

Aside from my crying, the room was silent. And then my little Heather, one month shy of turning seven, walked over to me, took my hand in hers, and said, "Don't worry, Mommy. She's gonna be just fine, because you're gonna take great care of her just like you take care of me."

HEATHER'S PREDICTION CAME TRUE. During three days in the hospital, while the doctors ran tests and waited for results, her little sister surprised everyone with her determination and ability to thrive. Aside from some minor and ordinary newborn complications, she proved to be perfectly healthy. As the doctors explained the extensive therapies that would be required to deal with her disability, I felt the importance of ensuring she was surrounded only by love, support, and positive energy.

It was clear she had her uncle's strong spirit, and we decided to name her Christiana.

PART FOUR

TRUTH

Rather than love, than money, than fame,
give me truth. I sat at a table where were rich
food and wine in abundance, and obsequious
attendance, but sincerity and truth were not;
and I went away hungry from the inhospitable
board. The hospitality was as cold as the ices.

—Henry David Thoreau, *Walden,*
passage highlighted by Chris

CHAPTER 15

ATTENTION POSSIBLE VISITORS

S.O.S.

I NEED YOUR HELP. I AM INJURED, NEAR DEATH,

AND TOO WEAK TO HIKE OUT OF HERE.

I AM ALL ALONE, THIS IS NO JOKE.

IN THE NAME OF GOD, PLEASE REMAIN TO SAVE ME.

I AM OUT COLLECTING BERRIES CLOSE BY

AND SHALL RETURN THIS EVENING.

THANK YOU, CHRIS MCCANDLESS

AUGUST ?

(Note written on the back side of a page torn from Louis
L'Amour's *Education of a Wandering Man*, found with Chris's
remains. His last journal entry was "Beautiful Blueberries.")

"CARINE!" JON KRAKAUER'S VOICE buzzed through the phone. "I finally found out what happened to Chris's backpack!" The news startled me to the point that I almost dropped the phone into the bath water I was drawing for Christiana.

Two and a half weeks after Chris had died inside Fairbanks 142, after not seeing or speaking to another human for one hundred and twelve days, six Alaskans found themselves in an unexpected meeting outside the derelict bus. An overwhelming stench of decomposition, along with an ominous note taped to a window glass, kept them from examining the interior. According to Jon's findings, one man who'd mustered the nerve to peer through the window to investigate further recalled seeing an expensive backpack among the rifle, paperback books, and other items that were found with Chris's body. But the Alaska State Troopers who had extricated Chris's remains from the isolated vehicle had not returned with a backpack for the coroner to turn over to his family. When Jon visited the bus for the first time, he recognized many items that remained there as having belonged to Chris, but his backpack was nowhere to be found.

Fifteen years after Chris's death, Jon received a call from one Will Forsberg. A dog musher from Healy, Forsberg spends serene winters with his wife and dogs in a cabin six miles south of where the bus rests. Jon had spoken with Forsberg while researching *Into the Wild,* and while he had not mentioned this previously, the Alaskan now claimed to have Chris's pack.

During the recent call, Forsberg had told Jon that he had visited the bus shortly after Chris's death. After noticing the pack had been left behind, he took it back to his cabin, where, after deciding it could be useful, he simply hung the backpack outside on a nail under the eave of his roof.

The mystery-solving phone call came to Jon after he had first learned, through the Internet, that Forsberg reportedly had the items. Having not heard back from Forsberg after several droning requests left on his answering machine, Jon phoned my parents and suggested they give it a try. When he offered them Forsberg's phone number, they declined. Jon's next call was to me. I called Forsberg as soon as I hung up with Jon, and after several phone calls between Forsberg, Jon, and myself, the backpack was on its way to my front door.

I understood why Jon had called my parents first with the opportunity to retrieve the backpack, and I appreciated why that was appropriate. Jon always struck me as a man of veracity, who accepted a natural order when it came to such things. I had witnessed him put forth great efforts to share a mutually respectful relationship with my parents, despite the irrational behavior they sometimes aimed at him.

I also greatly admired his belief in the importance of truth, even as I had asked him not to divulge my family's traumatic history. Jon had spent three years of his life following and researching Chris's journeys before publishing his book about them, and his fixation on uncovering and dissecting every detail could often be described as obsessive. Perhaps the greatest example of his zeal was his bullheaded determination to unravel the mystery of exactly how Chris had died.

Jon's initial approach to this question was to assume the accuracy of the coroner's report, which stated that Chris had starved to death. But as Jon examined Chris's journal entries and photographs of the food he'd hunted and foraged, Jon came to believe that the coroner's report failed to consider crucial evidence about the cause of his death. Further, determining the precise cause of Chris's death *mattered*, because it could potentially say a lot about how prepared—or foolhardy—he had been. Jon remembered his own youth filled with risk-taking adventures, and he queried other adventure seekers about their opinions of Chris. Was he just an ill-prepared, arrogant tenderfoot? Or was there something more to what drove him?

When visiting the bus, Jon cited Chris's blunders to his friend and travel companion Roman Dial, who by all accounts is an incredibly accomplished and well-respected outdoorsman in Alaska. Jon felt Roman's response was important enough to include in *Into the Wild*:

> *Sure, he screwed up . . . but I admire what he was trying to do.*
> *Living completely off the land like that, month after month, is in-*
> *credibly difficult. I've never done it. And I'd bet you that very few,*
> *if any, of the people who call McCandless incompetent have ever*
> *done it either . . . Living in the interior bush for an extended pe-*
> *riod, subsisting on nothing except what you hunt and gather—most*

*people have no idea how hard that actually is. And McCandless
almost pulled it off.*

According to Chris's terse journal entries, on July 30, 1992, he
suddenly fell ill—an illness that weakened him to the point that he
could not hike out or hunt or forage for food. These entries persuaded
Jon that starvation alone was not responsible for his rapid demise.
Chris stated unequivocally in his ninety-fourth journal entry, approximately eighteen days before his death, that his extreme illness
was the "fault of potato seeds." He added that he was "extremely
weak" and was experiencing "much trouble just to stand up." This
foreboding statement led Jon to explore a number of theories in an
effort to either prove or disprove Chris's claim.

After ascertaining that Chris had properly identified the wild potato and had not mistaken it for another, putatively toxic species, the
wild sweet pea, Jon sent seeds he'd gathered from the wild potato
plants growing around the bus to be tested for toxic alkaloids. When
an Alaskan chemist derisively announced, "I tore that plant apart.
There were no toxins. No alkaloids. I'd eat it myself," Jon explored
the possibility that a toxic mold had contaminated the seeds Chris
had stored in a dirty plastic bag before eating them. When that theory was also shot down, Jon sent the seeds to a lab in Michigan to be
tested for other, less obvious toxins. Finally, after several false leads
and months of expensive chemical analyses, Jon conclusively determined by means of liquid chromatography–tandem mass spectrome-
try that the seeds contained a toxic, non-protein amino acid known
to cause serious illness in both animals and humans.

And why did Jon spend tens of thousands of dollars, devote months
of his life, and subject himself to public ridicule trying to figure out
the precise cause of Chris's death? I believe that he did it for Chris.
I believe that Jon genuinely cares about the morality and necessity
of truth, as Chris did. And never does such a search for truth seem

more compelling, and more crucial, than when it involves probing the personal enigmas that exist within each of us. Some people need to seek that truth and share it, regardless of the consequences.

WITH THE MYSTERY of Chris's backpack finally solved, I was provided with definitive answers to a few lingering questions—questions I was often asked by those who remained skeptical about Chris's ultimate ambitions. When I spoke with Forsberg, he explained that several years after taking the backpack from the bus, he discovered Chris's wallet inside, zipped underneath the interior lining, which apparently was utilized by Chris as a makeshift hidden compartment. Inside the wallet, Forsberg found several forms of identification and three crisp one hundred dollar bills—further evidence that while Chris was determined to challenge himself to survive in the harsh wilds of Alaska, he fully intended to walk back out.

It remains unclear to me exactly why Forsberg did not report the discovery of the backpack and wallet to authorities. In the months after Chris's death, Forsberg, along with another cabin owner in the area, asserted his belief that Chris had most likely been the vandal who had trashed some cabins that summer—even though Chris's journal showed no evidence that he had traveled anywhere near the cabins and he was not considered a suspect by the National Park Service. What I did glean from my own conversation with Forsberg was that with the passage of time, he had come to understand that it was unlikely that Chris had been the culprit. As talk of the movie ambled through the media, and with the presence of the film crew in the areas of Alaska where Chris had been, the backpack that had been hanging idly on the side of Forsberg's cabin for so many years seemed to gain new life. He felt it was time to return it to Chris's family. For that kindness, I will always be grateful.

RECEIVING CHRIS'S BACKPACK through the mail, a decade and a half after his death, was a surreal experience. As I peered into the large box, my tears quickly began to dot the cardboard. The fatigued material felt rough and rigid between my fingers. I could tell it was a North Face pack, although no identifying information remained on the outside. I propped it up next to my own thirty-liter capacity pack, stood back, and estimated that it could carry slightly more. In the natural light coming through my kitchen windows, the pack's muddled charcoal color contrasted starkly with the deep rich black I had seen in the pictures that Chris took during his travels so many years ago. It spoke to me about exploration. It looked like it still wanted to go. I thought about everywhere it had been, the distance it had covered with Chris, the stories it could tell. I had never been jealous of an inanimate object before.

The once-bright accent colors were dull and faded: A drab vertical rectangle of teal green stood on the front like a well-worn badge of endurance. A half-inch strip of lightened purple ran around the base above where Chris packed his sleeping bag and strapped on his bed-roll. The hip belt and shoulder harness were torn in several places, evidence that it had put in many hours of service. It still smelled of dirt and weather and adventure.

As I wiped my blurred eyes and inspected further, I noticed a manufacturer's name imprinted on the ladder-lock buckles on either side of the upper pack straps. The raised print read ITW NEXUS, WOOD DALE, IL 60191. The irony of the letters caused me pause, because ITW is the acronym so often used for *Into the Wild*. I imagined Chris never noticed these tiny letters as he wrote in his many journals about his travels. An avid hiker myself, I considered how great it would be to carry my own gear in his pack on my next outing. But the foam surrounding the internal frame in the back panel was deteriorated, and considering myself to be a smart and efficient packer, I knew it had seen enough trails already and could no longer be a reliable and safe haul. Besides, I had my own trails to blaze.

I easily located and unzipped the interior lining, and there sat Chris's wallet. It looked similar enough to the deep red fabric trifold he had carried in high school that I wondered if it could be the same one. The Velcro closure came open with a high-pitched *shwick,* and as I removed the items and spread them neatly onto my counter, I was overcome with multiple emotions. Seeing Chris's birth certificate returned my eyes to a watery mess. It was tattered and illegible in spots but had been neatly folded and safely tucked in. The library cards he had obtained from several towns he'd passed through made me smile. There was his social security card, his voter registration card, an eyeglasses prescription, his ID from the state of Arizona, a food services health card from Las Vegas, and a small scrap of paper where he had recorded his bike lock combination in neat block letters. I had asked Mr. Forsberg for a suggestion as to where to donate the three hundred dollars, and we had agreed that Chris would want it to go to support nature conservation in Alaska.

I put my head down amongst the collection and wept.

AFTER MOM AND DAD LEARNED I had the backpack, they developed a sudden interest in it. To avoid the blame that would come from making such demands directly, I soon received a letter from my parents' attorney. He represented their recently formed Christopher Johnson McCandless Memorial Foundation, and the letter commanded that I immediately deliver to my parents the backpack, wallet, and all other items that at one time had belonged to Chris— including those that they had given me after my return from Alaska with his remains. The letter continued to say that I was in violation of my parents' legal entitlement to these items, because they had automatically conveyed to them upon Chris's death, since he did not leave behind a will. It was also made very clear that all photographs Chris had taken were the property of my parents. A personal note from my father further warned that my noncompliance would prevent me, and thus my special needs daughter, from benefiting from their considerable assets.

Aside from my anger toward such callous communication, it saddened me to see further evidence that they failed to understand their own son so terribly; to think that as he lay dying in the Alaskan wilderness, among his beloved books, torn jeans, broken glasses, kitchen utensils, backpack, camera, and unexposed film—after holding on to hope that someone might appear to rescue him while he was out collecting blueberries—that with his last remaining strength he would think it necessary to take pen to paper and scrawl a last will and testament to pass on rightful possession of such things.

It reminded me of when I had traveled up to Windward Key for the ceremonial spreading of Chris's ashes. My parents had told me the day's plan, which was for me, Mom and Dad, Aunt Jan, and Buck to board my parents' new boat, sail it out far into Chesapeake Bay, and let Chris's remains flow away with the current. As I made the drive, I wrestled with my emotions. I recognized they had the right to make this decision, but I felt it wasn't what Chris would have wanted. Upon arrival at the town house, I took my mom aside for the debate I had rehearsed.

"Mom, I don't understand why we're spreading Chris's ashes in the bay when he mentioned so often that he was afraid of being in deep water."

I thought I had prepared myself fully for the discussion, but her reply left me speechless.

"This isn't about Chris," she said. "We live on the bay. We sail on it almost every day now, and this way we'll feel closer to him."

My pity for her in that moment outweighed my anger. I remembered how I'd felt when I'd been handed Chris's ashes in Alaska. *This isn't all that's left of him,* I'd thought. I knew he had moved on, and I let it go.

———————

AS SOON AS I FELT Christiana was old enough to travel safely, she and I boarded a plane to South Dakota, where filming for *Into the Wild* was under way. I struggled to remain focused. My duties as a mother, my accountability as a sister, and the immense responsibility I felt toward Chris all churned inside me at once, making each day emotionally exhausting.

Soon after arrival, we met up with Shawna and Shelly. Shelly was particularly excited to hold Christiana, because she herself was only a couple of months away from giving birth to a son. That afternoon, we all caravanned with members of the cast and crew to a lake house for an impromptu gathering between filming sessions. Sean and his staff had ensured there was a peaceful spot set up for me, and after I finished nursing Christiana on schedule, we all visited for a while. Everyone wanted a turn holding the baby, and while she was in Shawna's arms, Sean led me out to a large two-level back deck overlooking the water and called to one of the film crew. A moment later, up the wooden steps trotted the familiar gait of Wayne Westerberg. Sean knew what had happened when I'd come to South Dakota with Fish ten years prior, and his compassionate expression prepared to take in the reunion as if it were an improvisational scene.

Wayne walked slowly but straight over to me. He looked me in the eyes and then down. While staring at his shoes, he said simply, "Hi, Carine." And then we slowly embraced, two people who shared a common loss riddled with confusion and regret.

Sean said nothing, but I'm pretty sure his subconscious shouted out, *Cut! That's a wrap!*

I didn't get to see Gail again on that trip. But I did have occasion to meet Tracy Tatro. In December of 1991, eight months before Chris's death, Tracy was camping with her parents in a remote location in the California desert east of the Salton Sea. Locals identified the hot, barren site as Slab City. A mature teenager, she was immediately smitten with a handsome, mysterious young man who was visiting with friends at the Slabs and who called himself Alex. From Tracy's account, they enjoyed an innocent romance of long walks and sunset gazing, peppered with serious conversations about books and what Tracy wanted out of life. She was dealing with issues of her own rough upbringing, and she opened up to him about what she was going through. Although Chris shared nothing with her about his own past, she sensed an understanding in his eyes as he listened intently.

She tagged along as my brother held himself to a strict regimen of calisthenics in preparation for his journey to Alaska. She swooned as Chris entertained a flea market crowd with an old portable electronic organ someone was selling. After less than a week in his company, Tracy was in love. Chris hit the road again soon after, but the strong feelings she harbored for him remained.

As I sat with her in an extra cast trailer as a new day of shooting began, she stared intently at Christiana sitting on my lap. We talked quietly about a young man we both missed terribly but knew by different names. Finally, in mid sentence, she asked hastily, "Can I hold her?"

"Oh sure!" I replied. "I'm sorry, of course you can."

The moment Tracy's hands touched Chris's namesake, tears filled her eyes and overflowed into quiet streams running down her face. I don't think she registered any further words that came from my mouth. She appeared to be completely engulfed with grief from the loss of someone she had known for only a short period. But I understood her silent keening. I had already been witness to unspoken connections that lead certain people to find each other in life, and to how the passage of time seemed to be an insignificant factor in what caused Chris's gripping effect on people.

And as I also now understood, Chris's story had the power to influence people he had never met. In nothing was this clearer to me than the film's soundtrack, for which Sean had commissioned Eddie Vedder, an accomplished musician and vocalist and front man of the mega band Pearl Jam. The rough edges of Ed's supple baritone merged beautifully with the spirit of the film. Whenever I had the opportunity to observe Ed amongst others, he consistently proved to be humble despite his celebrity, with a kindhearted and genuine character. After hearing the lyrics he had composed, I was blown away by how he had seemed to channel Chris so acutely, and I told him so. His reaction was not exactly what I'd expected. Knowing that he was an outspoken atheist, I was unsure how open he would be to borderline religious conversation. Yet he took me aside and shared how easily the words had come to him, and allowed that it was a beautiful and rare experience that he could not quite explain. It seemed we had found a mutual space somewhere within what I would call spirituality.

THROUGHOUT FILMING, Sean shared completed edits of footage with me. His film was cinematically stunning and I was overwhelmingly pleased with most of the content. But my enthusiasm came to a halt when I reviewed the final scene.

In the cut Sean shared with me, as Chris was dying he pictured himself running into our parents' arms at the house in Annandale. While I appreciated Sean's pure intent and his artistic and poetic explanations for why parents must have a presence at both the giving of life and the coming of death, I felt it was incredibly disrespectful to Chris. I wanted him to change it before the movie was finalized. Sean felt it signified forgiveness, and his own experiences led him to believe that the desire of the human spirit to forgive is never stronger than at the end of life.

"Carine, you weren't with him when he died," Sean reasoned. "You don't know what was going through his mind."

"Yes," I agreed. "But Sean, you didn't know him. I did. And I understood his reasons for leaving better than anyone else, because he shared that with me alone." I continued in tears, "I am telling you with my whole heart, I just know that at the end of his life—with his last few breaths on this earth, he would not have gone back to a place where he had felt so much pain after working so hard to get away from it."

We reached a compromise a few days later. Sean called me in Virginia Beach. I could tell he was driving, and I heard papers rustling in the background.

"Hey! Good, I caught you! Um, hold on . . . hold on just a sec. Let me pull over."

I imagined him driving with a cell phone pinned between his ear and shoulder, pen and paper in one hand and a cigarette in the other, knees most likely in charge of the wheel, and his hair in the crazed Don King–like stance I had come to recognize meant Sean was really concentrating on something.

"Okay, how about this? What if—when you see Chris running into their arms, eyes up to the heavens—you hear Chris's voice-over say, 'What if I were smiling and running into your arms . . . would you see then, what I see now?'"

It was the perfect concession, and I was so appreciative that he cared enough to make the change. "Thank you, Sean. That says everything it needs to say."

WORKING ON THE MOVIE was cathartic, and I was proud of my contributions to what I knew would be a beautiful film. But my obsession to ensure Chris's voice and legacy were fairly honored sometimes brought with it a strong mix of emotions. One night while working on narrative edits, I sat alone on my living room floor, script pages strewn all around me. It had been an exceptionally difficult day, and feeling overwhelmed, I broke down and sobbed uncontrollably. I had been dealing with the latest in the long line of my parents' manipulations, and as I drafted words onto paper that my character would soon divulge to audiences in theaters around the world, I struggled to find a comfortable space between truth and necessity—two words that I honestly believed should rarely be apart. Feeling astoundingly desperate, I called out to my brother in a rare plea for help. I felt a bit silly doing it, but the words still came out loud and clear:

"Chris, please! I just can't do this alone! Please, I need to know that you are here with me!"

I continued to cry until I ran out of tears, then staggered to the kitchen for a drink of water and went to bed before Robert and the girls had returned from a dinner outing.

The next morning I was in my bedroom folding laundry when the phone rang. I heard Robert answer, then call down the hall for me to pick up the line. "Hey, Carine. It's for you. It's . . . Tracy Moore Raborg?"

I shared the surprise in his voice, because she was an old friend from my auto repair shop days and we had not seen each other nor had we spoken for years. Tracy was a true southern beauty who resembled supermodel Kathy Ireland, with dark blond hair and striking eyes that seemed to morph from blue to green depending on her outfit. We used to have fun roving around town with a mutual group of girlfriends, at a time when our weekends consisted of going out to bars and dance clubs, flirting with and teasing men, collecting only smiles and phone numbers before always leaving together. The welcome lifestyle changes that came with marriage and children had long ago put an end to those escapades.

"Carine?" Her usually buoyant voice sounded heavy. "I'm so sorry."

"What?" I asked, perplexed. "What's wrong? Oh my God, who died?"

"Oh geez. No, I just . . ." she stammered. "This is going to sound crazy. I'm so sorry, Carine. I wasn't going to call you, but something is making me do this. I can't explain it. Something has been gnawing at me all morning to pick up the phone. Please don't be angry or think I'm crazy," she continued on in a worrisome whirlwind.

"It's okay, Tracy," I assured her through my complete confusion. "Just tell me what happened."

"Oh God. Um . . . okay." Her voice relaxed. "I had this really vivid dream last night . . ."

"And?" I prodded.

"I was sitting in a restaurant with a friend," she continued. "I didn't recognize this woman, but somehow I knew she was a good friend of mine. Kind of weird. Anyway, we're having lunch and chatting, and . . . and your brother walks into the restaurant. He sits at a table in a faraway corner, diagonally across the room from us." The tone of her voice lightened. "And . . . well, he was kind of flirting with me with those big brown eyes of his!" She giggled. Tracy had never met my brother, since he had died before she and I met. But she had heard me talk endlessly about him and had seen his pictures on the shelves of my old apartment.

"Okay." I laughed, finding it completely logical that Chris, even in dream form, would find Tracy attractive.

"So," she continued, "I say to my friend sitting across from me, 'Do you know who that is?' And she shakes her head no, and I say, 'That's Carine's brother, Chris.' Then right away he stands up and walks over to our table. He looks down to me, right into my eyes, and says, 'Do you know who I am?' And I answer him, 'Yes, you're Carine's brother.' And then he says to me, 'I need you to do me a favor. I need you to call her and tell her I am there with her.'"

I stood next to my king-size bed, stunned, the phone receiver in one hand and clean underwear in the other.

"Hello? Carine, are you still there?" Tracy's voice brought me back into the moment. "Oh, Carine, I'm so sorry if I've upset you. I had to call you. Are you mad?"

"Mad?" I replied. "No. No, Tracy. Not at all." I could barely get the words out while tears fell over my cheeks and into my mouth. I told Tracy the exact message I had asked of Chris the night before. Then she started crying, too. She didn't even know I was working on a movie about him, since most of my friends didn't find out until after it was in theaters. I thanked Tracy profusely, and she thanked me back. The experience brought me the peace I needed to keep moving forward.

CHAPTER 16

WHEN A CHILD comes into your life unexpectedly, it causes you to reevaluate your priorities. When a special needs child comes into your life, unexpected or not, it forces you to change your lifestyle.

In the first few months after Christiana's birth, it was tough not to compare her arrival to Heather's. While I hadn't known Heather as a baby, I knew the pregnancy that led up to her birth had not been a healthy one, yet she came into the world physically unaffected. Christiana was born, as are most children with Down syndrome, with very low muscle tone. She had to put forth great effort to achieve every developmental milestone that most babies achieve quickly and naturally. For her, every day was filled with a regimen—aside from the normal infant routine of eat, sleep, poop, repeat—of physical and occupational therapy appointments, exercises to help improve her oral function and motor skills, hearing and vision tests, and extra doctor visits. Christiana seemed to have an innate comprehension of why this remedial monotony was important, and I was amazed by her determination through every new task. At home I set up different play areas with various apparatuses of toys that helped focus her efforts on a particular goal: reaching, grasping, rolling over. I took pictures and kept notes to document our daily work and track her progress.

Between therapy exercises, I sat in my living room, nursing Christiana on a consistent schedule. I had imagined it would be tough for me to sit still for so many hours each day. When she was very young, Christiana didn't like to nurse with the TV on or when there was a book distracting her mommy. She preferred her surroundings nice and quiet. But occupying my time was never a problem; I could get lost looking at her almond-shaped brown eyes, her little low-placed ears, her amazing skin. Her fine light brown hair already shone with golden highlights.

As I stroked Christiana's hair, I remembered how as a little girl, whenever I was sick, my mom would pull out the footie pajamas and put me straight into bed. Then she would slather Vicks VapoRub on my chest and wrap me up tightly in a blanket. Though I hated how the cold goop felt under my cotton shirt, especially sticky under the weight of the shirt's buttons, I always looked forward to how she would then sing softly to me and run her fingers through my long hair. As her voice soothed me, her smooth nails gently lifted the bangs away from my forehead, then stroked across my temples and around my ears again and again, until I fell asleep.

On pretty days, as I nursed Christiana, my gaze traveled outside our large picture window and into the front yard, to the flower beds overflowing with multicolored blooms. And on rainy days, I sometimes examined the photos nearby, including the self-portraits Chris had taken on his travels. I longed to have him there, sitting in the living room with me, holding his namesake in his arms. I wanted it to be him telling us all about his adventures, instead of these silent images. I wanted him to know Heather and for her to know him. I was so proud of her, and of myself. I knew Heather was both the greatest gift and the most important opportunity to ever come into my life.

One day while driving Heather home from school, she asked how Christiana had done with her exercises that day. I told her I still needed to get them done—most of my day had been taken up by reading through narrative revisions for the movie, and I was feeling emotionally drained. We returned home, and before I had unloaded Christiana from the car, Heather disappeared into her room without a word. I was concerned that she was beginning to get jealous, and the thought of dealing with any complaining about it agitated me a bit, even though it was completely understandable. After having the majority of my attention for several years, Heather had comparably little time alone with me now. When my head wasn't buried in a script, her little sister was either attached to me nursing or in my arms canoodling, or I was hovering over her, working to achieve the day's therapy objectives.

As I prepared dinner, I practiced what I would say to Heather to explain how important it will be for her to resist being selfish and to understand that her sister, probably forever, was going to require extra care. A few minutes into my rehearsal, I saw Heather come down the hall with an old school binder. She walked over to where her sister was lying motionless on a large blanket in the family room. She gently rolled Christiana onto her stomach, laid down next to her, and then, slowly rising up on all fours, she began to demonstrate the art of proper crawling. She carefully manipulated her little sister's head and limbs, then paused to write in the binder.

"What's that you've got there?" I asked.

"It's a therapy journal!" Heather said proudly.

I walked over to sit beside my eldest daughter and saw that she had divided the binder into four sections, labeled in pink crayon: "arms," "legs," "mouth," "?"

"I can help you since you're always so busy. Once she starts moving around more I can add other stuff," she said, pointing to the blank pages. "What do you think, Mommy?" she looked up to me and asked.

I believe some people come into this world to learn lessons, and thus others must come into the world as teachers. Watching Heather with Christiana brought back visions of Chris as a young boy, taking me by the hand in the house on Willet Drive, running outside to play, keeping me ahead of any adversity that simply accompanied our existence. I could sense Heather would always look out for her little sister.

I told her I thought she was going to be a great teacher.

————————

EACH TIME CHRISTIANA finished nursing, I propped her up and gently patted her back to coax out a healthy burp. The low tone of her muscles made her core feel clumsy between my hands. Every time we repeated this routine, she would lurch forward and use all her energy to reach toward a large picture sitting on the end table next to the couch. It was Chris's senior portrait from high school. A remarkably knowing look always manifested in her features as she stroked his face, up and down. Sometimes the acquainted expression in her eyes was accompanied by a giggle or a coo as she seemed to enjoy her own private conversation with the image.

One afternoon, after this had continued every day for a period of weeks, I realized that she must be seeing her own reflection in the glass. A couple of hours later, before waking her to nurse again, I removed the glass from the frame so the matte photo paper would offer no mirror image. Yet when I sat her up again, she reached over to Chris's picture and continued to run her fingers across his face with the same definitive familiarity. At that exact moment, and for the first and only time in my life, I heard a distinct voice in my head. It wasn't an ethereal booming or an angelic whisper. It was a simple voice that just sounded like a friend, and it said to me:

He held her before you did.

————————

TOO OFTEN MY PEACEFUL nursing times with Christiana were interrupted by the view of my parents' Cadillac speeding into my driveway. Doors flung open, and the scene played out as it had at my shop, aggravated, of course, by whatever angst the pending release of Sean's film had loosed. But now the judge they sought had a tiny treasure to protect, and before they were even through the front door, my milk had seized and Christiana was crying.

"Please!" I would appeal to them, since they seemed completely oblivious to the needs of the additional screaming child in the room. "Don't you see what's happening? Whenever you two come around here with your fighting she can't nurse!"

Neither of them understood why I felt breast milk was so important for Christiana's health. That and the hand washing I insisted upon drew constant mockery and eye rolls.

"For God's sake! Why don't you just give her a bottle?" Mom snapped.

"Because she needs me right now!" I explained. "And I can't feed her when you guys bring this stress. My milk dries up instantly!"

"Oh give me a break, Carine!" she replied.

I began to wonder if my mom had lost all her maternal instincts. She had recently suggested that I intermittently place an ice cube against Christiana's protruding tongue to train her to keep it in her mouth. Due to her low oral strength and function, I was currently Christiana's only source of nourishment. Besides, I was forming such a wonderful bond with my baby, and nursing her was a huge part of that.

The breaking point came the day my mother arrived alone. She was quiet and somber, and she carried my father's laptop with her. The discussion began like so many had before. She had decided to really divorce my father this time, but the reason was much graver than before. She began to cry. She said she needed my help. I put my baby aside in her crib and sat down on the couch with my mom.

She explained that my dad was a porn addict, spending most nights in their penthouse loft alone with his computer. She was not very computer savvy but had found a website address scribbled down

in his office trash can. She showed me the note. We took his laptop
into the kitchen and pulled up the site. The picture that flashed up
on the screen was as gross as I had expected. I didn't need to look at
any more. A quick history search confirmed her suspicions, that this
was a consistent habit of his. We both knew what we needed to talk
about next, and surprisingly, she led the discussion as we moved back
to the family room couch.

"I know that you will be strong enough to do what I could not do.
I don't want to lose my granddaughters," she said.

Her chin was strong, her eyes set. Tears began to stream down
her face again. "I've walked in on him, and I saw the porn on his
computer. I think there could be illicit content on there. He and his
buddies from church go up to the Subway every day once school lets
out, and they sit there and ogle over these pretty young things from
high school in their little shorts. It's disgusting."

She told me that he was still violent with her, that he forced himself onto her. I had always suspected that I was conceived through
violence, and she confirmed that I was. Years ago, another woman
in the family had claimed Dad molested her, and now I asked Mom
if it was true. She said that she believed her but had stood by Dad in
his denial.

I told her that this was it. I would help her, but she had to follow
through and prove she really meant it this time before I dragged
myself, my husband, and my two little girls through the storm that
was to come. I was familiar with their financial trusts, because they
often reminded me of how rich I could be when they died. I assured
her she could live comfortably after divorcing him. We formulated
a plan, one that required her very first move to be driving straight
to the police station to turn over Dad's computer to be checked. I
explained to her how that could make her break from him easier and
safer. They already owned two units at a condo complex in Virginia
Beach, and she could move out immediately. I told her I would help

get her away from him. I held her. I cried with her. I said I was proud of her.

When I did not hear from my mother that night, I asked Robert if he thought I should drive over. "No," he said, definitively and wisely. "I'm tired of watching them do this to you, and now to our kids."

I'd given a lot of thought to why a resolution to my problems with my parents always seemed to reach an impasse. It reminded me of how the human body can often recover from one devastating stab wound from a clean, sharp blade—especially if the wound is tended to immediately, giving a surgeon clean and clear breaks to locate and repair. But it's different when a body is stabbed repeatedly by a rusty, jagged blade. Even if you can stop the bleeding, if the wounds are left unattended and uncared for, they begin to fester. They become infected. The contagion kills off the parts that are needed to recover, thus leaving nothing to repair, and the body dies.

The next day, my father arrived at my home. Everyone else was at school or work, so it was just me and Christiana, but I wasn't afraid of him. I let him in and we sat at my kitchen table. He's always had a gift for appearing wounded and helpless whenever he's done something particularly horrific. He said that he was going to get help. He would talk to their pastor. He said that it was only adult porn and nothing involving children. I said nothing.

He asked me to please not take his actions out on Mom and that he'd prepared a compromise. He wanted my girls to be able to come to their house for a visit alone or to stay the night—something I had already disallowed—while he stayed at the other condo or on the boat.

I recognized his wounded expression. It was the same one he'd worn the day we sat at the dining room table in Annandale, after he'd attacked me in the drunken rage that had caused me to be moved out to Windward Key.

"No," I said.

"What?" he replied. "What do you mean 'No'?"

"I mean exactly what I said, Dad. No." I continued, "If you sincerely care about Mom, then walk away. You have never been able to solve your problems together. Maybe it's time that you tried to work on things as individuals."

And with that, I welcomed him to leave my home. My mom called the next day to tell me they had decided to separate, but I was not to tell anyone. They would live in separate condos but still attend social functions together, including worship services, because they did not want to lose their good standing at church. She sounded very excited to implement this new plan and said she felt really good about it.

"So, what do you think?" she asked.

"Did you give Dad back his laptop?" was my only question.

"Well, Carine. You know that your father manages our investments on his computer. I had to! If something had come up he couldn't address right away, we could have gone bankrupt!"

"You have to know that's bullshit," I countered. "I just don't understand why you can't leave him, Mom."

"Oh, Carine, because he's your father!" With Chris no longer available to blame, I was next in line.

"Okay then, Mom, I'll give you my opinion," I obliged. "You have, once again, chosen your financial status and social reputation over your children, and now your grandchildren. Do not come to me for help again. I am done playing this game with you, and I refuse to install my own children as participants." I hung up.

Thirty-six hours later, Mom called again. When I asked her if she had changed her mind, she claimed to not know what I was talking about.

Over the next few months, both of my parents avoided any direct discussion about what had happened. But I still hoped that I could help them grasp the gravity of this situation and begin some healing, separately if not together. I told them they were welcome to come by and visit as long as their behavior was appropriate. I invited them to Heather's soccer games, and suggested that we could still have dinners together. But I had also set a firm boundary that I would never leave my daughters alone with them, for obvious reasons. All interactions would have to be on my terms. No negotiations. I told them that I would not play along with their latest perfect relationship fantasy, nor become part of the show when out in public together.

As had been their pattern, Mom and Dad began to spread rumors that I had invented the facts that surrounded our latest impasse, and claimed that I refused to allow them to see my children. If I saw them in person, they acted as if they were terribly wounded by my hurtful and disrespectful behavior.

One night, sickened by this devastating history repeating, I sat down and drafted a long impassioned letter to my parents. I apologized for sending it via email, but said that I felt it would be too stressful to deliver it personally and needed them to hear what I had to say right away. Just as Chris had done almost twenty years before me, I explained why I felt our relationship was at risk of complete disintegration. I took great care in my writing and worked hard to balance my pure and honest anger with compassion and logic:

> I am very upset with you both. The fact that you have not spent any time with Heather and Christiana over the past three months is appalling to me, and even worse is that you, as usual, have twisted the facts around in your minds that somehow this is my doing, ignoring the fact that these are choices you have made through your own actions. I will try to, once again, spell this out for you. But honestly as I do this now I feel that this is an exhausting exercise, knowing that this is probably futile. You have proven that you cannot take a hard look at yourselves in the mirror, and finally accept responsibility for the choices you have made over the past forty plus years that have led your children to feel this way. You will tell yourselves and each other, and your friends, and your church, and

your God, that we are all just ungrateful children that have cut you
out of our families' lives for no reason whatsoever—that you are
dismayed, confused and so very hurt that we could do this to you,
and that it must have something to do with money. Or you might
choose to dismiss my being upset with you as a result of my "emo-
tional state after giving birth." Ridiculous.

I included long personal notes to each, listing incidents from our
distant and recent history in a desperate attempt to connect on a level
that would allow some chance of reconciliation that had seemed possible so many times before. Then my letter continued:

Now with all of those years passed, the fault lies with you both
equally. You have both had plenty of opportunities to discontinue
this behavior and have CHOSEN not to . . . It has always
amazed me, although not surprised me, that losing Chris failed to
snap you both into the reality and understanding of how our child-
hood, while we agree was certainly not the worst ever experienced
(as you often point out), was still in fact very confusing, violent,
negatively dramatic, dishonest, and stressful (which you often ig-
nore). We have always understood and appreciated the good things
you did as parents and in raising us, but somehow in your minds
this cancelled out the validity of our feelings about the bad times.
Any attempts by us to discuss this honestly with you, while at that
moment in time seemed like a possible breakthrough, were always
predictably followed up with some sarcastic comment about us being
spoiled, difficult children to raise, or we just simply had a warped
recollection and you certainly don't remember it that way.
      Eight children remember it that way.
      Your refusal to acknowledge this, and continuation of the same
dramatic negative cycle, has <u>*pushed*</u> *your children and grandchildren*

away. No one expects the past to be rewritten. We just don't want it repeated again & again & again, and we do not want it to negatively affect our own children . . .

It makes me very sad that I do not feel comfortable calling you up to tell you that Christiana's therapy is going so well, to tell you to come over quick to see her rolling over, to hear her talking, or to see how cute she looks in her high chair eating cereal and even drinking out of a cup. You should be at Heather's soccer games and should not have to go up to the school to give her a present.

I will end with this. Chris told me once of the five-page letter he wrote to you both, in a last desperate attempt to get you to understand his feelings. His hopes that it would be worth all of that effort—his pouring out of his soul, his dragging back into the front of his mind the things he had safely tucked away into the back— were lost, when the only response he got from you was a sarcastic postcard from a ski resort . . . That is when you lost him forever. I hope you do not make the same choice again.

Please LISTEN & SEE!!! With love & hope, Carine

Soon after, I received their reply:

Carine,

You have been uncharacteristically uncommunicative for some time now. In fact, this isolation tendency has been growing significantly for at least two years, predating our present disagreements. . . . Your belated note to us merely exacerbates an already damaging situation.

They continued on, through various forms of communication: sometimes with a peaceful and loving tone, expressing dismay over our emotional distance and protesting that I had refused their attempts to mend our relationship; other times with sarcasm and vile threats, assuring me that due to my "despicable" actions, I was ruining Christiana's future by destroying her opportunity to inherit any of their money.

They always closed with the same sentiment—that regardless of how I was treating them, they would continue to pray for me to find my way to God's grace in hopes that He might have mercy on my soul, and that they would be waiting with loving hearts and open arms, for me to see the error of my ways.

I looked to my faith, and into my heart. I thought about Chris and the responsibility I felt to be a survivor. But that obligation—that instinct—had shifted from my role as a daughter to my accountability as a mother and a sister.

I thought about the importance of truth.

I thought about the meaning of shared happiness.

And that is how the war came to its end.

EPILOGUE

Let your life be a counter friction to stop the machine.
What I have to do is to see, at any rate, that I do
not lend myself to the wrong which I condemn.

—Henry David Thoreau,
Civil Disobedience

WITH THE WAR OVER, it was time for the history lessons. When Christiana was able to start a full day-school program, I accepted an invitation to join the Random House Speakers Bureau. Jon's book was now printed in more than thirty languages and had been required reading in schools across the country for over fifteen years. As I visited high schools and colleges, I saw how hungry the students were for a better understanding of Chris. They wanted to know what drove him to the decisions he made. Teachers and professors wanted to provide their students with a personal connection to Chris's life and death, so that his triumphs and his mistakes could be more than words in a book. I realized early on that something simple blocked that connection: the students didn't have the whole story.

I had helped perpetuate misunderstandings about Chris's life. I felt guilty that I hadn't been stronger and more willing to let Jon tell the whole truth from the beginning. But in gentler moments, I remembered I was only twenty-one when I met Jon and still hopeful that my relationship with my parents would take a different course. Chris had taught me to learn not only from their mistakes but also from my own. The important thing was that I tell the whole truth now.

From working with students and from the messages I received about Chris from people all over the world, I came to understand that his legacy could do so much more to help people if its primary focus was based on that which was most important to Chris: TRUTH—a word he'd carefully written in large block letters in one of his beloved books. Now I speak honestly about my part in hiding much of that truth. I have worked hard to forgive myself for that infraction, while fully examining the reasons that I did so and why I can do so no longer.

At the end of every lecture presentation, after every Q&A session, I can always count on at least one student straggling behind, waiting for the others to get their final questions answered. I always allow this last student to approach at his or her own pace while I pack up slowly. Perhaps the most powerful of these meetings happened on a visit to Westfield High School, the largest in Virginia, in the same town where Chris and I grew up.

"Excuse me, Ms. McCandless?" The young man's eyes finally met mine. "Umm . . . I just wanted to thank you for being so honest with us."

"Of course," I replied, looking into a young face carrying a familiar burden.

"I'm dealing with the same thing at home." We spoke for a while about his own struggles as a member of an abusive household. New occurrences like this kept domestic violence a part of my life, but now it was on my terms.

"Umm . . . just one last thing." He paused for a while, clearly gearing up to ask me something important. "I was wondering . . . have you ever been able to forgive your parents?"

I had spoken to thousands of students over the past several years. It was not the most personal question I had ever been asked, but it was by far the most difficult. And I was not sure that I could give him an honest answer, because I was still trying to figure that one out for myself.

I struggle with the definition of forgiveness. I debate with myself as to whether it is a matter of compassion, of understanding, or of simply being willing and able to forget. But with forgetfulness comes recurrence. I wrestle with my faith, which instructs me to show mercy to those who have not asked for it and pardon those who have not earned it. As painful and complicated as it is, the conflict dissipates when I look at my children. I know in my heart and soul that my primary responsibilities—above all else—are to protect them and to teach them. Through any adversity, against all odds, and until my last breath, I will measure myself on how well I serve this purpose.

As a mom, I've often used something I call the "Billie check" when struggling to control my anger and frustration. My mom rarely raised her hands to us as Dad did, but she was just as scary. Recently I came home after a grueling work week and noticed that Heather had yet to pick up her wet towel from the bathroom floor, she'd gotten mascara on the white counter, and the mortar-like remnants of a fruit smoothie sat in a glass on the back of the toilet. I could feel myself boiling over as I heard the TV on in the family room and pictured her sprawled out on the couch in front of it. *This is typical teenage stuff,* I said to myself as I did the Billie check. *Don't take your*

*anger—about taking on more work than you have time for, about your lack of
sleep, about how long it's been since you had time to sit in front of the TV—
out on your daughter.*

So, I didn't. "Heather?" I called down the hallway.

"Yeeees?" she answered, knowingly.

"Can you come here for a minute please?" I continued. She came
down the hall with an expectation of what was to come. I recognized
there was no fear in her eyes, and I was proud of myself for that.
"Hello there, sweetheart," I said with a hint of sarcasm. "Do you
recall me asking you to clean the bathroom this morning?"

"Yes," she answered, looking down just slightly, then around the
bathroom.

"And was I speaking English at that time?" I asked.

"Yes," she concurred, smiling a little.

"And is English still your primary language?"

"Yes, ma'am," she answered.

"Oh good! So, you *did* understand me. I was concerned the French
you're studying in school had taken over completely, and I don't remember much of it myself. Whew!" I walked to the kitchen, leaving
Heather to her cleaning, fully prepared that we'd have the same conversation again when it came to her room.

Christiana is thriving, and she and Heather continue to have a
close and protective relationship. Together they have already taught
me more than I can ever hope to teach them. When I look at them,
I think about Chris and me, but I also think about Sam, Stacy,
Shawna, Shelly, Shannon, and Quinn. My extended family today
is closer than ever. That family doesn't involve the people who biologically produced me; it includes those who molded me. We've had
cause throughout our lives as children, as adults, and now as parents
to band together time and time again. Perhaps the greatest bequest
that Walt and Billie have offered us, in the end, is how their actions
have brought us all together.

SEVERAL YEARS AGO I visited the area where Chris spent his last days, the purest and most peaceful days of his life. It had taken me fifteen years to emotionally prepare myself for the trip, and my brothers and sisters helped give me that strength.

I made the trip with Jon in the summer of 2007, right before the movie was due to hit theaters across the world. Just as Jon's presence was of great comfort to me throughout my experience with the book and film about Chris's life, it felt incredibly appropriate to have him beside me on the day that I would visit the site of Chris's death.

I wondered what was going through Jon's mind as we watched the ruggedness of the Alaskan backcountry spread out beneath us. I knew it was not in Jon's character to take the easy way in. My own adventurous side felt a bit cheated as we floated high above the thick spruce and alder in a safe and warm helicopter. I would rather have immersed myself in the challenge but only if it had made sense. Despite my deep love of nature and outdoor adventures, I had never visited the outback of Alaska before, nor had I hiked in similar territory. I accepted my level of naïveté, and since I did not take the time to properly train and prepare, I knew that I should not hike in. The most important goal of that trip was for me to get back home to Heather and Christiana, and Chris's voice in my head was my strongest reminder.

Glaciers were visible in the distance, but there was no snow on the ground as there had been when Chris hiked through this terrain. From up above, hearing nothing but the high-pitched hum of the aircraft's rotors and our pilot's conversant narrative through my headset, it was hard to imagine what Chris experienced. The pictures he had taken shifted through my mind. My chest tightened as Jon pointed out the Teklanika River. The churning waters were still brown with silt from the late spring thaw.

The skids touched down on the rocky banks of the much tamer Sushana River, the waterway that ambles beside the abandoned bus that Chris had made his base camp for more than one hundred days. We were still a short walk from where the derelict vehicle rests. The toes of my thick boots scuffed along the shoreline. I picked up a few small colorful rocks and examined them for their aerodynamic properties, then tossed them across the top of the water as Chris had once taught me to do, hopeful for the skip. But my skills were rusty and the rocks simply plunked into the cold, slow current to meet the river bottom once again.

As I made my way up the short trail, Jon allowed me the time and space I needed to digest what was waiting just beyond the overgrown vegetation. As I entered a clearing, I saw it, just to my right. Fairbanks City Transit System bus 142 was parked beside a thicket of aspen and scraggly clumps of fireweed with blushing blooms. The green and white paint was peeling from over forty years of battling the elements. Rust devoured the metal as it crept across each point where yellow primer was exposed. I slowly turned, full circle, taking deep breaths to soak in the pain and the peace. I could see what had attracted Chris to this serene and beautiful place, and I remembered how he could be alone without being lonely. But sadness returned as I recalled his journal entries that revealed he was lonely and scared toward the end. In front of the bus sat the chair in which Chris took his now infamous self-portrait—the sole image Jon used in *Into the Wild*—during a happier time here, one leg comfortably propped up on the other, his wide smile lighting up an expression of absolute content. I cemented the image in my mind as the memory I would take from this place.

The whining of mosquitoes at my ears motivated me to move on, and I asked Jon to show me the location of the cave where Chris tried in vain to protect the moose meat from hordes of flies and their maggot offspring. The bus sat about ten yards from a small cliff over-looking the Sushana. We scrambled over the precipice toward the water on a narrow and scarcely used trail. Despite the throng of in-sects that followed, it was a beautiful setting, with the soft sounds of water running over and between rocks, meandering through forest as far as the eye could see. I imagined Chris pausing to take in the secluded view as he hauled his bath and drinking water up and over the edge. A small opening appeared in the bedrock not far from the top, where Chris had removed enough of the compacted dirt for his improvised smoking pit. The weight of his despair bore down on me as I stood in the same footing where he would have agonized over the failure of his attempt.

Back atop the overhang, I stared across the clearing and steeled myself to examine the interior of the bus. As I entered, I looked di-rectly to the mattress where Chris took his last breaths. Tears blurred my peripheral vision as I walked slowly to the back. As I sat on the makeshift bed and cleared my eyes, I tried to imagine Chris here: stoking the fire in the oil-drum stove, having his meals, reading his books, and writing in his journal. Some of the windows were broken, some were missing, allowing the cool damp air and mos-quitoes inside. The floor was strewn with leaves and dirt. I felt the urge to clean it up. But not the energy.

As my gaze traveled upward, I saw graffiti covering the worn sheet-metal walls, much of it scrawled by pilgrims inspired by Jon's book to visit my brother's final resting place. Many had come from distant points around the globe. While the messages had their differences—some were quite heartrending, while others appeared to have been written with elation—they all led me to believe that what draws individuals to this place is not so much about connecting with some-thing they've found in Chris but rather to reconnect with something they've lost in themselves.

I heard Jon moving around outside the bus and it struck me that

I owed him a debt that I could never repay. The fact remains that if Jon had not written such an intriguing book, my family and I would have been able to just grieve in silence. However, the world would have lost the inspirational story of my brother. And I would be stuck only with every day's sadness, without the constant influx of gracious strangers and their stories to offset that grief.

I also would never have had the emotional strength to track my brother's journey and follow his path, as Jon did. There is so much I never would have known about the last years of his life and, perhaps most importantly, the last hours of his life. I would still be without the peace that I have in my own heart, from knowing the peace that Chris found in his, before his death. Jon wrote:

> *One of his last acts was to take a picture of himself, standing near the bus under the high Alaska sky, one hand holding his final note toward the camera lens, the other raised in a brave, beatific farewell. His face is horribly emaciated, almost skeletal. But if he pitied himself in those last difficult hours—because he was so young, because he was alone, because his body had betrayed him and his will had let him down—it's not apparent from the photograph. He is smiling in the picture, and there is no mistaking the look in his eyes: Chris McCandless was at peace, serene as a monk gone to God.*

The note Chris held was the one the coroner had given us so long ago. Chris had torn a page from one of his favorite books—Louis L'Amour's memoir, *Education of a Wandering Man*—and written in very neat, very large block letters:

I HAVE HAD A HAPPY LIFE AND THANK THE LORD.
GOODBYE AND MAY GOD BLESS ALL!

On the backside of this page were some printed lines that L'Amour had offered from Robinson Jeffers's poem "Wise Men in Their Bad Hours":

> *Death's a fierce meadowlark: but to die having made*
> *Something more equal to the centuries*
> *Than muscle and bone, is mostly to shed weakness.*
> *The mountains are dead stone, the people*
> *Admire or hate their stature, their insolent quietness,*
> *The mountains are not softened nor troubled*
> *And a few dead men's thoughts have the same temper.*

Although Chris addressed others in his final message, I believe that the act of writing it was more for himself than for the world. His final act of self-awareness. His final act of truth.

TO ME, LIFE IS LIKE A BOOK. We all have the same first and last chapters. What makes up the story of our lives, and the legacy we leave behind, are the pages in between.

It is tragic that my brother died so young. But although he dreaded his impending death, he still died at peace, because the paths he had chosen throughout his life had kept him true to himself. And in the end, whenever that end comes, isn't that the best any of us can hope for?

I believe Chris went into the wilderness in search of what was lacking in his childhood: peace, purity, honesty. And he understood there was nowhere better for him to find that than in nature.

At forty-two, I often feel like I am living for both Chris and me, as the span of his entire life has roughly been the first half of my own. He never had the opportunity to experience a long adulthood or to be a parent. I realize now that my adulthood is where I have sought out what was lacking in my childhood: necessary lessons of worth, strength, and unconditional love.

The legacy I leave behind will have little to do with famous stories, books, or movies. It will have everything to do with the love I feel for two little girls. Except for Shannon, all my siblings have kids, and I know they feel about their own kids the same way I feel about mine. Most of us were apprehensive about becoming parents, and we all delight in seeing each other be so *good* at it. In the decades since Chris's death, my siblings and I have come together to find our own truth and build our own beauty in his absence. In each other, we've found absolution, as I believe Chris found absolution in the wild before he died.

During my trip to the bus, I represented all of Chris's brothers and sisters by leaving behind a journal. Chris's siblings filled up the first few pages, but the rest remained for visitors to the remote location to leave their own stories about what brought them there.

"Follow your heart, follow your adventures," wrote Sam.

"Chris," wrote Stacy, "always the adventurer with a desire for knowledge. I know, I understand, and I love you!"

Shelly wrote, "Before my son was born I gave him a big McCandless-style party. Inside the invitation was this Hodding Carter quote: 'There are only two lasting bequests we can hope to give our children. One of these is roots; the other, wings.' I think in some strange way you played a part in sending me the greatest gift. I will always use you as a guide so I don't clip his wings. Always in my heart and soul."

I placed a picture in the journal of all of us together as young children. We're all standing side by side. When I look at the picture, I don't see our intermixed ages. I don't see half brothers and sisters. I don't see anyone missing. I see wholeness. I see a family. I see we are all smiling, and even Chris has a beaming grin from ear to ear.

That was a good day, and one that can never be taken from us. Beneath the picture I wrote, "The love of brothers and sisters never dies," and beneath that, I wrote a few simple words Shawna had contributed to the journal. Always the one to lay down roots in a storm, she added,

Eight of us stand as one.

And she's right.

AUTHOR'S NOTE

On September 30, 2012, I opened my front door to load some things into my Honda Pilot and saw my mom standing on my front porch. She hadn't been in my home for several years, and this visit had come without invitation. Shocked to see her there, my first thought was one of relief that Robert had the girls for the day. Heather was thirteen years old and Christiana was six—my youngest would not have even recognized her grandmother.

When I asked Mom what she was doing there, she flashed a disingenuous smile, which was all too familiar, then showed me a small package tied with a satin ribbon and said it was for my anniversary. She had never gotten me an anniversary gift before, and I knew she was well aware, through common acquaintances, that Robert and I had separated two years prior. I accepted the package—I don't know why—and she left. I waited for a while before examining the gift. It was an old novelty I remembered from its perch on a random shelf in the Annandale house; thick black backing in a cheap wood frame with a gold paper etching of two lovebirds cuddling in the center. I knew my mother's tactics too well for her message to be anything but crystal clear.

Whenever discussion about her decision to stay with Dad became uncomfortable, she always pointed out my failed marriages. She saw them as evidence of my flaws, while I saw leaving any situation where I was treated with disrespect as evidence of my courage. I wanted my daughters to learn that lesson of worth from me. Despite our marital problems, Robert and I rarely fought, and never in front of the girls. However, we were always honest with them about our situation, even when those talks were difficult. Some people find it strange that although we are no longer a couple, Robert and I still spend a lot of time together with the girls, at community or school events, having dinners together, even the occasional camping trip. They say it's just not normal. They're right. And I'm very proud of that. I wanted my girls to learn that lesson of strength from me. And together, Robert and I have shown them that our love for them both is unconditional.

My mother's condescending act that day, and the detrimental messages I occasionally receive from both my parents, only strengthened my resolve to complete this book. It is not my intention to portray them as monsters, because clearly they are not. They are simply human and make mistakes as we all do. But I am absolutely certain that my witness to their mistakes, as well as my own, can serve an important purpose. I want every reader to benefit from the evidence of my family's dysfunction in the hopes that it can help them make wise decisions to lessen these burdens in their own lives.

I have made my best effort in every way possible to be honest, fair, and forthright. Some persons' names and identifying characteristics were changed in order to protect their privacy or per their request. While most of the book is organized chronologically, there was a need to occasionally combine events to fit within the confines that come with writing for the page. While I have intended to represent Chris as I believe only I can, I was careful not to speak for him, because I think no one should. Anywhere I have quoted him in the book came from my direct memory of a discussion with him, from his letters written to me or to others, or from a recollection of several corroborating witnesses of a particular occurrence. I went by the same rule with respect to others in the book as well, and if I relayed an event that I clearly was not present to witness, I corroborated separately with several people who were in attendance in order for the retelling to be as accurate as possible.

There are places in the book, especially in the early chapters, where I was not yet born or just too young to recall the details of certain events on my own. For those instances, I relied on my interviews with family members and information found in old letters for accuracy. Where my powerful and emotional final break with my parents is concerned, I pulled from one specific email exchange, followed by letters and the spirit of discussions that happened over the phone or events in person and often witnessed by others, to summarize what ultimately severed our relationship.

I hope that my openness about these difficult circumstances can be of help to others; and perhaps with raw and selfish optimism, I am left to wonder if removing the final masks from my parents might also bring upon them some relief, and allow healing within my own family.

Carine McCandless
February 2014

AFTERWORD

Storms make oaks take root.

—Proverb

There's a well-known version of the birth of the Greek goddess Athena, and each time I read it or hear it, I think about the story of my family.

According to my favorite retelling, the most powerful Greek god, Zeus, is intimate with the goddess Metis. He becomes fearful immediately afterward, because it had been prophesized that Metis would bear children more powerful than their sire. Feeling threatened, Zeus *eats* Metis, believing he can simply consume that which he can't control.

It's too late for Zeus, however, because Metis is already pregnant. In time, Zeus suffers a terrible headache, such that his head has to be cleaved in two. And Athena, goddess of wisdom and philosophy, savvy in warcraft, with a purpose for justice, comes out of his forehead, fully grown, fully armed.

Zeus easily recovers, but Athena does indeed prove to be stronger than her father. He is powerful, yes, but he is also a megalomaniac. Athena has no tolerance for such ego and relies on her insight as her greatest defense.

Like Athena, my brothers and sisters have proven to be stronger than our father. We are armored with our experiences, which have bestowed reason and compassion. We broke the cycle of violence—every single one of us. We collected all the broken pieces and put them back together to create something strong and beautiful. Each family event where Walt's surviving kids gather, we revel in one another's company regardless of our differences or any disagreements, and we always put the children first. We are all focused on the next generation, as we should be.

Perhaps our loyalty to each other and our children is never more clear than when faced with crisis. On October 11, 2012, my little boy, who was five at the time, was diagnosed with a pediatric brain tumor. The surgery to remove his malignant tumor lasted fifteen hours, and none of my brothers and sisters left the waiting room. In the months since the surgery, it's been my brothers and sisters as well as my mom who have supported me as I've taken my son to chemotherapy treatments, therapy appointments, and body scans. From cleaning my yard so we could relax outside and enjoy some fresh air, to attending a group information seminar about coping with cancer, to arranging a steady stream of hot meals and keeping our village of support informed through our internet lifeline, they have all been there for me unconditionally.

Each time I'm at the hospital with my son, I notice the signs posted about domestic violence. DON'T SUFFER IN SILENCE, they read. Too many people still do. The violence often remains locked up tightly behind closed doors along with those experiencing it. We need to open those doors. I choose to acknowledge my past experience in the hope that it can help others find their own voice.

A few days after we had finally arrived home from the hospital following several surgeries, my son was playing with Legos and stopped suddenly. "Does Uncle Chris have a spirit?" he asked me. I told him yes, and, in the way that children do, he went back to playing with his Legos. I love my brother Chris, and though all these years have passed, I still miss him beyond words. But although he is no longer here in body, I feel the strength of his spirit with me every day, just as I felt the presence of all of my siblings in the hospital during my son's multiple procedures. Throughout any adversity, as on any given day, we stand together with unconditional love.

Sometimes in life we must endure specific challenges that are part of our journey to learn from and to teach by, and valuable lessons are gleaned from the effort. I know Chris would be so proud of Carine for bringing the truth to light, because in that spirit, some stories just need to be told.

Shelly McCandless
May 2014

ACKNOWLEDGMENTS

Writing this book highlighted for me how many people I am indebted to for their help and support throughout my lifetime. First and foremost, I thank God for this gift of life that I have sometimes failed to be grateful enough for. I thank my parents sincerely for their part in bringing me into this world and for the opportunities they provided to me. There are simply not enough words to thank my brothers and sisters, Sam, Stacy, Shawna, Shelly, Shannon, Chris, and Quinn, for being my family and support system. I love you all so much. Included in that family is someone whom I not only respect but *revere* for her great class and kindness—Marcia, I offer an endless thank you.

I want to thank my brother Chris for giving me my inspiration to gather the courage to complete this book, for being my strength as I relied on the imperativeness of truth to guide me, and for teaching me how to honor each day.

To my eldest daughter Heather—The amount of love my heart holds for you is beyond words. You have been an incredible gift, a remarkable teacher, and the most important opportunity I have ever received. I can never thank you enough for all that you have done for me, so I will dedicate my life to showing you how grateful I am. To my youngest daughter Christiana—My love for you is also indescribable. What a miraculous blessing you are. Always remember that your DNA does not define you. Rise up to every challenge that you are faced with and you will accomplish amazing things. You are beautiful, and you inspire me every single day. My deepest gratitude to you both for revealing to me the very best part of myself. I am humbled and honored to be your mom. Thank you for your patience in the years that it took to complete this book and forgive me for everything I was absent from during my travels or while strapped to my laptop on stressful deadlines. If I can sell a few books I promise we'll catch back up on fun missed and I won't edit paragraphs in line at Disney World ever again.

Robert—Although our marriage did not survive the stresses that come along as life changes, I am so thankful that our sincere friendship has endured. Thank you for some truly great memories. I appreciate how our common goals and priorities when it comes to our girls always remind us of the love we shared, and that the gifts from our union were well worth any costs.

A very special thanks goes to Pat and Steve Grzybowski and to Abbey Anderson, the Harper family, and the SMI Aunties for the love and care they have always given to the girls while allowing Robert and me to accommodate our demanding work schedules.

I am grateful to many family members who helped me dig through the history of our past in order to expose some very private things to the present. I know it was emotionally stressful at times, and I wholeheartedly appreciate your willingness to take the chance with me that the effort would be worth it and would do much to help others. To so many in my extended family who showed their support simply by sending hellos and messages from time to time to let me know that you were there, I thank you for your thoughtfulness.

To my best friend and surrogate brother, Pete—There is much in recent years that I could not have accomplished without your love and support. Thank you for believing in me and for always being there when I need help. You are an incredibly valuable part of my life.

Jon—With great respect I thank you for your faithful friendship that has lasted half of my lifetime. Your wisdom and constancy has made many difficult times without Chris easier to endure.

Ed—My deepest appreciation for your continued friendship, sincerity, real love, and all around great mojo. You truly rock.

I have so many more friends to thank for everything from lending their eyes to early drafts and their ears to comprehensive discussion to providing accommodations and a quiet space to write while I traveled, as well as loyalty and support, friendship, laughter and stress relief at just the right moments, the occasional glass of wine, and positive energy, thoughts, and prayers when I have needed them most: Doug Kennedy; Ashley Kunhardt Cronin; Amanda Aksel; Deni Brown; Chris Rossney; Greg Higgins; Mike Lim; Kimberley Maxie Guilfoy; Stacie Campbell Franks; Dave Reisch; Dan Mewhorter; Beth Hughes; Sean, Jenée, and Sam Farrell; Matt Gardner; Korey Johnson; Karen Jones; Amanda Shupe Webb; Tim, Brian, and Heather Johnson; Michael and Margaret Land; Brian Free; Adam Read; Steve and Heather Salmon; Allan Estivalet; the Khalsa family; Ryc Stine; Michelle Machay; Lisa McNew; Paula Berenson; Bob Fiedler; Chevonne Bertelson; Heather Perrine; Jennifer Purdy Mazur; Beth Handros Shubert; Holly Miller Vesilind; Heather McNeil; Michelle Barrett; Jennifer Crossman; Jolie Atkins; and Margie Arrivillaga. Additional appreciation for facilitating my sanity and judgment, inner peace, and complete fitness goes to Susan Giddings, Kat Cummings, and Carter Jones. And a special shout out to Betsy Arnaudin and all of the ladies of the United Methodist Women and Promise Circle.

Thank you to Daniel Hill for your genuine compassion and encouragement, your smart advice, your supportive voice, and for sharing the Nutella with me. Most of all for not just telling me, but for showing me, that everything you can hope for is truly possible.

Special thanks to my dear friends and Alaska hiking buddies from the Last Frontier Adventure Club: Erik and Jenna Halfacre, Jedidiah White-Mathany, Mike Kramer, Trevor Jones, Duke, Andrew Brooks, Jeremy Egger, and Brandon Martinez and Meranda Carter from the Wild Bones Project.

To my friends Sharon and Beth I offer my sincere thanks for allowing me to see things in a new light and for urging me to flip the switch.

Important contributions to the content of the book were made by Denise Barker Griffin, Janice Barker, Giti Khalsa, John Casagrande, Tracy Tatro, Tracy Moore Raborg, Julie Carnes Puckett, Carrie Carnes Kemper, Andy Horwitz, Lloyd McBean, Josh Marshall, and Mickey Mariner Hines. And a special mention to Chris Fish—I am honored by your openness, trust, and support. I feel blessed to have regained our friendship and am inspired by the person you have become.

A group thank you to all of my loyal employees, clients, and customers over the years who became my second family and that helped me get to this point.

My appreciation goes to the following for their help with all things preceding the book development and beyond: to Dominic Peters with ManyMedia for your exceptional photography, to H. L. Wilson III at Addrock Services for your creative web design ideas and skills, to Jayme White at Luna Spheres Designs for your thoughtful and clever logo creation, and to Kim Thornton Igenito and Kate Berner at the Penguin Random House Speaker's Bureau for your attentiveness and hard work.

I have also benefitted from the thoughtful direction and wisdom of Jack Ferrebee, John Midgett, and Tazewell Hubard. Thanks guys.

To Marie Tillman I want to say how much I value your spirit, your kind advice, and your careful suggestions that led me to the absolute right people to help me tell my difficult story with positivism and grace.

To Jenna Land Free with Girl Friday Productions—Wow. I'm not sure I can say enough to do justice to this epic experience we have taken together. This has been such a powerful and emotional project and I thank you for helping me through it all. Your remarkable talents as an editor, chapter architect, and writing coach far outweigh any misunderstanding you still retain of why hats are a stylish and practical fashion accessory. I could not have written this book without your guidance and friendship. Thank you. If I don't pull through for you on the other thing I will pray for the safety of dogs everywhere.

I am extremely grateful to many others who helped create these pages and who allowed this intense book writing process to remain enjoyable for me:

To Gail Ross, literary agent extraordinaire. You keep it brief and get it done, so I will too. You're simply awesome.

Huge thanks to my publishing editor, Nancy Hancock, for taking this project from our first meeting all the way to the presses. Your management, energy and spirit have provided such a valuable education. And I will never forget that giant burrito.

To my publisher, Mark Tauber—I am incredibly grateful for your passion and dedication to this book since day one. I am confident that the genuine connection you have with this endeavor will allow its message to reach many and will accomplish great things.

To the entire team at HarperOne, I offer my heartfelt thanks to all who I have spoken to and worked with in person, and to all those behind the scenes who might be unnamed but whose work is no less worthy. I sincerely appreciate your part in this effort: Michele Wetherbee, Dwight Been, Claudia Boutote, Terri Leonard, Noël Chrisman, Elsa Dixon, Elisa Rivlin, Dianna Stirpe, Tanya Fox, Ralph Fowler, Joan Olson, Kim Dayman, and Suzanne Wickham.

Special acknowledgment to Sharon Olds for being an invaluable asset to the narrative work on the *Into the Wild* film, for facilitating my voice with direction, and for allowing me to include excerpts from her poem *I Go Back To May 1937* in this book. You have done much to highlight the connectivity of strength, empowerment, and healing.

And to all those who I am forgetting to list who I have surely expressed my thanks to in person, you are no less important. My brain is just exhausted and my notes are somewhat illegible. When I read this as printed in the book and gasp at your absence I will call to apologize.

ABOUT THE AUTHOR

Carine McCandless is an entrepreneur, activist, and mother. She has been successfully self-employed since she started her first business at the age of nineteen. As a public speaker her presentations are featured in education and corporate venues across the United States. She is the sister of literary icon Chris McCandless and consulted closely with Jon Krakauer on his bestselling book *Into the Wild*. She also worked as a direct advisor and script contributor to Sean Penn for his film adaptation of the book. She lives in Virginia Beach, Virginia, with her two daughters.

www.carinemccandless.com